AF835049

# Art Therapy in In-patient Settings

Bringing together the voices of academics, art psychotherapists and service users, this unique volume explores the contemporary impact of Edward Adamson's pioneering work on art therapy practices in in-patient settings.

Drawing on both primary and secondary sources, as well as case studies, the book explores the extent to which Adamson's work has become a conceptual framework for art therapy in a variety of in-patient settings today. It describes how practice contributes to the shift in mental health provision towards a trauma-informed culture, and represents a research-led rationale for increased and reliable provision of arts therapies in in-patient settings as a vital contribution to patient experience and recovery. Chapters cover key elements such as the open studio model, the role of the art therapist, art therapy as personal narrative, art therapy in forensic settings and its use in supporting the wellbeing of staff in in-patient settings. The volume locates Adamson's legacy within a changing healthcare framework, reflecting on the future of art therapy in the context of evolving government policy, financial restraints and – in the UK – the changing face of the NHS.

This volume will be of interest to researchers, scholar-practitioners, psychotherapists and postgraduate students in the fields of arts therapies, the history of psychology and mental health provision and, more broadly, mental health nursing and policy. It will give senior leaders an opportunity to understand the contribution of arts therapists to improving the quality of care for service users and staff.

**Maggie Batchelar** is a Lead Art Psychotherapist in Norfolk and Suffolk NHS Foundation Trust, UK.

**Andrew Colley** is a former Senior Lecturer in Special Education, University of East London, UK.

## Routledge Research in Creative Arts and Expressive Therapies

This series provides a forum to discuss the latest research, debates and practice in creative arts and expressive therapies; including arts therapy, dance therapy, dramatherapy and music therapy.

**Intercultural Music Therapy Consultation Research**
Shared Humanity in Collaborative Theory and Practice
*Lisa Margetts*

**Reflections on Authentic Movement**
Theory, Practice and Arts-Led Research
*Eila Goldhahn*

**Space, Place and Dramatherapy**
International Perspectives
*Edited by Eliza Sweeney*

**Posthuman Possibilities of Dance Movement Psychotherapy**
Moving through Eco-feminist and New Materialist Entanglements of Differently Enabled Bodies in Research
*Caroline Frizell*

**Ethics, Identity, and the Dramatherapy-informed Classroom**
Processes of Identity Negotiation and Performance
*Jeanne Roberts*

**Art Therapy in In-patient Settings**
The Legacy of Edward Adamson
*Edited by Maggie Batchelar and Andrew Colley*

# Art Therapy in In-patient Settings

## The Legacy of Edward Adamson

**Edited by Maggie Batchelar and Andrew Colley**

Routledge
Taylor & Francis Group
LONDON AND NEW YORK

First published 2026
by Routledge
4 Park Square, Milton Park, Abingdon, Oxon OX14 4RN

and by Routledge
605 Third Avenue, New York, NY 10158

*Routledge is an imprint of the Taylor & Francis Group, an informa business*

© 2026 selection and editorial matter, Maggie Batchelar and Andrew Colley; individual chapters, the contributors

The right of Maggie Batchelar and Andrew Colley to be identified as the authors of the editorial material, and of the authors for their individual chapters, has been asserted in accordance with sections 77 and 78 of the Copyright, Designs and Patents Act 1988.

All rights reserved. No part of this book may be reprinted or reproduced or utilised in any form or by any electronic, mechanical, or other means, now known or hereafter invented, including photocopying and recording, or in any information storage or retrieval system, without permission in writing from the publishers.

For Product Safety Concerns and Information please contact our EU representative GPSR@taylorandfrancis.com. Taylor & Francis Verlag GmbH, Kaufingerstraße 24, 80331 München, Germany.

*Trademark notice*: Product or corporate names may be trademarks or registered trademarks, and are used only for identification and explanation without intent to infringe.

*British Library Cataloguing-in-Publication Data*
A catalogue record for this book is available from the British Library

ISBN: 978-1-041-01161-3 (hbk)
ISBN: 978-1-041-01162-0 (pbk)
ISBN: 978-1-003-61342-8 (ebk)

DOI: 10.4324/9781003613428

Typeset in Galliard
by SPi Technologies India Pvt Ltd (Straive)

# Contents

# About the Editors

**Maggie Batchelar** has worked in the NHS for 34 years, 32 of those as an art therapist. Once qualified from Sheffield University, she established a new art therapy service in a large, rural learning disability hospital in Northumberland, before moving back to East Anglia, where she has worked across the age range in community and in-patient mental health services, focusing on older adult in-patient settings. Her interest in working with older people has lifelong roots. Maggie is a lead art psychotherapist within her Trust; a member of the National NHS Arts Therapies Leads Forum and the Psychological Professions Council for the East of England. She has recently jointly established a BAAT Special Interest Group for art therapists working in in-patient settings, aiming to improve understanding of and access to arts therapies in this clinical field.

**Andrew Colley** is a former Senior Lecturer in Special Education at The University of East London. He has master's degrees from the Universities of Birmingham and Cambridge. This is his fourth book published by Routledge after *Inclusion is Dead: Long Live Inclusion* (2017), co-authored with Peter Imray; *Enhancing Wellbeing and Independence for Young People with Profound and Multiple Learning Difficulties* (2021), co-authored with Julie Tilbury; and *In-patient Mental Health Care from the Asylum System to the Present Day – a Lived Experience of Policy and Practice* (2024). He is the co-author with John Neil of *The Man Who Tested Parachutes: Charles Agate and the Development of Britain's Airborne Forces for D-Day and Arnhem* (Pen and Sword Books, 2025).

# Contributors

**Emma Allen** is an HCPC-registered art psychotherapist and the Professional Lead in arts psychotherapies at Rampton Hospital, one of the UK's three high-secure hospitals. Emma is also a Senior Art Psychotherapist for the adult mental health service in the South West Yorkshire NHS Foundation Trust and has previously held the position of Senior Lecturer in Art Psychotherapy at the University of South Wales. She is the founder of Forensic Sandplay and has two decades of experience within the criminal justice system, prisons, secure hospitals, units and youth offender institutes. Emma is a published author and active researcher.

**Jackie Edwards** is a UKCP-registered dance movement psychotherapist, working in mental health NHS services since 2008. She currently leads a team of ten arts psychotherapists. Jackie has written about her journey to becoming a dance movement psychotherapist following her experience as a parent of three adult sons, two of whom are autistic. Jackie has also worked as a family carer representative with the Department for Health, including the Autism Programme Board, chaired by Sir Norman Lamb from 2010 to 2015. Jackie has been studying at a postgraduate degree level, focusing on Dance Movement Psychotherapy and autism.

**Fiona Grainger**, MA, is an integrative arts psychotherapist with eight years of clinical experience in a London NHS Mental Health Trust. She provides both group and individual art psychotherapy within community mental health services and a locked male Psychiatric Intensive Care Unit (PICU). Her clinical and research interests focus on the implementation of trauma-informed art therapy within mainstream NHS mental healthcare. She is also dedicated to promoting equitable access to creative psychotherapies and expanding their reach across diverse socio-economic populations.

**Dr Val Huet** is trained in sculpture and as an art therapist in 1986. She later trained as a Group Psychotherapist and Organisational Consultant and completed a PhD on art therapy groups for work-related stress. Val was the Chief Executive Officer of the British Association of Art Therapists (BAAT) from 2003 to 2021. She was a Trustee of the Adamson Collection Trust from

2017 to 2025. She is a Visiting Professor at the University of Hertfordshire and at Ulster University. Her current clinical practice is with people who live with chronic pain and fibromyalgia.

**Dr Jed Jerwood** (MA Art Psych, PhD) is an Advanced Clinical Academic art psychotherapist at Birmingham and Solihull Mental Health Foundation Trust and Honorary Clinical Associate Professor at the University of Birmingham. His clinical practice is with adults with enduring mental ill health. His research interests lie in health inequalities, the relationship between physical and mental ill health and end-of-life and palliative care. Methodological interests include co-creation, participatory and art-based research methods.

**Dr Alan Johnson** is an Occupational Therapist at the PCLI Community Transition Team, Hunter New England Area Health, NSW, Australia. Alan has a creative arts background with a degree in Art for the Community and uses art and creativity in his everyday work. Alan completed his PhD in the School of Health Sciences at the University of Newcastle.

**Estelle Kane** is a registered dance/movement psychotherapist working within NHS in-patient mental health settings with experience in single sex, mixed, acute and intensive care wards. Estelle has a background in international and national research and policy development, having worked in Europe, Australia and the US. Estelle currently supports arts psychotherapies research and development in an NHS setting.

**Kate Lawrence** started her working career in the fashion industry before retraining as an art psychotherapist and then further developing her career by becoming an Eye Movement Desensitisation and Reprocessing (EMDR) practitioner and clinical supervisor. She now works in high-secure settings within the mental health directorate as well as with adults with brain injuries, the homeless and children and adults who have experienced mental, physical and emotional trauma.

**Siobhan Lennon** is an artist and art psychotherapist currently working with adults in acute in-patient mental health services. Siobhan has worked for many years in NHS healthcare teams in a range of criminal justice settings with children, young people and adults. She is interested in navigating the complex relationship of art psychotherapy within institutions and supporting people to contact the therapeutic potential of creativity within acute and restricted settings.

**Joanne Noble** qualified as an art therapist in 1993 from Sheffield University and gained a BA (Hons) in Fine Art in 1990 from Coventry Polytechnic. She has completed further training in both psychodynamic and systemic approaches. Joanne has worked in a Therapeutic Community with adults with learning disabilities and currently works in mental health within the NHS, in a hospital in the North of England. More recently, she has worked with service users to evaluate and understand how art therapy helps people while in hospital. Joanne is joint coordinator of the newly established BAAT Special Interest Group for art therapists working in in-patient settings.

**Runa Park** is a registered art psychotherapist (HCPC) and accredited interpersonal psychotherapist (IPT UK) with extensive experience across NHS, community and educational settings. She currently works as a senior art psychotherapist and digital lead within the NHS, in addition to her private practice. Runa's work focuses on integrating creativity and technology to enhance accessibility, participation and sustainability in therapy, underpinned by evidence-based practice. Her professional interests include digital clinical development and nature-based approaches to psychotherapy. She was highly commended in the NHS England 2024 AHP Digital Practice category for her contributions to digital innovation.

**Tess Rendoth** is a Lecturer and teacher educator in the School of Education, University of Newcastle, NSW, Australia. Throughout her career as a teacher and in community development, Tess has supported young people and adults with complex life-worlds using creative arts as a driver for relational connection, communication and community building.

**Poppy Tomkinson** is an art psychotherapist working with children, young people and adults in community, in-patient and forensic settings. Her clinical interests include reducing barriers to psychological interventions through increasing the accessibility of less verbal therapies. She is an advocate for patient choice and was one of the therapists who developed and delivered the pilot described in Chapter 12.

**Fiona Williams** trained in Fine Art at Goldsmiths College, London, and qualified in art psychotherapy at St Albans School of Art in Hertfordshire. She has worked in the NHS for 29 years across a range of client groups and settings, but mostly in adult in-patient services as a clinician and Arts Psychotherapies Service Manager. She currently works in two NHS Trusts as a Head of Profession for the Arts Psychotherapies and as Service Lead for a Complex Emotional Needs Service. She is a visiting lecturer on the Art Psychotherapy Master's training course at the University of South Wales and has a clinical supervision private practice.

**Dr Chris Wood** has been an art therapist for some 40 years. She felt lucky to spend time in her early career working at Netherne Hospital under the tutelage of Julia Gudjonson. She moved to work in the NHS in Sheffield, where she helped establish the art therapy training at the University of Sheffield, alongside John Henzell, David Edwards, Joy Schaverien and David Maclagan. For a time, she was the course leader. As times changed, the course was based on a partnership between the NHS and Leeds Beckett University. It has moved to Hallam University, where she now works as a part-time lecturer. Chris is also a research fellow at the University of

Sheffield, and her interests include pluralism in art therapy research, linking systematic research with the arts and humanities. She is particularly interested in what helps people facing episodes of psychosis and how historical periods and health inequalities shape the psychological experience of populations. She feels privileged to work with *Art Refuge*. Chris has published a range of papers and the Routledge book, *Navigating Art Therapy: A Therapist's Companion* (2011).

**Tim Wright** is a registered art psychotherapist (HCPC) and a Systemic Practitioner, and he is Professional Lead for the Arts Therapies at a London NHS trust. He has worked in acute settings since 1995. Tim was editor of the *International Journal of Art Therapy* from 2008 to 2014 and chair of the British Association of Art Therapists from 2014 to 2020. He has published several articles on art therapy and was the lead author of Wright, T., & Holttum, S. (2020). *BAAT Guidelines on Art Therapy for People with a Psychosis-related Diagnosis*. London: British Association of Art Therapists.

# Acknowledgements

We are particularly grateful to the Adamson Collection Trust and Wellcome Collection for their support, as well as to the following, who have either contributed directly to this book or have influenced the work of the chapter authors:

Matt Adams
Mark Adamson
Robert Ayres
Andrea Core
Anthony Drew
Michael Edwards
George and Pat Frogley
Stephen Gaskell
Amanda Glynn
Gillian Goodchild-Colley
David Gussak
David Gwyther
John Henzell
Professor Susan Hogan
Karen Huckvale
Hunter New England Local Health District
Kevin Jones
John Neil
Nana-Kofi Okyere, SEND Consultant.
Holly Peel, Image Services Manager, Wellcome Collection
Lianne Rees
Therese Richardson
Joy Schaverien
Braddon Snape
Jane Watt
Lindy Zubairy

Thanks also to all the service users who have added their voices to this book.

# Introduction

*Siobhan Lennon with Andrew Colley*

As a student of Fine Art almost 20 years ago, I spent many glorious afternoons in the university library, an architectural and educational gem of 1930s London. Here, I would peruse the shelves, indulging in any title or cover image which caught my eye, always finding something new and wondrous to flick through. I was free to let my attention wander and settle where it chose.

At the same time, though, I was feeling a deep frustration in contextualising my emerging art practice, and the same questions tormented me across the three years of my studies:

*What was I making and why?*
*Who was it for?*
*What did it say and to whom?*

One afternoon as I was browsing those library shelves in my final year, I came across a book called *Art as Healing* by Edward Adamson (1911–1996). The title, the cover image and the book itself immediately captivated me, and it was within its pages that I finally discovered a more comfortable relationship with the critical questions which had plagued me. I found an ease and authenticity in the artwork created by Adamson's patients as well as a practical sincerity in the professionalism with which Adamson treated their art making. His words struck a deep chord:

> The visual arts are more than a palliative – under the right guidance they can be a vital form of self-help which allows Nature's healing powers to restore balance and harmony to the troubled mind.
>
> (Adamson, 1984, p. 5)

*Art as Healing* is a bold and beautiful testament to the healing power of art and to the intuitive knowledge that creative expression can be a salve for our wounds. The book became a sort of mirror to me, reflecting a purpose for my own art-making: granting it permission and laying foundations for a psychic home. In that final year of fine art studies, my dissertation focussed on

DOI: 10.4324/9781003613428-1

exploring the connection between art, art making and psychological/emotional healing in both the individual and the group, as well as the potential for the therapeutic use of art in prisons and psychiatric institutions. Through the process of writing and research, I had discovered the profession and practice of art therapy.

From then onward, *Art as Healing* has been a faithful companion on my journey of becoming a qualified art therapist. It is always near to hand and has also perhaps been a prototype: resonating with my belief in art making, and in art therapy. This journey has taken me through various institutions, within which I found systemic difficulties in acknowledging patients as complete people in need of holistic care. *Art as Healing* has provided a counterbalance to this, an alternative narrative resonating with the aspirations I hold for these institutional spaces in which art is made: illustrating the necessity to have a space, a studio, a therapeutic home to nurture the work of the service users.

Edward Adamson's extraordinary work at Netherne Hospital in Surrey in the second half of the last century, and his pioneering contribution to the development of art therapy as a practice and as a profession, cannot be underestimated, and yet there is little academic research into the enduring impact of his work in contemporary in-patient settings. That impact and the legacy of Edward Adamson are explored in this book by leading academics and practitioners from a range of in-patient and other settings.

The book is in three parts. Part I is principally empirical in style and content, serving as an introduction to Edward Adamson's early life and the context of his work with patients at Netherne Hospital over nearly 40 years. We gain a sense of how Adamson shaped and managed the studio spaces at Netherne, what these spaces permitted the patients to create, and the impact of their creativity on their recovery and well-being. Part I concludes with a chapter discussing the Adamson Collection, which holds thousands of pieces of artwork by Adamson's artist/patients as well as works by Adamson himself, and we explore the ethics of collecting and exhibiting artworks made in a therapeutic context by people experiencing psychological distress.

The second part of the book is primarily research-led and discusses to what extent Adamson's work has become a contemporary conceptual framework for art therapy in acute and intensive care in-patient settings, as well as in wards for older people and high security facilities. There is a focus on the environments where art therapy takes place and on the evolving role of the art therapist, followed by chapters addressing art therapy as a collaborative enterprise between staff and service users and as a means to support staff wellbeing. Part II also includes powerful service user voices, including those from a pioneering art therapy project in New South Wales, Australia, and a discussion around the common language of all arts therapy modalities. The final chapter presents two innovative approaches to measuring impact and outcomes.

Part III begins with a powerful chapter proposing that art therapy has a vital role to play in in-patient care, through increasing access to psychological therapy for those who are unable to engage in a cognitively based approach.

We then ask how the key role of art therapy, and of Adamson's focus on the need for time and space, can be sustained in the context of evolving Government policy, financial restraints and the changing face of the NHS. The book's concluding chapter discusses how the themes and issues explored throughout the book have implications for the arts to contribute significantly to the improved well-being of the population as a whole.

In the UK and around the world (Gilburt and Mallorie, 2024), the number of beds available in psychiatric settings has decreased whilst the demand for them has continued to rise, and this pressure on beds drives a priority to expedite discharge from hospital. People may be admitted far from home or have long waits in Accident and Emergency services or other inappropriate environments before a bed is found for them. And yet, the Royal College of Psychiatrists Culture of Care Programme (2025), which is part of NHS England's Quality Transformation Programme, sets out a priority to 'support wards to provide safe, trauma informed, therapeutic and equity-focused care'. This book highlights the valuable contribution art therapy brings to achieving this priority and is a timely opportunity to offer a comprehensive overview of the growth and clinical relevance of art therapy in contemporary in-patient care. Edward Adamson's legacy and his vision for art as therapy reverberate through this book, through the development of art therapy over more than 40 years and are perhaps more relevant than ever today.

## Editors' Note

Nathan Filer in *This Book Will Change your Mind about Mental Health* (Faber and Faber, 2019) reminds us that 'there is no uncontroversial language when talking about mental illness' (p. 5). This, of course, includes how we refer to people who are in the care of the mental health services. Currently, the terms 'client', 'service user' and 'patient' are all used in the UK, and in this book, our chapter authors have used whichever term is most common in their setting. Similarly, the terms 'art therapy' and 'art psychotherapy', which are both state-registered protected titles, are used interchangeably and the term 'arts therapies' is used to refer to all four modalities of art therapy, dramatherapy, music therapy and dance movement psychotherapy.

## References

Adamson, E. (1984). *Art as Healing*. London: Coventure Ltd.

Filer, N. (2019). *This Book Will Change your Mind about Mental Health*. London: Faber and Faber

Gilburt, H., & Mallorie, S. (2024, February 21). *Mental Health 360*. The Kings Fund. https://www.kingsfund.org.uk/insight-and-analysis/long-reads/mental-health-360

Royal College of Psychiatrists. (2025). *Culture of Care Programme*. https://www.rcpsych.ac.uk/improving-care/nccmh/culture-of-care-programme

# Part I

# Edward Adamson

# 1 Edward Adamson and Netherne Hospital

*Chris Wood and Andrew Colley*

In 1980, I had recently trained as an art therapist at Goldsmiths College in London when I began working at Netherne Hospital in Surrey. I did not meet the pioneer art therapist Edward Adamson as he had already retired, though I did work alongside two artist/patients who had worked with him in his studios, and my relationships with them are described a little later. I did occasionally hear that Adamson had visited the hospital to retrieve artworks from his curated collection of over 60,000 pieces of art, made by people who passed through his studios at Netherne between the 1940s and the mid-1970s. This would become The Adamson Collection, which is discussed in Chapter 3.

Netherne Hospital was built at the start of that century on a hill east of the main London to Brighton railway line on extensive farmland (Wills, 2021). It was accessed by a long lane that meandered through fields and woods. The hospital grounds were well-cared for and especially beautiful in the autumn when the leaves along the lane were golden. The main part of the hospital was built around a large semi-circular corridor. This long corridor was immaculate – polished daily by staff and 'patients' – as they were called then - with doors leading to different wards. Even in the 1980s, whilst I was working at the hospital, the prospect of living in the main part of this 1,000-bed hospital on some of the long-term wards was frightening for many. There was little privacy, and some sights, sounds and treatments could be terrifying.

Everything in the large main building was sturdily built, and I think we all had the impression from the very fabric of the building that this was a place that had stood the test of time, and that hospital life would continue. We could not have anticipated the dramatic economic changes that would come to shape the UK mental health services, some of which arguably have not represented progress.

I worked as an art therapist mainly at John Reid House, the admissions unit at Netherne. It was much smaller than the main hospital: a two-storey building with residential wards on the second floor and meeting rooms, offices, a kitchen and a dining room on the ground floor. Stays in the unit typically lasted for a few months, unlike the long years that people had languished in the main hospital. Importantly, John Reid House contained a lovely old art

DOI: 10.4324/9781003613428-3

studio with three high bay windows. It was at the end of a long corridor. So, just as John Reid House was apart from the main hospital and the sights and sounds of those long-term wards, the studio was also set apart. I remember being impressed by its size and light when I first saw it. Patients and staff seemed to enjoy visiting that room.

In 1985, Andrew Colley was admitted as a patient to John Reid House. He remembers meeting a kindly psychiatrist who reassuringly suggested that if he stayed for a few months to rest, exercise, do a little work within the hospital, and perhaps visit the art studio, he and his staff could help him return home. In his book *In-Patient Mental Health Care from the Asylum System to the Present Day. A lived experience of policy and practice* (2024), Andrew describes the legacy of Edward Adamson's influence as he experienced it and suggests that Adamson had brought about a quiet revolution using art therapy on psychiatric wards during his 30-year tenure at Netherne:

> Edward Adamson's presence … was still there in the hospital's large art rooms. Almost every day a few of us would shuffle into one of these – a room full of light from the tall windows, and on the walls paintings, drawings and collages made by patients long discharged or dead. We would sit where we wanted – at a table, an easel or an armchair – drink tea, smoke, and talk, to each other a bit but mainly with the art therapist, who listened. We were never told what to do … and sometimes we did nothing at all, but often we would paint a little or cut out shapes and stick them on paper, or mess around with charcoal … The art therapist at Netherne in 1985 would look, and sometimes comment very softly but never judgmentally, and always listen. In retrospect, nearly 40 years later, I can see that there was a kind of gentle alchemy going on in that room.
>
> (p. 24)

Similarly, my memories of working at Netherne in a system that offered precious time and studio space to work as an art therapist have served me well. Working at Netherne provided a solid foundation for my later practice and research. This is particularly important when thinking about what circumstances in contemporary times offer a secure base (Bowlby, 1988) for art therapy practitioners and their clients.

Born in 1911, Edward Adamson studied at Bromley School of Art. Although he trained as a chiropodist in the 1930s – mainly at the behest of his parents – he only practised briefly during his service as a non-combatant conscientious objector with the Army Medical Corps. This experience, as we will see in the next chapter, would be pivotal in shaping his future work at Netherne Hospital, but he was an artist, and he remained an artist for the rest of his life and it was as an artist that a connection with the Red Cross Picture Library took him to Netherne for the first time in 1946 to give an illustrated talk to the patients.

> I must confess the idea filled me with a certain apprehension: I had never visited an 'asylum' before. Nor were my fears quelled when, having passed through long corridors and many locked and relocked doors, I was ushered into a large hall containing about a hundred people ... many of the inhabitants underwent major brain operations, and consequently many were shaven headed. Others were swathed in bandages and were disfigured by post-operative bruises and black eyes.
>
> (Adamson, 1984, p. 1)

That first lecture was a success, and the hospital asked him to return. He discovered that some patients had been drawing for years, using whatever materials they could find. One of these had produced large numbers of drawings on semi-transparent toilet paper using charcoal from the ends of matches (Adamson, 1984). Some of these images are reproduced in Chapter 3.

When he started working at Netherne in 1946, he was under the auspices of Dr Eric Cunningham-Dax (1908–2008) and Dr Francis Reitmann (1905–1955). These psychiatrists were interested in how art might help patients. Both had previously been involved in experimental research in mental health and neurosurgery, and they wanted to use similar empirical methods to research the impact of artwork on patient health (Cummings, 2017; Waller, 1991). This meant that initially the parameters of Adamson's work were constrained, even to the very details of how studios were furnished and used, because his work was seen as being part of a controlled psychiatric experiment.

From 1950, however, Dr Rudolf K. Freudenberg (1908–1993) became hospital superintendent at Netherne. He was at the cusp of the transition in psychiatry, as it moved from mainly medical intervention (he had been an early proponent of insulin therapy) towards social psychiatry. He became an advocate of liberal approaches to the organisation of psychiatric hospitals (Becker & Bennett, 2000) and appears to have approached the organisation of Netherne whilst it was still a 2,000-bed hospital within the historical tradition of Philippe Pinel (1745–1826), who wrote the psychiatric treatise *Traité* (1809). Pinel's work drew on ideas of human equality from the French Revolution of 1789, in the same way that the father and son psychiatrists, Eugene Bleuler (1857–1939) and Manfred Bleuler (1903–1994), were also influenced by the French Revolution in treating their patients with straightforward care, attention and respect. The York Retreat had used Pinel's ideas with some success in the 1830s by introducing 'Moral Treatment'. This is sometimes mistranslated. The French word 'moral' means spirit or feeling, and Pinel's version of Moral Treatment implies treatment through emotions, kindness and respect and not notions of moral mental hygiene.

These changes in the management and ethos of Netherne Hospital from the 1950s meant that Adamson had more freedom to choose how he organised his studios, the artmaking and his work. He established at least five art studios at the hospital, some shared, one of which was a converted army hut which comfortably accommodated twenty patients, and some for individual artists. The individual studios were home to artists such as the Canadian William Kurelek (1927–1977), the Hungarian printer and engraver George Buday (1907–1990) and the remarkable Gwyneth Rowlands (1915–2009), who painted faces on hundreds of flints she found in the hospital grounds. It is possible to see one of Rowland's works in Chapter 3.

The establishment of these studios shows Adamson's commitment to creating the conditions for patients to be accepted as artists. He increasingly operated an open-door policy, where patients were free to drop in to one of the studios, paint or chat and stay as long as they could. As he told an interviewer from the Cambridge Jungian Circle in 1994: *For some patients, the studio was the one place they could rely on.*

Adamson also opened a large gallery for patient artwork at the end of the hospital's long central corridor. David Gwyther, a technical assistant at Netherne in 1970 during Adamson's tenure there, used to visit the gallery. When interviewed for this book, he said:

> *I had no idea what to expect, but I can remember being profoundly affected by the quality and images of the paintings, and their meaning. My lasting impression of Netherne has been the exposure to the paintings of the art gallery, in particular the ranges of subject matter involving conflict between hope and despair as depicted by the many artists.*

A painting given to David by one of the artist/patients working with Adamson at Netherne in 1970 is shown in Chapter 12 of this book.

During the first few days of working as an art therapist at Netherne, I was asked to visit a young woman of a similar age to me. I think someone had thought that our ages might mean we could relate to each other. Details like this show staff compassion even though the system at that time strictly distinguished between patients and non-patients. I had to make my way to a closed ward in the main building, and it was a stark change in culture between John Reid House and the main hospital. I remember finding my way through corridors and staircases and eventually entering a small area through several unlocked and relocked doors. I met a young woman I will call 'Dina', who, after a severe trauma, was in the middle of a psychotic episode.

Dina and I got to know one another in that closed ward, and she made some intense drawings alongside me. She gradually made her way back to herself, and hospital staff agreed she could come to the studio at John Reid House. Initially, she worked with me alone and then started attending open studio sessions with others. She was flamboyant and often worked very rapidly, creating collages that covered the floor, which we had to roll up like carpets at the end of each session. Those collages helped me, other staff members, and her to understand more about what had happened to her. Patients and staff liked and appreciated Dina. Her journey from the main hospital to the more open setting of John Reid House was possible because philosophies about mental health treatment were in flux and becoming more relaxed.

Nevertheless, Adamson would have known the constraints I found on Dina's ward in the main hospital. Indeed, his work would have mainly been to help those in the main hospital who lived in large, strictly controlled wards. This makes even more impressive the enabling approach he seems to have established in his studios.

In the Surrey History Centre archive, I found an old photo from 1959 that shows Adamson, smartly dressed in a suit and tie, but in a relaxed stance, with his artist/patients in one of the studios. Perhaps as hospital governance changed, it was possible to be more relaxed and less constrained by the conditions of the 'experiment' (Image 1.1).

When I began working at John Reid House, I was encouraged to join the nurses, occupational therapists and psychiatrists in morning community meetings with patients. This was a therapeutic community approach (Rapoport, 1967; Campling, 2022) that involved genuine efforts to work collaboratively, honestly and more permissively than traditional approaches to recovery. Adamson was aware (Hogan, 2000), as was Freudenberg (Becker & Bennett, 2000), of the burgeoning development of therapeutic communities and group

*Image 1.1* Edward Adamson in his studio, circa 1959.

Reproduced by permission of Surrey History Centre.

work from the end of World War II to the 1970s. Indeed, society became increasingly permissive from the 1960s. It is hard to imagine that this did not influence the context for Adamson's work and his approach, even when working alongside long-term patients who lived in large, crowded wards.

Adamson's descriptions of his life's work in his 1984 book *Art as Healing* intimated Jungian ideas about depth psychology and the centrality of creativity in healing processes:

> The hospital residents who came to the studio were accorded the dignity of helping to cure themselves.
>
> (p. 2)

Nevertheless, the different views about Adamson's approach in the art therapy profession suggest it was hard to categorise. Diane Waller (now Professor Emeritus) spoke in a 1978 lecture at Goldsmiths College, of Adamson's approach being based on a milieu-therapy model. I understand this to mean providing settings that facilitate a person's development through well-considered provision of space and time. Peter Byrne (1996) regarded Adamson's work as 'a-theoretical' (p. 32), whereas some aspects of what Adamson writes in *Art as Healing* (1984) suggest a collaborative approach born out of experience of working alongside people he increasingly saw as artists and not what Byrne described as 'very sick and disturbed people' (Byrne, 1996). Hogan (2000) saw Adamson's work as 'non-interventionist' (p. 169), which is different from 'a-theoretical'. She points to Adamson's affinity with Jungian ideas rooted in the Withymead community, which had been based on using various art forms alongside analytic psychology. There will be further discussion of Adamson's links to the Withymead Community in the next chapter.

When trying to categorise Adamson's approach, it is essential to remember that he worked at Netherne for more than three decades, and so his approach to practice would have evolved and changed. He began as a traditional lecturer, speaking to rooms full of patients about works by well-known artists, and then it seems that he took, at least in part, the approach of an art teacher. This may explain a memory of the person I have called 'Bryn' below, who told the art therapist Kevin Jones that Adamson occasionally drew on artwork made by people in the studio. Only gradually, it seems, did Adamson consolidate a sense of an 'art therapist' identity.

From what I heard from patients and colleagues who had worked with him, Adamson's approach to patients was always kind. As he became more skilled in his practice, he gradually became less prescriptive in setting out easels and materials. Bryn told me Adamson simply asked him: *would you like to do some painting?* He also asked people to work quietly. This quietness would have been a balm for those living on noisy wards.

Adamson moved on from his initial fear of the hospital as described above to a skilled acceptance of it and of his own work. The analytical psychoanalyst and art psychotherapist Joy Schaverien (1943–2025) worked alongside him at

St Albans College. She told me that he was engaging and playful, which may partly explain his ability to enable so many who came to his studios.

Bryn had lived in the hospital since the 1940s and visited me regularly when I worked in the John Reid studio. He thought of Adamson as a kind person. Bryn talked gently and with humour. He was studious in making his artwork, and he quickly established a place for himself in front of one of the bay windows in the studio (Image 1.2).

The artmaking absorbed him, and he seemed able to inhabit himself when it went well. But there were times when he came to the studio feeling low and hardly able to function. He spoke about the sheer number of years he had lived in the hospital, and he wondered what his life might have been like if he had not ever been admitted to Netherne shortly after the Second World War.

I also knew Rolanda Polonsky, another person who worked alongside Adamson. We do not need to conceal her name here, as her work is now well-known, and she was a celebrated artist before being admitted to Netherne with a diagnosis of psychosis. Adamson is said to have found her cleaning floors in the hospital. Rolanda made only a small number of visits to work with me in the John Reid House studio. She liked to draw to music played on our

*Image 1.2* The table where Bryn worked at Netherne Hospital circa April 1981.

Photo: Chris Wood.

old studio record player. She preferred not to talk much whilst drawing so sometimes, when there were a lot of people in the studio, she would come to collect art materials and take them away to work quietly in a studio created for her by Adamson that she shared with another client in the hospital grounds.

In the British Film Institute's *Rolanda Polonsky, Sculptor* (1971), filmed at Netherne, Rolanda tells the history of Christianity from a female perspective. She also worked outside alongside Adamson whilst casting the 14 sculptures of her *Stations of the Cross*. That they worked together outdoors, casting those large sculptures, adds another dimension to an understanding of Adamson's work. The sculptures demonstrate the collaborative range of his work. He did not simply sit as a passive enabler within indoor studios. He recognised those he worked alongside, and he valued their art.

It was evident from how Rolanda spoke about Adamson that she felt valued by him. This facilitated her sense of herself, her artmaking and her thinking. She lived at Netherne for 35 years before returning to live with her family in Paris and then moving to a convent in Italy, where she died in 1996.

I also benefited from the legacy of Adamson's studios and what they meant to me in being able to offer time, space and respect to the people who used them. Those who visited Adamson's studios could use art to look at what troubled them. However, extracting his work from the living context in which patients, staff and hospitals existed is not credible. Adamson's contributions, like those of all at the hospital, are pieces of a jigsaw, and no one piece can claim to be the cause of healing, though they were surely a valuable part.

Andrew Colley's memories of being a patient at Netherne Hospital more than forty years ago are in sharp contrast to his experience of admission to a modern mental health setting in 2020. His writing and research (Colley, 2024) enable him to piece together an understanding of what was helpful and what was not, and he describes powerfully the deterioration of many aspects of psychiatric in-patient treatment. His writing suggests that he understands why, during his second admission in 2020, he saw staff members in tears as they tried to comfort one another. During that admission, his seclusion room was nightmarish.

> One door with an observation window. Someone sat on the other side of that door and watched me all day and all night. No other windows, so I had no sense of time.
>
> (Colley, 2024, p. 92)

He does not suggest that the asylum system was in every way better than what we have now, and acknowledges that in the grounds of Netherne, there were what he describes as:

> villas…sinister places around which swirled rumour and innuendo about what they were for and what went on there, but if there were issues with restraint and confinement, even abuse, they were out of sight,
>
> (p. 26)

but the restricted space and clinical environment he found himself in 35 years later was markedly different from the time, space and understanding that Adamson had fostered at Netherne Hospital and substantially different from the time, space and understanding we all need when we are troubled.

In this chapter, we have drawn on our memories of Netherne Hospital, our research and our experiences of shifting mental health approaches to begin exploring the extent to which Adamson's work at Netherne continues to resonate in art therapy today, whilst acknowledging that today's in-patient settings are significantly different. Between the end of World War II and the present, there have been changes, some of which have not represented progress, but some which provide hope for the future. The next chapter, *Adamson in Context*, continues this exploration.

## References


Adamson, E. (1984). *Art as Healing.* London: Coventure Ltd.

Becker, T., & Bennett, D. (2000). Rudolf Karl Freudenberg — From pioneer of insulin treatment to pioneering social psychiatrist. *History of Psychiatry* 11(2), pp. 189–211.

Bowlby, J. (1988). *A Secure Base: Parent-Child Attachment and Healthy Human Development.* New York: Basic Books.

Byrne, P. (1996). Obituary: Edward Adamson and the experiment. *Inscape* 1(1), pp. 32–36. DOI: 10.1080/17454839608413025

Cambridge Jungian Circle (1994). *Visit to the Edward Adamson Collection* (May 29, 1994).

Campling, P. (2022). *Don't Turn Away: Stories of Troubled Minds in Fractured Times.* London: Elliott & Thompson.

Colley, A. (2024). *In-patient Mental Health Care from the Asylum System to the Present Day. A Lived Experience of Policy and Practice.* London: Routledge.

Cummings, C. (2017). The science of therapeutic images: Francis Reitman, schizophrenia and postwar psychiatric art at the Maudsley and Netherne Hospitals. *History of the Human Sciences* 30(2). https://doi.org/10.1177/0952695116687226

Hogan, S. (2000). British art therapy pioneer Edward Adamson: a non-interventionist approach. *History of Psychiatry* Xi, pp. 259–271.

Miskin, L. (Director). (1971). *Rolanda Polonsky, Sculptor.* British Film Institute.

Pinel, P. (1809). Traité médico-philosophique sur L'Aliénation mentale. (H. D. Gordon Hickish and L. Charland, Trans. second ed.). Paris: J. Ant. Brosson.

Rapoport, R. (1967). *Community as Doctor: New Perspectives on a Therapeutic Community.* London: Tavistock.

Waller, D. (1991). *Becoming a Profession: The History of Art Therapy, 1940–82.* London: Routledge.

Wills, C. (2021). Life pushed aside. *London Review of Books* 43(12), pp. 21–30.

# 2 Adamson in Context

*Chris Wood*

Adamson worked throughout times that ushered in huge social, cultural and political change in the UK. The infrastructure of the postwar welfare state in the UK was built on the nationalisation of education, health, social care and public transport (Loach, 2013), and in culture, there was a sense of democratisation (Byrne, 2002) and acceptance of art made by people outside the established art world (Dubuffet, 1949). This chapter places Adamson's work at Netherne Hospital in the context of these changes and explores their impact on the development of art therapy in in-patient settings. The first part of this chapter discusses the historical context of Adamson's life, before examining the shared context and history of those who were patients at Netherne.

## The Context of Adamson's Life

Although this book is not a biography, it does consider how the circumstances of Adamson's life may have influenced his work and its development at Netherne. This is part of gauging how Adamson's legacy continues to influence the work of art therapists today. As a non-combatant conscientious objector during World War II and a homosexual, Adamson was not a stranger to the potential for societal disapproval. Many conscientious objectors were treated hostilely in the press, by their families and on the streets. Any person who would not fight on grounds of conscience had to attend a tribunal. A few were sent to prison for the duration of the war and could not vote for ten years. Others were assigned a non-combatant role in the army. Adamson was assigned to the army medical corps, where he used his training as a chiropodist and in that role, he would have seen and heard what soldiers from the frontline had to face, and this almost certainly gave him some ideas about how to help them psychologically. Interviewed for this book, Adamson's great nephew, Mark, who was close to his great uncle, offers this insight into the impact this work in the medical corps had on Edward:

> *He told me something interesting: whilst undertaking his 'feet' related duties, he became very aware of the pent-up boredom and frustration on the wards full of returned and injured fighting men. This frustration led to*

DOI: 10.4324/9781003613428-4

> *everything from withdrawal, depression and fights. On seeing this, and as a trained artist, he introduced and encouraged the men to sketch etc. I think at this stage it was principally to fill their time, but he saw the calming effect. This developed into an Art Club and the rest is history.*

Adamson's friend, Adrian Hill (1895–1977), had served in the Artillery during the First World War from 1914 to 1917, and he was then appointed an official war artist for the Imperial War Museum. His book *Art Versus Illness* (1945) describes the benefits of art making for his own struggles with leukaemia and those of fellow patients, and the term *art therapy* is attributed to him. Around the same time, groups known as *The Northfield Experiments* were being used with former soldiers grappling with the trauma of war at Northfield Military Hospital in Birmingham. Accounts of the experience of soldiers in those psychological groups (Harrison & Clarke, 1992) provide a powerful indication of the intense post-war trauma faced by former soldiers, those trying to help them and the population at large. Hill used art to help returning soldiers from both World War I and World War II, and for a time, Adamson volunteered to work alongside him. It was through Hill's connections with the Red Cross Picture Lending Library that Adamson found himself in 1946 giving that first talk to psychiatric patients at Netherne about famous artworks from the Red Cross collection.

In an early article in the journal *Mental Health* (1965), Adamson acknowledged that when he started his career at Netherne, the surroundings were very different, but as the environment changed under more progressive approaches, so did the response to art created by the patients:

> As the treatments and restrictions changed, the 'Prinzhorn type' of drawing gradually disappeared, and a much freer type of work resulted, almost as a corollary to the abolition of padded cells and bars. Now, I work in a different world to the one I first entered, but it is a freer world.
>
> (Adamson, 1965, p. 274)

This reference to padded cells and bars is a stark reminder of conditions in psychiatric hospitals just after World War II. Hans Prinzhorn (1886–1933) was a psychiatrist who collected rich examples of art made in mental hospitals across Europe. He was fascinated by patient artwork and his collection included extraordinary works by artists such as August Natterer (1868–1933), Else Blankenhorn (1873–1920), Karl Genzel (1871–1925) and Adolf Wölfli (1864–1930). Their work was remarkably detailed, suggesting considerable time had been spent on it. So, although we do not know what exactly Adamson thought of as a 'Prinzhorn type' of drawing, and we know that he had not visited a psychiatric hospital before arriving at Netherne in 1946, we do know that the concept of extraordinary art collections was part of his experience and lexicon.

For the remainder of his working life, as we have seen in the previous chapter, Adamson helped the patients at Netherne Hospital find their own vivid expression for their inner world, and he became skilled at encouraging people in a wide range of psychological states to find expression in making art. In contrast, his own private life as a homosexual had to remain closeted. It was only in 1967 that the Sexual Offences Act partially decriminalised homosexual relationships, and before this, he and his partner risked imprisonment or unemployment if they came out. This, alongside his earlier experience as a conscientious objector, may have heightened his sensitivity and responsiveness to the lives of people hidden from society in Netherne's locked wards.

Adamson was also undoubtedly influenced by the work of Irene Champernowne (1901–1976) and her husband, Gilbert (1892–1959), who developed the Withymead therapeutic community in a large Georgian house with outbuildings several miles outside Exeter in Devon. The community functioned in a number of studios and a pottery, using Jungian principles and a belief in the healing qualities of wide-ranging forms of artmaking (Stevens, 1986). Hogan (2000) records that Adamson became friends with Irene Champernowne and introduced the art therapist Rupert Cracknell to work alongside her at Withymead.

The approach to art in the studios at Withymead was recorded by the art therapist, Norah Godfrey, as follows:

> A little group began painting in the loft of the outbuildings or in the garden. The loft was old with rugged walls and wooden beams, dusty and a place for playing or finding solitude as much as for painting.
>
> (Hogan, 2000, p. 262)

Adamson will have taken sustenance from this approach to studios and from what another art therapist working at Withymead, Michael Edwards (1930–2010), told me was the respect shown to pieces of artwork made by community members. Indeed, Adamson's own creation of multiple welcoming studios at Netherne, along with his respect for the artwork as evident in his collection and publications, is a strong part of his legacy.

## The Psychological Aftermath of War and the Great Depression

A range of psychological approaches emerged in response to the social, economic and cultural conditions of those times. In 2021, the analyst Giuseppe Civitarese reviewed the third volume of D.W. Winnicott's *Collected Works.* Donald Winnicott (1896–1971), the celebrated paediatrician and psychoanalyst, wrote extensively about the centrality of play in human relationships (Winnicott, 1971) and is much appreciated by art therapists. He also wrote in lay language and made radio broadcasts (Wellcome Foundation, 1949–1964) to help families cope with the psychological aftermath of World War II. Civitarese helpfully speculates that Winnicott's approach to psychological safety was, in part, a response to a broader societal need following the War. He writes that the element in Winnicott's work that reoccurs repeatedly is a response to the plea for a sense of safety. Adamson too understood the need to offer safe places in studios set apart from the main hospital, and this may have arisen from elements of his own experience and a sensitive response to what the people in the hospital had endured: the complex experiences of people post-war and post the great depression.

Throughout the world, people in Europe, and indeed the patients at Netherne, had suffered from the hunger, homelessness and poverty of the Great Depression (1929–1939). They had been shocked by the barbarity of World War II and the discovery of the concentration camps. The grief, loss, death and economic hardship of those times were pervasive. In Ken Loach's film *The Spirit of '45* (2013), we are offered a glimpse of a celebratory post-war period. Well-constructed documentary film clips convey the fear that post-war populations had of returning to the hardships and mass unemployment of the inter-war years. People are recorded as feeling that after the war, they became their brothers and sisters' keepers: they welcomed the 1942 Beveridge reforms, they applauded the creation of the National Health Service and the nationalisation of transport. Many dwellings were constructed, and amongst other reforms, school education was made free. Although another of Ken Loach's films, *Cathy Come Home* (1966), shows that reforms were slow, and some people continued to live precariously through no fault of their own.

Nevertheless, when Adamson began working, it was not usual to think beyond the pathology of the individual. Some patients at Netherne would have struggled through periods of unemployment, homelessness and hunger during what was a severe economic depression between the wars, and the resulting strain could have been the cause of admission. The period leading up to the mid-twentieth century witnessed an increase in the number of people admitted to mental hospitals, a phenomenon known as passive accumulation, resulting in approximately 150,000 admissions by the mid-1950s (Houston, 2020). Those admitted experienced stigma and prejudice, and the prevailing attitude was that mental health problems were incurable, so psychiatric hospitals were highly structured and institutionalised (Warner, 1985).

Adamson's early exhibitions of patient art at Netherne provided information about diagnoses, and initially, he viewed this information as part of his educational role. In contemporary times, however, it has gradually become recognised that social and economic circumstances, in combination with the trauma in a person's life, are central to mental health (e.g. Campling, 2022; Marchi et al., 2024; Read et al., 2020; Warner, 1985). We will hear later in this book about the place of art in trauma-informed therapy.

## Patients or Artists?

As we have seen, individuals who created art as part of their association with psychiatry were increasingly recognised by Adamson and others as artists in their own right, and as we know, Adamson curated and collected about 60,000 artwork pieces created by patients throughout his career at Netherne.

In the same timeframe as Adamson was making his collection, Jean Dubuffet (1901–1995) in Europe was gathering examples of what he named *Art Brut* (using the word *brut* to imply exceptional in the way that fine wine is described) by people untrained in the traditional arts. Dubuffet's collection was purposely different from those made in mental hospitals, but it aroused similar curiosity and imagination. The circularity of connections is seen in the fact that Dubuffet visited and engaged with Prinzhorn's collection of patient artwork. Dubuffet almost certainly shared a version of Prinzhorn's view (1972) that the extraordinary artwork (whether made inside or outside hospitals) did not offer a means of diagnosis, but evidence of the creative urge.

> Prinzhorn's desire to treat the works under consideration as true artistic products led to the decision to treat their makers as individuals.
>
> (Rhodes, 2000, p. 66)

The idea of treating the makers of such work as sentient individuals with life experiences, minds and imaginations spread. In the UK, Roger Cardinal's book on such artwork was initially to be titled *The Art of the Artless*, but his publisher did not think the title would help the book sell. As a result, the title *Outsider Art* (1972) was ultimately agreed upon. Agnès Cardinal, his wife, spoke after Cardinal's death (Jennifer Lauren Gallery, 2020) about the core of his interest being based on surrealism, and then, through his life, developing into what he saw as an exploration of 'innocent' artistic motivation. Cardinal was particularly moved by the artwork of Madge Gill (1882–1961) because of its fascinating and elegant detail. Gill spoke with Roger Cardinal about how spontaneous artwork had helped her find ways to stay alive in the challenging circumstances of being brought up in one of the Barnardo Care Homes (Cardinal, 1972).

The art therapist David Maclagan (2009) traced the emergence and understanding of outsider artworks. In a thoughtful analysis, he wrote that one of the purposes of Dubuffet's collection was 'to free these works from any association with psychopathology and to recognise them as examples of uncompromising individual forms of creativity' (p. 13).

As mental health approaches changed, and possibly as tangential knowledge of *Outsider Art* increased, people admitted to mental hospitals were recognised as having agency. The complexity of viewing and understanding the artwork they made was intertwined with a growing sense of their dignity and human rights. Also, cultural forms were expanding to include radio, music, magazines, newspapers, cartoons, cinema and TV. All of these were food for imagination, and they gradually found their way into mental hospitals. Adamson lived and worked throughout these evolving times, and his life partner, John Timlin, wrote a loving obituary in *The Guardian* in 1996, suggesting that Adamson increasingly viewed his patients as artists.

The interest in art making of psychiatrists Dax and Reitman discussed in the previous chapter was new and came at a time in psychiatric history when in huge, carefully controlled institutions, insulin therapy, electroconvulsive therapy (ECT) and lobotomy were still common psychiatric practices. As seen in Chapter 1, from the 1950s, Adamson came under the auspices of the psychiatrist R. K. Freudenberg, and his reforming approach gradually began to foster different approaches to the way patients were viewed, and slowly, some consideration of how the *people* who were patients might help in their own recovery took shape. Warner's seminal work (1985) considers the effects of the economy on treatment methods throughout the twentieth century and finds that history has tended mistakenly to associate the reforming approaches to psychiatric wards of people like Freudenberg with the advent of anti-psychotic medication. In fact, Warner demonstrates, in Northern Europe, the introduction of social therapies preceded and rivalled antipsychotic medication in their impact on the rehabilitation of patients, and he cites the work of Freudenberg at Netherne Hospital, who observed a general improvement in care during the period from 1945 to 1948:

> ...The changes for the better being evident from the larger number of open wards, the increased freedom patients are able to enjoy, the abolition of restraint and strong clothing, and the diminution of seclusion, aggression and incontinence.
>
> (Freudenberg et al., 1959, p. 159)

In Chapter 1, it is noted that Adamson himself increasingly operated an open-door policy, allowing people to drop in to the studios. One of my Sheffield teaching colleagues, Therese Richardson, told me she had fond memories of Adamson from when she was training under him as an art therapist at St Albans College. She remembered him hosting relaxed studio sessions for students and how she was asked the same question as 'Bryn', who was introduced in the previous chapter. *Would you like to do some painting?* At Netherne, the permission to drop in to relaxed, quiet studios must have been a stark contrast for patients, who were more accustomed to noisy wards and strictly structured institutional days at that time.

## Art as Therapy

During the 1960s and 1970s, Adamson disseminated some of his ideas about his work through several publications (e.g. 1965). Additionally, he became involved in promoting the creation of a profession of art therapy. John Henzell had worked as a lecturer at St Albans before joining the course team in Sheffield (Henzell, 2019). He smiles when remembering Adamson, from the time of setting up the British Association of Art Therapists (BAAT). It appears that early meetings were coloured by drama, and Edward Adamson was frequently involved in heated discussions alongside others who were attempting to establish BAAT. John remembers one occasion when Adamson stormed out of a meeting with a parting comment over his shoulder: *I am art therapy*! Adamson was to become the first chair of BAAT in 1963. However, it was not until 1984, in his book *Art as Healing*, that he wrote more extensively about his work.

Verhagan (2021) suggests that it is an injustice that too many people do not have the time and space to reflect on their lives, describing this lack as a source of inequality and dysfunction. Encounters in mental health services, including art therapy, might be some of the few times working-age and older adults are offered a sense of legitimate time to reflect upon their lives and the struggles they have faced. In art therapy, individuals may discover delight in ways to value their imagination.

During Adamson's work in the hospital, institutionalisation gradually relinquished its hold. The Mental Health Act of 1959 began to liberalise the conditions under which people were detained and give more weight to treatment approaches that involved the patient. There have been efforts to liberalise treatment approaches further, but although there have been genuine efforts for reform and the introduction of community care, many involuntary admissions continue because the funding from mental hospital closures did not necessarily follow services into the community (Barham, 2020). In May 2024, the UK's Mental Health Services were ranked by the Global Mind Project (2025) as the second-worst in the world.

Epidemiologist Kate Pickett writes in a blog post:

> ...That all aspects of what constitutes a good life must be considered holistically, whether it's access to health care and education or a strong sense of connection to one's community. It is growth in wellbeing that we need, and growth in mature, evidence-based debate or what works, not growth in outmoded GDP.
>
> (Pickett, 2023)

Whilst acknowledging that the profession is small (with some 6,000 HCPC-registered arts therapists in 2024), art therapists have found themselves needing to adapt to various restricted service settings, including psychiatric hospitals, forensic services, schools, community provision and work at international borders with refugees. As some of the chapters in the remainder of the book will demonstrate, art therapists have been successful in adapting to changing sets of circumstances. There appears to have been a core value in art therapy since World War II of trying, alongside other professions, to respond to the plea for safety and help with finding space to think, create and make a life. This is because, as in Adamson's time, the world remains a tumultuous place for people to live. Nevertheless, a positive feature of the contemporary period has been the increasing acknowledgement of the client voice. The shape of art therapy is widely shown to be reflecting this shift (Lloyd et al., 2018; Springham & Xenophontes, 2021; Wood, 2011, 2020).

One key idea from Warner's research is startling:

> Antipsychotic drugs appear to be more effective for the psychotic patient who is living in an inadequate setting and to be less valuable where the environment is designed for his or her well-being.
>
> (Warner, 1985, p. 86)

It highlights the importance of Adamson's legacy in offering adequate time and good places to meet with the human beings we encounter in art therapy, and this theme of creating *enabling spaces* for effective art therapy will be discussed extensively in Chapter 4 and elsewhere in this book. The next chapter, though, and to conclude Part I, will explore issues around curating, collecting and exhibiting artworks by people in in-patient wards – practices embraced by Adamson but which since then have often proved to be complex and controversial.

## References

Adamson, E. (1965). Review of Plokker, J. H. "Artistic Self-expression in mental disease: The Shattered image of Schizophrenics". Charles Skilton Ltd. *Mental Health* 24(6), pp. 272–274.

Adamson, E. (1984). *Art as Healing*. London: Coventure Ltd.

Barham, P. (2020). *Closing the Asylum – The Mental Patient in Modern Society*. London: Process Press.

Byrne, P. (2002). *Art Therapy: A Developmental Narrative. From Symptom and Theory to Cultural Paradigms*. [Unpublished doctoral dissertation]. The University of Edinburgh.

Campling, P. (2022). *Don't Turn Away: Stories of Troubled Minds in Fractured Times*. London: Elliott & Thompson.

Cardinal, R. (1972). *Outsider Art*. London: Studio Vista.

Civitarese, G. (2021). The collected works of D. W. Winnicott: Volume 3. 1946–1951. *Journal of the American Psychoanalytic Association* 68(6), pp. 1143–1154. https://doi.org/10.1177/0003065120980137 (Original work published 2020).

Dubuffet, J. (1949). Art Brut preferred to the cultural arts. In Weiss, A. S. (Ed.) *Art Brut: Madness and Marginalia [Art & Text 27 Special Issue, December–February 1988]*, 198–202. Manhattan Beach, CA: Epilonian Books Published by City Art Institute, 1988.

Freudenberg, R. K., Bennet, D. H., & May, A. R. (1959). The relative importance of physical and community methods in the treatment of schizophrenia. In Fussli (1959) *International Congress of Psychiatry*. Zurich, pp. 157–178.

Global Mind Project (2025). Mental state of the world in 2024. *Sapien Labs*. www.sapienlabs.org/global-mind-project/researcher-hub

Harrison, T., & Clarke, D. (1992). The Northfield experiments. *British Journal of Psychiatry* 160, pp. 698–708.

Henzell, J. (2019). Psyche Nullius: reflections on art psychotherapy and psychiatry down under. In Gilroy, A., Linnell, S., McKenna, T., & Westwood, J. (Eds.) *Art Therapy in Australia: Taking a Postcolonial. Aesthetic Turn*. Leiden/Boston: Brill Sense, pp. 115–133.

Hill, A. (1945). *Art Versus Illness*. London: George Allen and Unwin Ltd.

Hogan, S. (2000). *Healing Arts: The History of Art Therapy.* London and Philadelphia: Jessica Kingsley Publishers.

Houston, R. A. (2020). Asylums: The historical perspective before, during, and after. *The Lancet Psychiatry* 7(4), pp. 354–362.

Jennifer Lauren Gallery. (2020, October 28). *Recorded Conversation about the Late Roger Cardinal.* https://www.jenniferlaurengallery.com/news-press-media/roger-cardinal-interview

Lloyd, B., Press, N., & Usiskin, M. (2018). The Calais Winds took our plans away: Art therapy as shelter. *Journal of Applied Arts & Health* 9(2), pp. 171–184. https://doi.org/10.1386/jaah.9.2.171_1

Loach, K. (Director). (2013). *The Spirit of '45* (Film). British Film Institute.

Loach, K., & Sandford, J. (1966, November 16). *Cathy Come Home. Wednesday Play: 16:11:1966*, 90 minutes, black and white. BBC TV. British Film Institute Screenonline archive.

Maclagan, D. (2009). *Outsider Art: From the Margins to the Marketplace.* London: Reaktion Books.

Marchi, M., Alkema, A., Xia, C. et al. (2024). Investigating the impact of poverty on mental illness in the UK Biobank using Mendelian randomization. *Nature Human Behaviour* 8, pp. 1771–1783 doi: https://doi.org/10.1038/s41562-024-01919-3. Epub 2024 Jul 10.

Pickett, K. (2023, February 2). Will governments prioritise wellbeing? Equality trust. *Blog InequalityTrust.*https://equalitytrust.org.uk/news/blog/will-governments-prioritise-wellbeing-or-let-inequality-damage-mental-health/

Prinzhorn, H. (1972). *Artistry of the Mentally Ill* (Translated by E. von Brockdorff). New York: Springer Verlag.

Read, J., Morrison, T., & Waddingham, R. (2020). Traumas, adversities, and psychosis: Investigating practical implications. *Psychiatric Times* 37(7), 48–50.

Rhodes, C. (2000). *Outsider Art.* London and New York. Thames and Hudson.

Springham, N., & Xenophontes, I. (2021). Democratising the discourse: Co-production in art therapy practice, research and publication. *International Journal of Art Therapy* 26 (1–2), pp. 1–7. https://doi.org/10.1080/17454832.2021.1912939

Stevens, A. (1986). *Withymead: A Jungian Community for the Healing Arts.* London: Coventure.

Timlin, J. (1996, February 12). *Art as a Panacea: Edward Adamson Obituary.* London: Guardian.UK

Verhagan, M. (2021). Making time. *New Left Review* 129, pp. 97–106.

Warner, R. (1985). *Recovery from Schizophrenia: Psychiatry and Political Economy.* London and New York: Routledge Kegan Paul.

Wellcome Collection. (1949–1964). The child and the family: The original BBC talks by Dr. D. W. Winnicott. No. 1. https://wellcomecollection.org/works/rvfggcsv

Winnicott, D. W. (1971). *Playing and Reality.* London: Pelican.

Wood, C. (2011). *Navigating Art Therapy: A Therapist's Companion.* London: Routledge.

Wood, C. (2020). Hearing voices movement and art therapy. *Art Therapy* 37(2), pp. 88–92. https://doi.org/10.1080/07421656.2020.1756138

# 3 The Adamson Collection and Its Relevance to Contemporary Art Therapy Practice

*Val Huet*

## Introduction

For 35 years, Edward Adamson provided a space where residents of Netherne Hospital were treated with care and respect, and made thousands of artworks under his watchful, but non-interfering, presence. There is no way of knowing how many of these drawings, paintings, sculptures and three-dimensional artworks were produced and stored in Adamson's studios, but although many were lost through different events, thousands remain. For instance, when Dr Cunningham Dax, the Netherne medical superintendent who employed Adamson in 1946, moved to Australia in 1952, he took with him many of these artworks to start his own collection now sited in Melbourne (Ostrowska, 2015). Additionally, although many artworks were thrown away following Adamson's retirement in 1981 (O'Flynn et al., 2018), 2500 drawings and paintings are currently stored at the Wellcome Library in London. The Adamson Collection is a rich resource for anyone interested in outsider art, art therapy and twentieth-century psychiatric care, but its merit is not limited to historical legacy, and this chapter will reflect on the Collection's relevance to contemporary art therapy practice.

Psychiatric asylum residents were often marginalised, and the collection's artworks are a vivid testimony to how they used art to have a voice and tell their stories. These artworks ensured their lives were not forgotten, and in the first part of the chapter, I will explore how this resonates with the contemporary context.

The collection also raises ethical issues on the ownership and public exhibition of artworks created in art therapy, and in the second part, I will explore past and current practice around collecting and exhibiting, as well as the legal framework governing the ownership of artworks and the naming of the artist.

Finally, I will reflect on how Adamson's practice of exhibiting residents' artworks disappeared for a while, which coincided with a dominance of psychoanalytic theory within UK art therapy. The contemporary resurgence of this practice reflects a growing confidence in our art roots, mirrored by the growth of art therapy in galleries and museums. Exhibitions of service users'

DOI: 10.4324/9781003613428-5

artworks now also highlight a strong commitment to a co-production ethos within art therapy practice.

## Forgotten Lives: Then and Now

I started my art therapy career in 1986 at Warley Hospital in Essex in the UK, a large Victorian psychiatric institution that provided day services and long-term wards for people who had spent most of their lives as in-patients. 'Care in the Community' was about to be rolled out, a process still unfolding when I took up an art therapy post at Springfield Hospital, in Tooting, London, in 1991. Then, people who had hardly had a life outside of an institution were on 'rehabilitation' wards to prepare them for their new circumstances. They were the last of a group of institutionalised clients who would soon be moved to small group homes, where promised improvements in their quality of life did not always materialise (Colley, 2024). Many of them were from pre- and post-Second World War generations and had been initially admitted because of mental health issues, or for breaking social norms such as having a child out of wedlock, or being gay, as had been the case since Victorian Times (Wise, 2014).

Both Warley and Springfield hospitals had large art therapy studios: Warley's was in a disused bakery, and Springfield's was in an airy and well-lit space, reminiscent of art school studios. The permanence and size of both rooms enabled a rich array of art materials to be offered, and artworks could be stored for long periods of time, as there was little pressure on space. Clients could make messy art without feeling inhibited by, for instance, a carpeted space. Studio groups in the style and approach developed by Adamson were a regular feature of the art therapy programme. They were popular and well attended by people who, like Adamson's clients, made innumerable artworks.

Most service users did not have anyone who had shared their childhood or who had been a consistent presence in their adult lives. Their life stories were held in clinical notes, and often limited to a list of diagnoses, admission dates and medications. How and why they were initially admitted was often in the form of a text copied from one document to the next. However, within the art therapy room, service users' stories came alive in their artworks, and significant experiences were represented and shared with me and with other group members. It did not matter if recollections were at times jumbled and confusing: the artworks were taken seriously by all, and service users were given time to describe them when they wished to do so. During this time, I became aware of the power of art in helping people find purpose and significance in marginal and often forgotten lives. This experience highlighted how artmaking mediates a profound human need to communicate, be understood and feel connected to others, especially when reality feels fragmented and confusing, and that need is prominent today: it is still rare for service users with longer term needs to maintain connections to friends and family. The resulting isolation and loneliness have devastating consequences, as highlighted in a Nuffield

Trust report (2024): over a quarter of suicides between 2010 and 2021 involved mental health service users.

Although made in a different social and cultural context, the Adamson Collection artworks resonate powerfully with themes of alienation, and many depict movingly the anguish of experiencing mental health distress. They also reflect how people used art to keep parts of themselves intact through creativity, rebellion and humour. Adamson (1984) described how, when first visiting the locked wards at Netherne Hospital, where no artmaking facilities were provided, he was given drawings made by patients on torn book pages and lavatory paper, using burnt matchsticks, such as those made by 'a very ill man who had been in a locked ward for many years' (p. 9). One strip of paper references 'J.J. Beegan, Sculpterer' (*sic*), but this may not have been his real name (Image 3.1).

Although I do not know his intention or the meaning of his artwork, my response is one of admiration for a proud claim to an artist's identity, and for his determination and resourcefulness in producing art with no access to materials, in what could be a rebellious response to circumstances.

These life- and identity-affirming artworks, often infused with rebelliousness, are a familiar feature of contemporary art therapy practice and continue to challenge stigmatising perceptions of mental health service users.

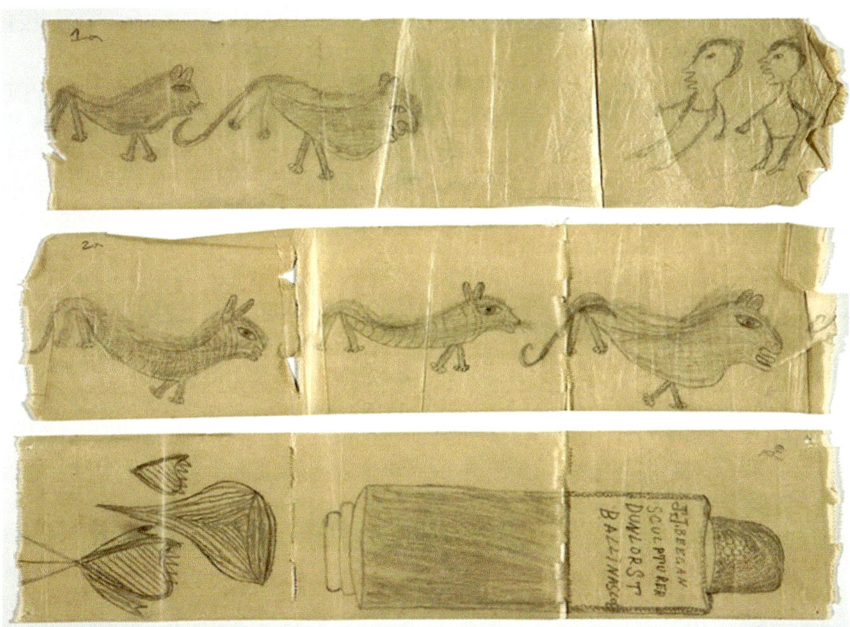

*Image 3.1 Graffiti on Lavatory Paper*, all undated. Creator known as JJ Beegan (c. 1946), match charcoal on Izal Medicated Toilet Tissue.

Courtesy of Wellcome Collection. Image copyright: Adamson Collection Trust.

## Whose Art Is It Anyway?

All of the artworks in the Adamson Collection were significant to the makers. However, it is unclear if at the time they were considered to be the owners of their artworks or were consulted about their storage, disposal or use in exhibitions (Ostrowska, 2015).

The issue of ownership of clients' artworks is still live within contemporary art therapy practice. Adamson and his colleagues practised in different cultural and legal times, and it would now be deemed unethical to keep and display clients' artworks without their knowledge and informed consent. Dedicated art therapy space in healthcare settings has become increasingly rare in the NHS since the early 2000s (Morrison & Anderton, 2007), and storage of artworks is becoming problematic during and post-therapy. Currently, most art therapists assume that service users own their artworks and usually offer them the option to take these home after therapy ends. If service users leave artworks uncollected, the British Association of Art Therapists (BAAT) advises that these should be disposed of following guidelines on disposal of confidential material (BAAT, 2018). The issue of keeping physical artefacts has also evolved, as most service users now have smartphones and prefer to keep a digital record of their artworks. During assessment, art therapists often explore with them the issue of posting artworks from art therapy on social media platforms and the potential impact of negative or uninformed responses to their posts.

Some organisations may take the view that as they fund the art therapist, the materials and the space, then the artworks themselves ultimately belong to them. In July 2017, the Wellcome Collection, in partnership with the Adamson Collection trustees, hosted a series of public consultations on ethical issues linked to the collection, and the first event explored the artworks' ownership. The Adamson Collection trustees considered themselves to be the caretakers of this body of work (O'Flynn et al., 2018), now legally classified as 'abandoned chattels/goods' (O'Flynn & Schupbach, 2019, p. 25). A consensus emerged that the makers, and not the institution, should own the artworks (O'Flynn et al., 2018), a view largely shared by UK art therapists in their current practice, as stated above. This issue remains, nevertheless, a live concern: a group of lawyers, art therapists and arts in health practitioners, in consultation with service users, are currently developing a guideline, *Who owns outsider art? Good practice in attending to visual artworks made in Art Therapy and Arts & Health.* (Pavis et al., 2025). The project is Wellcome Trust funded. As well as interviewing service users and practitioners, they are consulting the Health and Care Professions Council's statutory arts therapies standards of proficiency (2025a) and of conduct, performance and ethics (2025b) and the legal framework in England and Wales. However, although this guideline will be helpful when completed and published, and despite a general consensus that the makers own the artworks, the legal basis of ownership of artworks will not be unequivocally established until tested in a court of law.

Naming the artists and making their identity public is also a live issue in contemporary art therapy practice and was explored in the second public consultation at the Wellcome Collection. Adamson recorded the artists' names on most artworks, a practice taken up by most art therapists. This enabled the trustees to identify several artists and contact surviving relatives who may have wanted to claim the artworks (O'Flynn et al., 2018), a task requiring care and tact. It was not possible to know the artists' wishes on revealing their identities, and some participants felt that, since they had not been consulted in their lifetime, they should remain anonymous and their artworks should not be displayed. Indeed, a letter by Gwynneth Rowlands, well-known for her prolific and striking pebbles and flints paintings (Image 3.2), requesting to remain anonymous, was found posthumously, and too late to honour her wishes.

However, a consensus emerged on how important it was to name people who had been dehumanised in psychiatric institutions and had lost their identity as a result.

*Image 3.2* Untitled (Woman and Child). Gwyneth Rowlands. c.1962–1982. Poster paint, Indian ink and varnish on flint.

Courtesy of Wellcome Collection. Image copyright: Adamson Collection Trust.

## Exhibiting Service Users' Artworks

Adamson (1984) thought that artworks produced in the studios should not be displayed on the hospital's walls, as this would be too reminiscent of schoolrooms. Instead, he set up a gallery space within the hospital, where residents' artworks could be viewed by appointment and also used as part of healthcare professionals' training. It is unclear how these artworks were selected, and residents were not consulted on exhibiting their artworks, or aware that these were shown not only within the Netherne gallery but also in other national and international settings (Ostrowska, 2015). Adamson also displayed the artworks anonymously and did not name the artists. The gallery remained open until Adamson's retirement in 1981, when, to Adamson's great disappointment, it was turned into a physiotherapy suite (Colley, 2024).

Exhibiting clients' artworks early on in the development of art therapy may have been the foundation of a thriving approach to practice that would have grown to integrate a contemporary ethical and consultative framework. However, from the mid-1980s, British art therapy became increasingly influenced by psychoanalysis (Brown & Omand, 2022) and many, including Adamson, felt that the art was being left behind. This 'psychoanalytic turn' (Brown & Omand, 2022, p. 14) was investigated by Brown and Omand (2022), who, having interviewed art therapists mostly supportive of a psychoanalytic approach, found no evidence of a detrimental effect on studio practice and the perception of its value. This teleological conclusion contrasts with evidence published at the time: influential studies by McNeilly on group analytic art therapy (1984, 1987) were critical of theme-based, directive art therapy and of the art therapists who used this approach. The fear that anything other than non-directive, psychoanalytic-based was not 'proper art therapy' (Springham, 2013, p. 11) may have 'established a form of censorship (…) inhibiting the development of art therapy'. (Springham, 2013).

Indeed, this was echoed in my experience as a visiting lecturer: colleagues offering practice placements in the 1990s and early 2000s often apologised for offering studio and open groups and *not doing proper art therapy.*

Worryingly, artworks seemed to disappear from art therapy spaces: colleagues who espoused a psychoanalytic 'hardline' argued for removing posters, art books and any trace of other clients' artworks from their practice space so as to not influence any potential transference issues. Art produced in art therapy sessions was deemed to be seen only by the art therapist and their supervisor, but never shared with team members. The notion that service users may wish to share their artworks and benefit from exhibiting these became an alien concept.

It is, therefore, reassuring to witness a return to Adamson's practice of exhibiting service users' artworks, done within a contemporary framework of informed consent and using a co-production approach (Springham & Xenophontes, 2021).

In 2009, in my previous role as the Chief Executive Officer of the BAAT, I organised a conference and an exhibition on art therapy and physical conditions. The exhibition, in the Together Gallery near Old Street, London, was co-produced with service users and art therapists, and included artworks and written comments and reflections from both. Service users were given a choice of sharing their identity or remaining anonymous, and were supported by their therapist to reach the decision that felt right for them. Richardson (2009) reviewed the event and noted that exhibiting service users' artworks remained a contentious issue in art therapy. He described the exhibition as reflecting a process of self-discovery through art making for service users, and concluded that, rather than continuing to avoid the issue, the exhibition 'began a long overdue process of engaging with how work can be shown in a way which respects it, the person who made it, and the therapeutic process from which it derives'. (p. 11). One of the service users exhibiting her artworks was interviewed by Richardson and shared how, since she had no formal art background, she found it strange to be described as an artist. Nevertheless, she was inspired by this and planned on trying new media and developing her art practice.

It can be said (Coles & Jury, 2020) that the growth of art therapy practice in art galleries and museums reflects a new confidence in our art roots and identity. In 2009, a seminal conference at Tate Britain, organised in partnership with Oxleas NHS Trust and the BAAT, asked: *What is a gallery for?* (BAAT, 2009) and explored several strands, including the *Gallery as Mind*, where art therapists and curators collaborate to improve access to museums and galleries for people who experience complex psychological issues, and the *Gallery as Community*, where service user-led groups can work together with curators on art-based projects.

There are a growing number of examples of exhibitions of service users' artworks, either within an art therapy studio (Martyn, 2022), an art gallery (Armstrong, 2022) or a host organisation (Richardson, 2022), and in Chapter 6 there is an account of the innovative *Bounceback* project in New South Wales, Australia, which exhibits art by service users from mental health settings. Exhibiting service users' work is also seen as an opportunity to support social change by increasing viewers' empathy (Potash et al., 2013). Armstrong (2022) describes transgender people's experiences of 'Transitioning into visibility' (p. 116) in their Northern Canadian community when deciding to exhibit their artworks in an art gallery. The 'client-artists' (p. 120) were actively involved in selecting and presenting their artworks, setting the artworks' sale prices and choosing to disclose their identity or remain anonymous. Armstrong stated that 'the purpose of the art therapy groups was not to learn coping skills to exist within the oppressed and marginalised community that they live in but to create change in the culture of Yukon Territory'. (p. 124).

Retrospectively, it feels that much was lost in art therapy when Adamson's practice of exhibiting service users' artworks was abandoned on his retirement. This included opportunities to challenge stigmatising views of mental health amongst professionals and the public, and to influence social change. Sadly, rigid views on confidentiality led to confusing barriers as boundaries, and the art therapy room was often seen as having a perpetually closed door (Learmonth, 2002). As stated above, our current ethical and legal framework now ensures that service users are consulted and actively involved in decisions on their care, including art therapy, and when given the opportunity and the right support, many choose to exhibit their artworks.

## Reflections

In this chapter, I have focused on The Adamson Collection's relevance to contemporary art therapy practice: artworks made between the 1950s and 1980s by people experiencing emotional distress reflect the devastating impact of isolation and loneliness, and the need to communicate and connect with the self and others. They can also be humorous and rebellious, and challenge a view of service users as being narrowly defined by their mental health conditions. They also ensure that their lives are not forgotten and erased.

Important ethical questions are raised by The Adamson Collection and link to contemporary practice, including the ownership of artworks, naming the artist and exhibiting clients' artworks. However, art therapists are increasingly practising in galleries and museums, and co-producing exhibitions of artworks with their clients. As a result, they are actively engaging with complex issues and developing approaches that are ethical and beneficial for service users.

Adamson, as was discussed in Chapter 2, was a gay man at a time when homosexuality was illegal. He, too, had to live his life marginally and within a hostile culture that did not tolerate difference. He will have been painfully aware of the devastating impact of suppressing identity:

> In the stark dormitories, the long rows of iron beds offered no seclusion, as they were not curtained off from each other. The practice of taking communal showers afforded no personal dignity, neither was there any privacy in the bathrooms. (…) Under such conditions, it as not surprising that the studio gradually became an oasis for each person to express that individuality that had suffered such erosion in this desert of sameness. Painting gave expression to the uniqueness of each human being.
>
> (Adamson, 1984, p. 2)

In Part I of this book, we have seen that Adamson's unique contribution to art therapy cannot be considered in isolation from his identity, and is reflected in his affinity as a gay man with marginalised people, in the person-centred culture of the Netherne art therapy studio, and in the foundation within art therapy of a non-judgmental stance towards service users and their art.

Part II, *The Enabling Space*, will take a research and practice-driven approach to the practice of art therapy today in a variety of settings and explore Adamson's enduring legacy.

## References

Adamson, E. (1984). *Art as Healing*. London: Coventure Ltd Publishers.

Armstrong, Z. (2022). Transitioning into visibility: Exhibiting art from a therapeutic group for the intended purpose of knowledge sharing, education, social action, and social change in a northern Canadian community. In C. Brown & H. Omand (Eds.) *Contemporary Practice in Studio Art Therapy*, pp. 117–125. London: Routledge.

British Association of Art Therapists. (2009). Advancing art and mental health: What is a gallery for? *British Association of Art Therapists News Briefing*, Spring Issue, p. 100.

British Association of Art Therapists. (2018). *Artwork Disposal and Note Keeping after the End of Art Therapy*. Guideline Accessible to BAAT Members. Downloaded from www.baat.org

Brown, C., & Omand, H. (Eds.) (2022). *Contemporary Practice in Studio Art Therapy*. London: Routledge.

Coles, A., & Jury, H. (Eds.) (2020). *Art Therapy in Museums and Galleries: Reframing Practice*. London: Jessica Kingsley Publishers.

Colley, A. (2024). *In-patient Mental Health Care from the Asylum System to the Present Day – A Lived Experience of Policy and Practice*. London: Routledge.

Health & Care Professions Council. (2025a). *Standards of Proficiency – Arts Therapists*. https://www.hcpc-uk.org/standards/standards-of-proficiency/arts-therapists/

Health & Care Professions Council. (2025b). *Standards of Conduct, Performance and Ethics*. https://www.hcpc-uk.org/standards/standards-of-conduct-performance-and-ethics/revised-standards/

Learmonth, M. (2002). Painting ourselves out of a corner. *Newsbriefing, Newsletter of British Association of Art Therapists*, June Issue, pp. 2–5.

Martyn, J. (2022). Exploring experiences of exhibiting artwork from a therapeutic art studio for refugees and asylum seekers. In C. Brown & H. Omand (Eds.) *Contemporary Practice in Studio Art Therapy*, pp. 184–193. London: Routledge.

McNeilly, G. (1984). Directive and Non-Directive Approaches in Art Therapy, *Inscape, The British Association of Art Therapists Journal*, December, pp. 7–12 (Article first published in 1983 in The Arts in Psychotherapy).

McNeilly, G. (1987). Further Contributions to Group Analytic Art Therapy, *Inscape, The British Association of Art Therapists Journal*, Summer, pp. 8–11.

Morrison, V., & Anderton, S. (2007). Healing spaces versus multi-functional rooms. *British Association of Art Therapists Newsbriefing*, Winter Issue, pp. 22–28.

Nuffield Trust (2024, September 11). *Suicide in Mental Health Service Users*. https://www.nuffieldtrust.org.uk/resource/suicide-in-mental-health-service-users

O'Flynn, D., & Schupbach, W. (2019). The art of those with lived experience: excavating the Adamson Collection. *Journal of EAHIL* 15(4), pp. 23–38.

O'Flynn, D., Szekir-Papasavva, S., & Trainor, C. (2018). Art, power, and the asylum: Adamson, healing, and the collection. *The Lancet Psychiatry* 5(5), pp. 396–399.

Ostrowska, A. (2015). The Adamson Collection: Illustrations of mental illness or a testament to spontaneous artistic expression? *Journal of Visual Communication in Medicine* 38(3–4), pp. 196–202.

Pavis, M., Huckvale, K., & Barton, T. (2025). *Who Owns outsider Art? Good Practice in Attending to Visual Artworks Made in Art Therapy and Arts & Health*. Reproduced from unpublished draft shared with permission of authors.

Potash, J. S., Ho, R. T. H., Chick, J. K. Y., & Yeung, F. A. (2013). Viewing and engaging in an art therapy exhibit by people living with mental illness: Implications for empathy and social change. *Public Health* 127(8), pp. 735–744.

Richardson, S. (2009). The healing mind: Art therapy and the body. *British Association of Art Therapists Newsbriefing*, Spring Issue, pp. 10–11.
Richardson, S. (2022). Making space: Art, the studio, and exhibition in homelessness services. In C. Brown & H. Omand (Eds.), *Contemporary Practice in Studio Art Therapy*, pp. 204–214. London: Routledge.
Springham, N. (2013). Calling an art therapy Amnesty. *British Association of Art Therapists Newsbriefing*, December 2013, pp. 11–15.
Springham, N., & Xenophontes, I. (2021). Democratising the discourse: Co-production in art therapy practice, research and publication. *International Journal of Art Therapy* 26(1–2), pp. 1–7.
Wise, S. (2014). *Inconvenient People: lunacy, Liberty and the Mad-Doctors in England.* Berkeley, CA: Catapult.

# Part II

# The Enabling Space

# 4 Enabling Spaces

*Maggie Batchelar and Kate Lawrence*

## Introduction

The societal and cultural changes since Adamson was at Netherne have been well documented in the previous three chapters. The impact of these changes is evident in contemporary healthcare provision, both in the physical spaces and the services provided within them. There is now substantial evidence that healthcare environments benefit from the inclusion of artworks and that this promotes greater well-being and recovery.

Comparing and contrasting with the 'enabling spaces' created by Adamson at Netherne Hospital, there will be descriptions in this chapter of the spaces in contemporary in-patient mental health wards where art therapy is now offered. We will also discuss how the closure of the large asylums, often, like Netherne, with expansive grounds, meant the loss of access to nature for patients and staff. It is now well evidenced that connections to the outside, to the natural world, are of benefit to us all and particularly for people experiencing the restrictions of being in hospital. As contemporary hospital settings rarely have such green spaces, there will be consideration of how artworks in hospital spaces and art therapy today can help to create bridges to the outside and to nature to benefit those in hospital.

Finally, the chapter will present two contrasting spaces – an older person's NHS mental health in-patient ward and a secure forensic setting. We will show how these spaces are navigated and enacted by the art therapist to ensure that, despite the challenges of the spaces and environment, art therapy can be an impactful and effective intervention for people in these settings.

## Art and Healthcare Environments

In 1860, Florence Nightingale observed the impact of the environment on well-being in her *Notes on Nursing*:

> Variety of form and brilliancy of colour in the objects presented to patients is the actual means of recovery.
>
> (p. 34)

DOI: 10.4324/9781003613428-7

More than a century later, in *Art as Healing* (1984), Edward Adamson described his own response to the bleakness he found when he first arrived at Netherne Hospital:

> I wanted to create a cheerful and stimulating environment, so the walls of the long corridors were painted in different colours to break up the monotony...I used a shocking pink for a small porch at the end of one corridor, and the mud brown varnish of the heavy pine doors was removed to reveal the natural beauty of the grain.
>
> (p. 13)

Today, some of the old Victorian asylums are still used for in-patient services, but more often, there are now new, purpose-built units and wards, often located near or within the grounds of general hospitals in towns and cities. These are, in general, 'wards designed not unlike the wards of the nearby medical units' (Colley, 2024. p. 69) and this design alignment was at least in part motivated (Hardcastle et al., 2007) by the drive to bring mental health care in line with physical health care, enshrined in law by the Health and Social Care Act 2012 as *Parity of Esteem*: the principle by which mental health must be given equal priority to physical health.

However, despite the downsizing of mental health in-patient estate provision over the last half century, there continues to be a legacy of the principles of the British Red Cross Picture Library Scheme, which first brought Adamson to Netherne in 1946, as well as of the Paintings in Hospitals organisation,[1] which in 1959 had started displaying artworks in waiting rooms and wards in general hospitals. These initiatives were driven by a belief in the 'healing potential of artists' creative endeavours' (Paintings in Hospitals, 2025) and that people's reactions to artworks communicated how important art could be to our well-being:

> From waiting rooms to wards, surroundings have an impact on the way we think and feel. Art can transform stark clinical environments into compassionate care spaces filled with inspiration.
>
> (Paintings in Hospitals, 2025)

In 2007, the Department of Health Review of Arts and Health Working Group found that arts and health should be firmly recognised as being integral to health, healthcare provision and healthcare environments, and in 2017 The All-Party Parliamentary Group on Arts, Health and Wellbeing Inquiry Report *Creative Health: The Arts for Health and Wellbeing* stated that:

> Patients and staff alike appreciate health and social care environments which are well designed and animated by the arts.
>
> (p. 11)

There are now many examples of artworks in healthcare spaces, not just providing visual stimulus and pleasure, but also having significant impact on how we feel. In 2013, for example, the musician, composer and artist Brian Eno designed ambient music and changing panels of colour, called *77 Million Paintings*, in the reception area of the privately run Montefiore Hospital in Hove, with the aim of reducing anxiety and creating a calming space for visitors (Middleton, 2013). Clive Parkinson, the director for *Arts for Health*, commented on the project in a BBC news article in 2013:

> *There's evidence that projects like this can even reduce pain. It's impressive stuff – and part of a growing international movement.*

Bringing artwork into healthcare spaces is included in the recommendations from the 2013 Department of Health's *Health Building Notes*, which offer best practice guidance on the design and planning of new healthcare buildings and on the adaptation or extension of existing facilities. There is recognition that considered artworks can support orientation in otherwise non-descript, clinical spaces and that images of nature are considered to contribute to a more relaxing environment. Improvements continue to be made to healthcare environments as part of the NHS modernisation programme, with recognition of the impact of the environment on how we feel, particularly when unwell (Kings Fund, 2021).

In 2021, a radical new child and adolescent mental health in-patient service (CAMHS) unit opened in Edinburgh. This design differed from typical mental health in-patient provision as it focussed on therapeutic use of colour, design, light, open communal spaces and more private meeting places, away from individuals' own bedrooms. The design aimed to create bright, welcoming spaces, minimising the clinical feel, offering privacy whilst maintaining visibility and safety. The projects office director for the organisation Building Better Healthcare offered the view that this new provision demonstrates that whilst NHS funding is hugely overstretched and projects can be limited by legislation, building designers can create environments which improve well-being, by consulting and listening to service users and their families (Building Better Health Care, 2021). More recently, the July 2023 report, *NHS England acute in-patient mental health care for adults and older adults*, acknowledges the importance of attractive and engaging shared spaces, as well as the extensive evidence base in support of the use of artworks in these environments.

One of the most innovative recent developments echoing this recommendation was the founding of the arts charity Hospital Rooms[2] in 2016, by artists Tim Shaw and curator Niamh White. Hospital Rooms has now worked in collaboration with mental health units across the country. Commenting on the project, Christopher Bailey, Arts and Health Lead, World Health Organisation, said this:

> The Hospital Rooms project is one of those rare initiatives that seamlessly combines first-rate artists and real engagement with the patient and

caregiver community to go beyond mere pleasant decoration. They transform austere patient holding areas into nurturing and healing environments, respecting not only the art and the science, but the essence of compassion which unites the two.

(Hospital Rooms, 2024)

Service user feedback also reflects the benefits:

*It's helped me take my mind off the reasons I'm here in hospital.*

*People managed to focus on the artwork rather than each other which is often the way on the ward.*

*I like it because it makes me think differently*

*It's like being in the Tate Gallery in here, I love it!*

## Outside Spaces

In an interview with Susan Hogan in 1994, Edward Adamson noted that *even the walk to the studio across the hospital grounds was of therapeutic benefit.* Yet one major impact of the changes in the buildings and locations of mental health in-patient services has been a loss of easy access to the outside and to nature. In 2011, for example, St Clement's, a large Victorian hospital in spacious grounds with mature trees located in Ipswich in the East of England, was closed down. In-patient services were relocated to a new purpose-built unit on the site of the town's general hospital, now surrounded by car parks rather than trees and grounds. There was a desire amongst many people who worked at the old hospital to commemorate the loss of this building, its beautiful grounds and its long history. In response to this, an arts project was devised by a community artist and art therapist who had worked in the original hospital. A textile project offered workshops for current and past service users and staff to make fabric containers, with prints and rubbings from the building walls, inspired by the grounds, and to write poetry about the space. One participant reflected: *I liked being here because of the fields of green,* and another commented:

*The textile project will have very happy memories for me, being here in the Main Building and grounds of St Clements – this fine example of old-fashioned British architecture and landscaping.*

The project also served as a testament to the 150 years of psychiatric in-patient care and the unspoken accounts and stories of people who had admissions there.

*Red Rose Chain,*[3] an Ipswich-based theatre company, researched and developed a play about the history of mental health in-patient provision, which was performed in the old refectory in the hospital grounds. This project, marking the closure of the hospital, demonstrated how the arts can be a powerful means of telling stories, holding history in mind and ensuring that there was representation for people who had not had their voices heard.

Since the Covid-19 pandemic, hospitals have focussed on infection control, but this has resulted in spaces that are arguably even more clinical and stark, (ONS, 2021) and an increasing loss of connection to green spaces and to the outside. Art, then, and art therapy in particular, have an ever-greater role to play in creating bridges to the outside. Within the art therapy profession, nature-based art therapy practice is a growing field that is exploring the benefits of strengthening connections to outside spaces and to nature, with a special issue in 2025 of the *International Journal of Art Therapy* dedicated to this expanding practice. Stuart-Smith (2020) observes that 'The majority of hospitals designed in the second part of the twentieth century prioritised functionalism, inflection control and technology' (p. 257) and describes the buildings as lacking in daylight, fresh air and greenery, with most UK wards excluding gifts of flowers as a precautionary infection control measure. Florence Nightingale in *Notes on Nursing* (Nightingale, 1860) recognised the importance of fresh air and daylight and her understanding of the power of patient surroundings to influence physical healing:

> I remember a nosegay of wildflowers being sent me, and from that moment recovery becoming more rapid.
>
> (p. 34)

Stuart-Smith, in her chapter *View from the hospital*, cites Roger Ulrich, a pioneering environmental psychologist and his findings that 'paintings depicting natural scenery in a Swedish psychiatric hospital, were never damaged' (p. 261), arguably because imagined outside spaces in the artworks invite relief from the clinical environment. Stuart-Smith also writes of her own experience of being in hospital and how she was helped by the invitation into the natural world through a postcard of a painting, depicting a window looking out onto a garden:

> Like a picture within a picture, this glimpse of vivid green grass, blossom covered trees and yellow flowers compensated for the dismal wall outside my real window.
>
> (p. 257).

She concludes that 'the truth is that in connecting with nature we connect with ourselves, sometimes to the very core of our being' (p. 269).

Considering the loss of access to nature in most contemporary in-patient provision, we now focus on how art therapists find, adapt and cultivate spaces inside wards. In this setting, art therapy can provide what Sacks (1984) called an 'in-between' place (p. 138), a 'quiet place, a haven, a shelter to gradually regain confidence and health' (p. 135) for people removed from their lives and in the limbo of hospital admission, and which British actress Dame Judi Dench, in her foreword to Frogley and Welch's *A Pictorial History of Netherne* (Frogley & Welch, 1993) defines as 'a sanctuary or place of refuge, protection'. British Psychiatrist Anthony Stevens (1933–2023), in his own foreword to *Art as Healing*, described the studio space created by Adamson at Netherne as a *temenos*, which is a Greek word referring to a sanctuary or holy place, largely due to the uninterrupted and respected environment and atmosphere Adamson enabled there. We will now explore how art therapists create similarly reflective and gentle spaces in in-patient units today and how this influences and shapes practice.

## Art Therapy Spaces on Wards

Few contemporary mental health in-patient wards benefit from dedicated studios, summer houses or gallery spaces of the type developed by Adamson at Netherne in the decades after World War Two. Cavaliero (2022) suggests that 'there are probably only a handful of bespoke art studios in psychiatric hospitals still in existence' (p. 155) and it is likely that art therapists working on wards today might struggle to provide the conditions for art therapy as described by art therapist, Malcolm Learmonth:

> The art materials and paints, the easels and mess-friendly tables and floor, look and feel like an invitation to use the paint, the clay, the charcoal and modelling wire – in short, to get creative. It is a studio not a consulting room.
>
> (Learmonth, 2005, p. 18)

Contemporary in-patient art therapy provision might be in a designated room, but more commonly, it will take place in multipurpose spaces. Art therapists might have access to a room with a sink and storage off the ward, in another building, use an art room on the ward, or hold groups in the open spaces of the ward day areas, or in outside spaces, courtyards or gardens. The suitability of the spaces used is in response to the availability of spaces in the building and ward but also to patient need and presenting risks.

Despite the compromises of available spaces on wards, the authors propose that art therapists can still offer supportive, reflective and 'enabling' spaces, for people in high levels of distress and disturbance. To understand how art therapists find and create these spaces, it is helpful to consider what the in-patient ward environment looks and feels like today. At any one time a ward may be quiet, or it may be very noisy with loud voices, shouting and alarms. Doors will generally be locked, both into and within the unit. There are communal, institutional spaces for eating and watching TV whilst patients will in general have their own bedrooms and usually bathrooms. Some patients may be on close observations with members of the nursing team and unable to leave the ward.

The spaces patients arrive into on an in-patient ward are a visual communication that has impact, particularly for a first admission. Colley (2024) describes his first impression of an in-patient ward:

> A long corridor stretching either side of the nurses' station: female one end, male the other, with bedrooms on either side, 20 in all, and other rooms: storerooms, activity rooms. All locked. Sterile, neutral colours, and clean, hard edges. Some display boards in reinforced cabinets.
>
> (p. 45)

Mumford (2022) reflects on the impact of this on patients:

> The environment of the modern-day mental health ward has been reduced to a series of bland, flat and unadorned surfaces, but at what cost to the well-being of the people who have to stay there?
>
> (p. 22)

Curating spaces for art therapy on in-patient wards seems a fitting description; the derivation of the word *curate* is the Latin word *curare*, meaning to *take care of*. Art therapists take time and care in shaping the spaces and conditions for art therapy on the ward. Changing part of the ward into a temporary art therapy space becomes a familiar weekly ritual and creates a welcoming area, which can offer respite from both the exposing, clinical space of the ward and from the distress of one's internal world: somewhere to 'be', to 'be together, think, feel and create' (Brown & Ormand, 2022, p. 6). Within these spaces, the art therapist provides a range of art media, natural objects and photographs, magazines and postcards of the natural world and of contemporary and historic artworks. These images can offer windows onto other spaces and stories that can engage and invite connections to individuals' lives and experiences.

The 'Community Table' model developed by the charity ArtRefuge offers an adaptive, inclusive and welcoming space for shared creative activity:

> the shift in power dynamics at the table (…) makes way for a more democratic environment. More than ever we need to be gathering around real and imagined tables, talking to each other and seeking creative responses (…) with people from different perspectives, cultures, ideologies, socio-economic and political backgrounds and identities.
>
> (Art Refuge, 2024)

In an in-patient provision, people from diverse backgrounds, ethnicities and privileges find themselves sharing the same space, and by the nature of being in hospital, have reduced autonomy and agency. The art therapists who developed the community table approach state that 'the arts can support a place to pause, reminisce, remember and recalibrate' to support people's resilience (Lloyd and Usiskin, 2022, p. 104). The democratic, being alongside, relational approach invites a different power dynamic for patients from the passivity that can be experienced in a hospital. In a 1989 interview for BBC *Night Network* Adamson summarised this as follows: *They aren't being dictated to, they are completely free in the studio.*

We will now explore how the environment is enacted and the space enabled in two contrasting settings: an in-patient ward for older adults and a provision in a secure forensic setting.

## Setting up a Group on an Older Adult In-patient Ward

In setting up an art therapy group on an older adult ward, particular consideration needs to be given to access, due to the physical health needs of many patients. Within this population, there can also be significant anxiety, hopelessness, passivity, fear, distrust and varying levels of cognitive decline and impairment, including dementia. For these reasons, consistency and reliability of the group and of the art therapist are crucial. Micus (2020) reflects on the challenge of the environment on a ward for people with dementia:

> Establishing the space in which to facilitate the art therapy group and feeling content with a decision was a lengthy process. People living with dementia can be sensitive to external stimuli, so it is important to consider sounds, temperature, smells and other environmental conditions.
>
> (p. 46)

Micus suggests that there is a need for art therapists on a dementia ward to adopt a nomadic approach: 'A dementia ward is not static and therefore, to establish stability and safety within movement, it is important to flow with the dynamics. Becoming a nomad, in part, refers to the therapeutic space moving within the unit' (p. 46–47). Micus also reflects on her art therapy training, and the ideal space she imagined as a student was 'consistent, contained, uninterrupted and therapeutic'. (p. 46) and she suggests that it is the therapist who becomes the 'protective, safe and containing boundary' (p. 46), that a dedicated room might otherwise provide. Micus speaks to the need to assess the ward space and population, to locate the group in an optimally accessible space within the ward.

The art therapy group on the older adult ward presented here has been established for some years, in a space within the communal day area, chosen to optimise ease of access. Likewise, Adamson organised the studio space at Netherne with consideration of how he felt the space could be most beneficial for patients:

> I saw to it that everyone who came to paint had a chair, an easel and a small side table to hold paints, brushes and water. Each art unit was a little island where the person could feel their privacy was respected.
>
> (Adamson & Timlin, 1984, p. 14)

Whilst Adamson offered each person a separate space within the studio, in the older adult ward, the art therapy group is offered as a space to be 'grounded in relational connection' (Lloyd & Usiskin, 2022, p. 105). There is a ritual to setting up, which begins with placing a long table in the same space in the main ward area, with chairs from the dining area placed around it, seating six comfortably, additional chairs brought in if needed and space made for wheelchair access as required. Some large armchairs are located apart from the table, which can be used if people need to manage their proximity to others. The table is only used for the art therapy group and stored away during the week. It has become, as shown in Image 4.1, an art piece in itself, with the traces of art making over many years of the group.

The table is often remarked upon favourably by patients and is an integral part of setting the scene for the group, denoting a different type of space on the ward, which is otherwise fairly typical of in-patient wards: functional dining tables, PVC-covered chairs and notice boards.

In preparing the space for the group, a large portable whiteboard is placed across the opening to the extended communal space, creating a temporary 'wall'. It has a sign on the board facing outwards to the rest of the ward space with a notice stating the time of the group and requesting no interruptions

*Image 4.1* The Table: An Artwork in Itself.

Photo: Maggie Batchelar.

unless necessary. This is a communication to staff about the nature of the group: that patients are being offered time and space without expectation or pressure. The portable quality of the whiteboard enables the group space to remain accessible to patients for whom exercising choice about approaching and staying for any duration in the group is encouraged. The reverse of the board faces inward to the group and is used to place images, with individuals' agreement, for the end of group reflection. This is described as a space for shared looking and reflecting, creating physical, emotional and aesthetic distance from artwork, which, within the group, supports reflection and facilitates connection between people. The benefits of this are discussed in more detail in Chapter 5. The ritual continues by setting the table with a range of art media, including found objects such as shells, feathers, as well as art books and magazines with photos of the natural world. This array of materials arouses curiosity and draws people towards the table. The space where the group is held has double doors which can be opened onto a small courtyard area and, although covered by CCTV, the table is not overlooked, creating a sense of privacy in the space, which is valued. Patients remark on the calm and gentle feeling of the space and that it is better when not interrupted, which cannot be guaranteed in this setting. Far from being the separate space which Adamson provided and where 'many people said how they appreciated the natural silence of the studio' (Adamson & Timlin, 1984, 1984, p. 3), the group is subject to the noises and activity of ward life, though this can also be helpful as it can connect patients to the 'ordinary', everyday life of the ward, to which they return after the group has ended.

The ritual of creating the art therapy group space continues into ending the group, clearing away, restoring the day room back as it was. Discussion about whether patients would like to keep a piece of their artwork from the session can offer patients some connection to the group in the intervening week between the sessions and provides another imaginative space. Patients have described this as a helpful focal point when ward life and their own internal world is challenging. This contrasts with the status of artwork made by patients in Adamson's studio spaces as discussed in Chapter 3, where they were generally not considered patients' property, as has been discussed in more detail in Chapter 3.

Art therapists working in in-patient wards today must consider how patients' artwork is treated on the ward; what the options are for storage, and who has access to it. Some patients might feel that showing their artwork to the Multi-Disciplinary Team might invite greater understanding of their difficulties. As Cunningham-Dax noted of the work Adamson's patients created, artwork was to be 'kept as carefully as his case notes' (p. 20). Micus (2020) speaks of the impact for patients with cognitive impairments or dementia, of keeping their artwork:

> People with dementia will have often experienced a great amount of loss especially once they have been admitted into hospital and, as a result, may feel increased lack of control and power. By keeping their images,

> they may attain a sense of empowerment and ownership. Often, they may want to show their work to relatives, experiencing a sense of pride and esteem.
>
> (p. 47)

In the older adult ward, loss is a dominant theme: bereavement, home, relationships, changes in physical and mental capability, loss of independence and hope. With this in mind, it seems counterintuitive to keep artwork out of sight, stored away, but to offer the choice for artwork to be kept by an individual, or to be displayed in a ward 'gallery' space. This visibility brings the person into view from a different perspective, other than being a patient, and the artwork can become a currency of communication with other patients and staff.

The art therapy group in the older adult ward is visible and accessible within the ward space, reducing both physical and psychological barriers for patients in approaching the group. If the group took place in a group side room, through two sets of heavy doors, needing to be opened by staff, the movement in and out of the space and the relationship of patients to the space would entirely change. The transition of moving into and out of the group space enables patients to find their own way and approach into the group and back into ward life afterwards. Patients often initiate helping to pack away, taking some ownership of the space and are frequently visibly energised by the connection and agency the conditions of the group can generate.

## Establishing Spaces for Art Therapy in a High Secure Setting

High secure hospitals in the UK offer individualised care for patients who are detained under the Mental Health Act, due to the significant risk they present to themselves and others. These provisions offer a high level of care and support, with an ethos towards recovery, and the average stay in hospital is around 5–7 years.

The UK Government *High Security Psychiatric Services Directions* (2019) place legal requirements on the hospital's procedural, relational and physical security. Of relevance to the art therapist, restrictions are placed on items which can be used by patients in hospital, though each ward has found a way to create its own culture, with artwork, soft furnishings and dedicated spaces to be creative.

The inclusive, quiet studio space Adamson describes in *Art is Healing* is something that can still be achieved on a busy ward, with adaptations, even with the high levels of risk and security required in these buildings. Art therapy can be adapted to a range of spaces and conditions, changing the functional, austere spaces with the introduction of coloured paper, paint, inspirational books and postcards. The ward is the patient's current home, and their monthly community meetings are an ideal space to introduce art therapy and the therapist and make the group a welcome space.

Setting up the room before a session is imperative to change its use from a primarily physical to a relational space (Brown & Ormand, 2022). On some wards, tables can be pushed together, whist in others, furniture may be fixed to the ground. In an environment where choice is limited, giving the patients the option to sit together or on their own can be significant. The door to the room is left open, due to security constraints, but patients can come and go as they please, and the space becomes one of warm acceptance and interaction with those who are quietly making art. This also encourages conversations about art that interplay between patients and visitors: conversations about memories, hopes and aspirations which can offer some relief from the physical restrictions of being detained in a high secure hospital. Often, patients who do not want to make art come into the session to read, play chess or just sit and enjoy the atmosphere of calm. There can be interruptions to the session, even with the best preparations. Acknowledging this when it occurs seems to preserve the sanctity of the space even in the nosiest of times.

Some patients can only leave their room with a high staff-to-patient ratio, sometimes as much as 5:1, and for these patients, a 'drop in' model of art therapy has been developed. Patients who are willing to engage are invited to attend an art therapy session for as long as they can manage with their allocated staff ratio. The recovery model adopted by the hospital encourages patients to progress from this high staff-to-patient ratio to eventual participation in meaningful activities with a balance of therapeutic work, alongside leisure activities and rest. Staff members are encouraged to actively participate in the session, reflect and respond to the art making and so model the framework and boundaries of the sessions, its ethos and rhythm. This therapeutic space can be the first step towards recovery, hope and acceptance for many patients, and in some cases, the first time they have touched a drawing implement for years.

The model demonstrates to the patient the therapist's commitment, reliability of the therapy session and considers that there may be some weeks that the patient is too unwell to participate. Where a patient is unable to access the available space, or there are not enough staff available to facilitate a drop-in, then 'hatch work' is an option. The word 'hatch' here refers to a small lockable door into their room, through which items can be passed. Negotiating this as a therapeutic space can be a challenge. Paper, cardboard and coloured pastels are passed through the hatch. Drawing whilst standing without a conventional table or desk requires some adaptation; cardboard provides a sturdy, lightweight support, enabling patients to prop up their paper and work comfortably whist standing. It also allows for flexibility – patients can move their work around as needed and choose the way they wish to position themselves during the creative process. The art materials are risk assessed with the staff team, with the understanding that if the patient refuses to hand them back, then the items can do little harm to self or others. Images made can be shared through a small window in the door. This joint attention on an object presents a subtle shift to the patient's interaction with clinical staff, who observe them every 30 minutes. This is an opportunity to look together, patient and therapist, at art made, and share meaningful reflections which engenders a gentle way to build rapport, confidence and consistency. It is a unique space, where the usual boundaries and frame of therapy are shrunk to an exchange from one hand to another. One cannot avoid touching the hands of the patients as the materials are passed through at the beginning and end of the session; a simple act of trust on both sides of the door. This point of contact, where a physical and psychological contract begins, is the enabling space for art therapy.

As there is a door separating therapist and patient, conversations are not always private due to the presence of other staff, or there is a necessity to raise a voice to be heard through the door. Whilst these conditions present challenges for the art therapist, it does have its own positive by-product. The gentle noise of conversation from the session can be heard by other patients whose history of trauma and abuse compromises their ability to build trusting relationships (Deljavan et al., 2025). Regular and consistent presence on the ward by the art therapist can allay fears, lower anxieties and highlight the benefits of art making, whilst giving the opportunity for the patient to witness other patient–therapist interactions. This witnessing encourages engagement at the drop-in sessions and can provide the very first step into a therapeutic space for the more reluctant participants. These enabling spaces, from hatch work to drop-in with staff and then to open groups, often parallel a patient's recovery journey through the hospital.

Maintaining connection to the outside and to nature is essential for people in in-patient wards and particularly in a high secure setting where patients may be detained for many years. In a high secure unit, grounds access is limited until much later in the treatment pathway, when patients can join in with horticulture, walks around the grounds and football. Until this time, they will only experience the outside by feeling the breeze from windows, waiting for swallows to arrive or watching the trees sway. Bringing objects from nature into the therapy space supports people to remain connected to the world outside the hospital, to their lives, their stories and their memories and fuel imaginative life through art and art making to sustain a sense of place.

## Conclusion

This chapter has shown that art therapy in contemporary in-patient settings is shaped and informed by the need to adapt to a range of physical spaces that are available, suitable and safe to work in. The art therapist's stance, approach and relational skills shape these meeting places, and it is a testament to the resilience of art therapists that they can adapt practice to work in a range of different spaces, often in the least therapeutic conditions, enabling encounters with patients who might otherwise struggle to have access to other psychological therapies.

In the introduction to this book, art therapist Siobhan Lennon wrote vividly about her discovery of Edward Adamson and her journey as an art therapist. To conclude this chapter about the environment where art therapy takes place, Siobhan reflects on her own practice in an in-patient setting:

> *It is only in the past year that I have held a role working on an acute in-patient ward in a purely mental health setting. My previous experience has been in secure institutions: adult prisons, young offenders' institutes, secure training centres and secure schools, so it is interesting to consider the differences in the physical spaces whether permanent or temporary I have experienced.*
>
> *The Art Therapy studio comes in many guises, existing in varied physical forms shaped by the context of the therapy. A studio maybe a purpose-built, intentional space or a multi-functional, shape-shifting room. Perhaps an art studio by morning and a karaoke venue in the afternoon. Or perhaps it is not even a room. These temporary, flexible 'studios' meet the context and needs of the situation and offer a space where therapy can unfold. As Kalmanowitz and Lloyd (1997) state, it is due to the experience and knowledge of the therapists that therapeutic integrity can be maintained and containment offered despite the adaptions of the therapeutic framework.*

In Chapter 5, there will be a more detailed account of how art therapists in in-patient settings work flexibly to relate to people in their current crisis and distress and offer relief, psychological safety and opportunities for finding meaning in the reasons for their hospital admission, in the way Adamson was able to do in the very different environment of Netherne Hospital.

## Notes

1 www.paintingsinhospitals.org.uk
2 www.hospital-rooms.com
3 www.redrosechain.com

## References


Adamson, E., & Timlin, J. (1984). Art as healing. *Therapy*, *1*, 32–36.

All-Party Parliamentary Group on Arts, Health and Wellbeing. (2017). *Inquiry Report Creative Health: The Arts for Health and Wellbeing* (Second Edition). Oxford: National Centre for Creative Health.

Art Refuge. (2024).

Brown, C & Ormand, H. (Eds.). (2022). *Contemporary Practice in Studio Art Therapy.* London: Routledge.

Building Better Healthcare. (2021, June 14). Special report: Re-imagining mental healthdesign. https://buildingbetterhealthcare.com/special-report-re-imagining-mental-health-design-177180

Cavaliero, A. (2022). Terms of engagement, Aspects of facilitating open art therapy groups for adults in a psychiatric setting. In C. Brown & H. Ormand (Eds.) *Contemporary Practice in Studio Art Therapy*, pp. 155–156. London: Routledge.

Colley, A. (2024). *In-patient Mental Health Care from the Asylum System to the Present Day, A Lived Experience of Policy and Practice*. London: Routledge.

Deljavan, S., Zimmermann, K., Scott, A., Allen, K., Neil, R., Evans, C., Moghimi, E., Dell, C., Williamson, L., & Canning, C. (2025). Building capacity in patient-oriented research: Reflections on cultivating relationships within a high-secure forensic mental health hospital. *Research Involvement and Engagement*, 11(1), p. 18. https://doi.org/10.1186/s40900-025-00691-6

Department of Health (DoH). (2013). *Health Building Note 03-01 – Adult Acute Mental Health Units*.

Dreaper, J. (2013, April 19). *Brian Eno Branches out Into Hospital Work*. https://www.bbc.co.uk/news/health-22189774

Frogley, G., & Welch, J. (1993). *A Pictorial History of Netherne*. East Surrey Health Authority.

Hardcastle, M., Kennard, D., Grandison, S., & Fagin L. (Eds.) (2007). *Experiences of Mental Health In-patient Care Narratives from Service Users, Carers and Professionals*. London: Routledge.

Hogan, S. (2001). *Healing Arts: The History of Art Therapy*. London: Jessica Kingsley Publishers.

Hospital Rooms. (2024). *Our Impact*. https://hospital-rooms.com/our-impact/

Kalmanowitz, D., & Lloyd B. (1997). *The Portable Studio: Art Therapy and Political Conflict: Initiatives in Former Yugoslavia and South Africa*. London: Health Education Authority.

Kings Fund. (2021). *Celebrating Achievement: Enhancing the Healing Environment Programme*. London: TSO.

Learmonth, M. (2005). Changing our mind. *Open Mind* 134, pp. 18–19.

Lloyd, B., & Usiskin, M. (2022). The community table: Developing art therapy studios on, in-between, and across borders. In *Contemporary Practice in Studio Art therapy*, pp. 101–116. London: Routledge.

Micus, Y. (2020). On becoming a nomad: Setting-up and adapting an art therapy group on an acute assessment and treatment unit for people with dementia. *The British Psychological Society Psychology of Older People: The FPOP Bulletin No. 152*.

Middleton, K. (2013, April 21). *Brian Eno Launches Art Installation at Hove Hospital*. https://www.theargus.co.uk/news/10369883.brian-eno-launches-art-installation-at-hove-hospital/

Mumford, J. (2022). Therapy beyond good and evil. *The New Atlantic*.

NHS England (2023, Oct 30). *Acute Inpatient Mental Health Care for Adults and OlderAdults*.https://www.england.nhs.uk/long-read/acute-inpatient-mental-health-care-for-adults-and-older-adults/

Nightingale, F. (1860). *Notes on Nursing: what it Is and What it Is Not*. New York: D. Appleton and Company.

ONS (Office for National Statistics). (2021, April 26). *How Has Lockdown Changed Our Relationshipwith Nature?* https://www.ons.gov.uk/economy/environmentalaccounts/articles/howhaslockdownchangedourrelationshipwithnature/2021-04-26

Paintings in Hospitals. (2025, September). *Our Story*. https://paintingsinhospitals.org.uk/our-story/

Sacks, O. (1984). *A Leg to Stand On*. New York: Simon Schuster Inc..

Stuart-Smith, S. (2020). *The Well Gardened Mind*. London: William Collins.

# 5 Finding a Meeting Place

## Art Therapy Practice in In-patient Wards

*Maggie Batchelar and Joanne Noble*

### Introduction

Chapter 4 explored the spaces used for art therapy in contemporary in-patient wards and the need for an adaptive, flexible approach. This chapter continues this discussion, drawing on theories of creativity and the arts from a psychological and evolutionary perspective to propose how art and art making and the ways in which art therapists relate, can alleviate emotional distress and psychological disturbance. We will consider how the art therapist's approach retains the core values held by Adamson and describe the ways in which art therapists have had to adapt their practice in accordance with contemporary in-patient provision.

The chapter focusses on art therapy groups in in-patient wards and describes why this space is helpful to people in this setting. There is also consideration of the art therapist's wider role within the in-patient Multi-Disciplinary Team (MDT) and their contribution to a psychologically informed understanding of patients. We also reference the work art therapists undertake with staff: reflective practice, debriefs and staff support, noting that Chapter 9 *Art Therapy and Staff Wellbeing* covers this in more depth.

### Art Therapists' Response to Patients

'For the new admission, hospital life is punctuated with a strange new regimen, entirely different from home life' (Adamson 1984, p. 16). This remains relevant today. People can often be in crisis when admitted to a ward, and admission can entail what can be a confusing and often traumatic pathway into hospital (Colley, 2024). Once on the unit, there are locked doors, and many people are detained under the Mental Health Act (1983). As Woods and Springham (2011) describe:

> Just at the height of vulnerability and distress, one encounters new surroundings with others who are equally distressed and may be acting bizarrely.
>
> (p. 60)

DOI: 10.4324/9781003613428-8

Although many in in-patient settings will be admitted formally under The Mental Health Act (1983), some people will have come into hospital informally: they have agreed to come into hospital for their own well-being, and therefore can come and go as they wish providing there are staff to let them in and out of the ward. Colley (2024) notes that 'the reality though in my own and others experience is that movement to and from the ward environment is so tightly controlled that informal patients cannot easily enact their rights' (p. 79). Bella Jackson (2025) reminds us that staff do have the privilege to come and go. 'It's easy to walk in and out of a locked ward and forget the significance of that power'. (p. 7).

Responding sensitively to how people might be feeling on arrival to the ward is a starting point for the therapeutic relationship. Rothwell and Grandison (2016) explain that 'working towards developing and maintaining a therapeutic relationship is paramount' (p. 181), and Berwick, as cited in Jarrold (2018), explains that when working with service users, we can try 'to shift from the patient as a guest in our service to us as the guest in the patient's life' (p. 76). Art therapists' training equips them to be relationally skilled and to have a gentle, consistent and flexible stance which echoes Adamson's personal qualities and approach as described by Anthony Stevens in his foreword to *Art as Healing* (1984):

> His comfortable, avuncular presence, his gentle courtesy, patent integrity and the rich humour of his eyes, combined with a warmly affectionate nature.

Art therapists consider all aspects of their communications with patients from the first contact in order to build a therapeutic alliance and create a sense of relational safety, which is crucial for more exploratory work to take place. Springham and Huet (2018) state that

> Human interest is a necessary agent in attachment and this calls for an emotionally involved stance from the therapist (…) human beings make unwitting disclosure through body language. Clients are sensitized to these disclosures as ways of judging trustworthiness because it matters so much.
>
> (p. 9)

Using non-medicalised language is central to the art therapists' approach, appealing to patients as people experiencing distress and difficulty, rather than focusing on symptoms of mental health diagnoses, echoing Adamson (1984) who sought to respond in a respectful and equal way to patients:

> I try to avoid the word 'patient', or the medical terminology so beloved by some, which denies the person his essential individuality, and distances him, like a specimen.
>
> (p. 7)

The language of psychiatric diagnosis can also be confusing, as one service user put it in 2025:

> *There's a lot of technical words used and you're not really well enough to take it in.*

The dominant framework for naming and treating mental health problems is psychiatric diagnosis, based on the DSM (*The Diagnostic and Statistical Manual of Mental Disorders*, 2025, APA, 2013) and the ICD (*International Classification of Diseases*, 2019, WHO, 2022). Art therapists need to familiarise themselves with this diagnostic language in order to function as part of the ward team; however, there has been a debate in recent years about the legitimacy and utility of diagnosis:

> The single most damaging effect of psychiatric diagnosis is *loss of meaning*. By divesting people's experiences of their personal, social, and cultural significance, diagnosis turns 'people with problems' into 'patients with illnesses'. Stories of trauma, abuse, discrimination and deprivation are sealed off behind a label as the individual is launched on what is often a lifelong journey of disability, exclusion, and despair.
>
> (Johnstone, 2018, p. 2)

Art therapy aligns with the premise of psychological formulation, which is gaining understanding as an alternative to psychiatric diagnosis and is supported by the British Psychological Society as a trauma-informed, narrative framework. Many people admitted to a ward may have experienced trauma and may have a diagnosis of psychosis, and the case for a trauma–psychosis link is consistently supported by research that reports high rates of sexual abuse in childhood, in addition to other traumatic experiences (Shevlin et al., 2008) With this in mind, art therapy is recommended in the *Guidance for Psychosis and Schizophrenia* (NICE, 2014), as it supports self-expression, helps people find ways of relating and is tailored to the individual. The BAAT *Guidelines on Art Therapy for People with a Psychosis-Related Diagnosis* (Wright & Holttum, 2020) also outline art therapists' trauma- informed approach and techniques to support emotional stabilisation and increase feelings of psychological safety.

## Models of Art Therapy

The relatively short lengths of stay in mental health wards today inevitably mean that art therapists have less time to work with people and need to take a more proactive stance than described by Adamson (1984), who spoke of the 'fullness of time which occurs in both Art and healing' (p. 7) and acknowledged that 'sometimes it is often weeks, months or even years that we are both obliged to wait for someone's creativity' (Adamson 1984). Art therapists today need to work within the time constraints of the admission. Rothwell and

Grandison (2016) propose that brief acute art psychotherapy work can support patients 'to develop a capacity to link thoughts, feelings, and experiences and to manage dissociation or outbursts derived from internal trauma triggered by current events' (p. 185), and art therapists must avoid making assumptions about what people might need. Woods and Springham (2011) state that:

> Art therapists may work with an assumption, whether internal or external (or both), that they should be trying to change something. But there is something very important about staying with and reassuring a service user that you can be with them as they are and there are no expectations that this has to change in that moment. If we can give back to our service users representations of themselves in the here and now to help them modify and regulate what they are experiencing we are helping them to feel accepted, valued and understood.
>
> (p. 66)

The art therapist's approach needs to be highly adaptive and flexible; therapeutic encounters do not just take place in an individual or group art therapy session, but in the day-to-day exchanges with service users. Luzzatto (1997) and Allen (1983) explain that flexibility is central in adapting to the different needs of the service users and advise that therapists should take an accepting stance. Woods and Springham (2011) suggest that 'it seems very possible that relating to service users as fellow human beings in distress, rather than a highly professional stance, is a more effective approach to alliance building on the ward'. (p. 67). Patients are subject to the unannounced presence of medical and nursing staff, who are required to assess both mental and physical health for admission, whilst art therapists can build rapport without this expectation: negotiating how and when to meet with patients invites a collaborative approach, appealing to an individual's sense of agency and choice. Taking art materials to use in conversations with patients outside of groups or individual sessions can also be helpful as signals that there may be other ways of being together without reliance on the spoken word. Trainee art therapists on placement on wards are challenged to rethink their ideas about art therapy in this context: The boundaries and confidentiality of therapy need to be contextualised within the frame of the ward, team and the wider service.

Noble and Hackett (2023) discuss the components of an art therapy approach in acute in-patient settings. These include the space and environment, the art materials, the therapeutic relationship and opportunities for reflection. Emphasis is placed on the service user leading the process at a level which suits them, with how much they participate depending on how they are feeling. Woods and Springham (2011) recommend implications for practice when art therapy is offered on in-patient wards. This includes 'if a service user is unable to regulate their own thoughts and feelings, something very concrete and basic needs to be provided before art therapists can consider (if at all) working at a deeper level' (p. 67). They advise communicating 'a sense of ordinariness and hope', and that 'interactions can take place outside the room' (Woods & Springham, 2011).

## Art as an Agent of Change

Anthropologist and writer Ellen Dissanayake (2003) describes the function of art as having 'the intent to affect individuals emotionally – to bring their feelings into awareness, to display them' (p. 20). Despite the universality of art across all cultures, and that in making art 'we are tapping into the same root capacity for re-imagining and for problem solving that were the difference between life and death for our ancestors' (Learmonth, 2005), many patients can feel estranged from their creative capacity, and expressing a lack of entitlement to use art materials or fear of judgement is common.

> Many clients referred to art therapy have experienced art as alienating, whether in their schooling or through contact with the art world.... Thus, a client's initial reencounter with art requires careful attention from the art therapist.
>
> (Huet, 2012, p. 7)

Malchiodi (2020) states that expressive arts therapy 'is used to help identify and ameliorate the body's experience of distress' (p. 52), without reliance on communicating experience verbally, 'normalizing the body's reactions to trauma as adaptive coping rather than pathology' (Malchiodi 2020). In response to the disconnection many people describe feeling in relation to art, it can be helpful to describe art making as a universal human behaviour:

> When we make art, we're working with capacities for imagination, dreaming, playing and working with feelings.
>
> (Learmonth, 2005, p. 18)

Using art media requires motivation and is active rather than passive, which can help mobilise patients who might be feeling helpless and withdrawn. Art materials can also stimulate imagination and invite what Mithen (1996, p. 168) calls 'cognitive fluidity', or changing our minds through the use of metaphor and symbols. This in itself can enable more flexible thinking:

> Working with art helps our minds to become fluid again, to be open to different understandings.
>
> (Learmonth, 2005, p. 19)

Art making creates a space between feeling and reacting and has a moderating effect on heightened emotional states, offering a means of safe ventilation of frustration, agitation and distress. Huet, interviewed by The British Association of Art Therapists in 2017 as part of its Creative Cuts series of programmes put it like this: *It's so difficult to find the words (to say it), when we're upset* and Noble and Hackett (2023) describe how service users reported a reduction in anxiety and feeling calmer after attending art therapy and noted that attending art therapy made talking easier, citing one service user as saying,

> *with art you can just draw, and you may be saying things that you don't even know that you're saying.*

Guidance from the National Institute for Health and Care Excellence (NICE) states that art therapy 'helps people to express themselves and to organise their experience into a satisfying aesthetic form. It can help people to accept and understand feelings that may have emerged during the creative process' (NICE, 2014, p. 37), and Adamson, in his foreword to *Art as Healing* (1984), describes this as 'the opportunity for the patient to real-ize what lies within himself – to discover inner resources and give them form in outer reality'. More recently, musician Brian Eno (2025) describes art as, 'a name we give to a certain type of experience. It's the name for a kind of engagement we have with something' (p. 13) and goes on: 'art helps us identify the sources of feelings or anxieties and gives us a way of locating them and sharing them' (p. 99). Adamson (1984) also highlights how many of his patients used art to share their feelings and noted that 'painting out these feelings is often followed by a tremendous sense of relief' (p. 17).

Art Therapists understanding of the potential of art making to connect to personal meaning is central to their practice. Art making, though, can evoke strong feelings, and vulnerable patients need to be helped to use art safely (Springham, 2008). Mental Health & Justice Project Artist Dolly Sen reflects that creativity helped her to express difficult feelings and that 'art became the roadmap back to myself'. (Cutler, 2020, p. 3).

## Art Therapy Groups

It is established practice for art therapists working on in-patient wards to offer groups, which do not exist in isolation (Yalom, 1995) as they exist as part of a wider ecosystem within the ward and the hospital.

Historically there has been some variation in how the in-patient group model has been provided and understood, as discussed by Cavaliero in *Terms of Engagement* (2022), but in facilitating all groups, preparation is essential to maintain physical and psychological safety.

Providing consistency and reliability by the group taking place on the same day and time each week is essential and creates a secure point of reference in the week of ward life. Groups can be held in the communal areas of wards, a side room or another room off the main ward, as discussed in Chapter 4. A space to make art on the ward may seem deceptively simple, but can: 'involve the therapist negotiating complex institutional dynamics; spaces just to "be" and to "be together", to feel and think and create are rare and may be resisted by a defensive institution' (Brown & Omand, 2022, p. 6). Art therapy open groups are offered as inclusive and welcoming spaces and can meet the needs of people on a ward who are unable to sustain proximity to others for any length of time. They offer a different group space to other groups run by psychology and occupational therapists, for example, which tend to have a focus and be more structured.

The primary aim of art therapy open groups is to be inclusive of any patient who approaches the session, with no pre-conditions for engagement, but with the art therapist managing risk and maintaining a safe space. This group approach supports patients to self-regulate, exercise choice and agency over their approach and to be welcomed unconditionally into the group space. Patients can come for any length of time within the designated time frame of the session, including leaving and returning during the session. The restrictions patients are subject to in hospital can increase feelings of frustration and powerlessness, so the freedom of the group space invites some autonomy. Allen (1983) stresses the flexibility of this approach:

> Patients with different needs, different behaviour, patients who came only to watch, patients who came only to paint, patients who came mainly to talk are allowed to coexist.
>
> (p. 3)

Similarly, there is an invitation from the art therapist for patients to choose when and how they use the art materials, without risk to self or others. In his foreword to *Art as Healing*, Dr Antony Stevens describes this as 'the art of letting things happen' so that patients 'discover inner resources and give them form in outer reality'. Within this framework, the art therapist holds positive regard for each individual and each artwork without judgement or pressure, as expressed by this service user in 2025: *my artwork was very rudimentary, but the art therapist never commented on that, but just accepted the message it conveyed*, and another shows how valued this lack of expectation or pressure is:

> *The art therapist let us get on with art without interfering. We were free to express ourselves and discussed what we had done only when we indicated that we wished to do so. If we didn't want to, that was fine.*

People may work in silence or talk with each other using art media to connect with their interests and values, because open art therapy groups are essentially a gathering of individuals around a shared table, materials and other resources. The art therapist's demeanour is integral to how people experience this group space, as Deco (1998) explains:

> Although there may be no direct interaction between the group members in the open group, they all have awareness of each other and are

> influenced in some way by the presence of others. Patients are acutely aware of the art therapist's communications with other patients in the room. It is therefore necessary to remember that something said to one patient is a statement to the whole group. Even if it can be barely heard, the tone of voice and general tenor of the communication has an influence on those around.
>
> (p. 105)

Some art therapists might offer themes in groups, but more usually the sessions align with Adamson's view:

> I considered it my role to facilitate, rather than direct. I never suggested what anyone ought to paint, because it seemed essential that the idea should be entirely theirs.
>
> (Adamson, 1984, p. 3)

The art therapist's welcoming approach is highlighted by service users in the BAAT *Guidelines for Psychosis* (Wright & Holttum, 2020) as being an essential feature of the art therapist's manner when working with people with a psychosis-related diagnosis. The NICE Guidelines for Psychosis and Schizophrenia in Adults: prevention and management CG178 (2014) recommend offering arts therapies in a group setting. They suggest that these groups are 'unstructured and led by the service user' and that this can enable people to 'experience themselves differently and to develop new ways of relating to others' (p. 38).

Deco (1998), describes the group space as an 'unduly demanding relational environment' (p. 101). Winnicott (1958), as cited in Deco (1998), explains how patients can have 'the experience of being alone while someone else is present' (p. 104). Patients can feel less isolated, which can contribute to reducing their risks. Fostering patients' confidence in communicating their distress enables the art therapist to bridge this understanding to the ward team:

> *Everything was really foggy and blurred and I had no outlet for that when I was on the acute ward, I think art is maybe a way for people to just express themselves without having someone saying so, how are you feeling today?*
>
> (Service User, 2025)

In addition to a range of art media, providing a range of natural objects can support patients' external focus, increasing exteroception (connecting to our senses and grounding in the present), which can support emotional regulation, self-awareness and a connection to the natural world outside the ward. Postcards of artworks can invite curiosity and engagement without the expectation to originate artwork and can reduce feelings of exposure in producing art. The views into other spaces and artists' interpretations of experiences can ignite a gentle curiosity and connect to memories, and the art therapist needs to be receptive to the explicit and implicit communications in response to the objects and art media. Adamson noted that 'many people loved to paint the things that were important to them and which they obviously missed when they came into hospital' (Allen, 1983, p. 13) and in Chapter 3 there was an acknowledgement of the agency art gave patients at Netherne, in finding a voice and sense of identity and being able to communicate distress through rebellion and humour.

## Art Therapists Making Art Alongside

In a video interview with Ed Lawrenson & Pia Borg, July 9, 2001, John Timlin recounts a story Adamson told him about one of his formative experiences in the art studio at Netherne Hospital. The hospital patients were working quietly – painting or drawing – and Adamson was wandering amongst the easels and desks observing, smiling, very occasionally offering words of encouragement. Then, out of the blue, one of the artists said:

> *We're all sitting here doing stuff, Mr Adamson. If you're so clever, why don't you start?*

So he did. He took out his sketchbook and started drawing the patients as they worked, and he continued to do so throughout the rest of his years at the hospital. Thousands of exquisite, sensitive drawings are now held in the Wellcome Collection in London. One, from 1954, simply titled *Man Painting*, is included at the end of this book.

Today, making art alongside service users is an increasingly common practice amongst art therapists. This practice, which Marshall-Tierney (2014) describes as being 'marginalised in UK literature' (p. 96), is now seen to have benefits for service users attending art therapy because 'therapist art making is a way of navigating fluid relationships without being controlling' (p. 105), and he concludes that 'art making can help art therapists become more attuned to their patients and more able to hold them in mind'. (p. 105). Patients may initially watch the art therapist use art materials and find the sound of another person drawing soothing. Watching is often a safe way of approaching the group space and is welcomed. Art therapists making artwork can prevent the gaze of the art therapist being solely on the patient, which may feel too intense and uncomfortable:

> *If you weren't art making and would just sit and watch me, I'd feel uncomfortable. It seemed to create a bond between us, that we were using the same art materials.*
>
> (Service User, 2025)

Adamson (1984, p. 4) believed that art therapists should first be artists, as they 'are on familiar terms with the inner self', which enables more understanding of patient's relationships to their artwork and Springham and Huet (2018) offer the view that art therapists need to have an authentic relationship with art:

> Art therapists might offer art because they themselves have high familiarity and epistemic trust in it. We need this fascination with art to be genuine because genuineness shows; it opens up contingent mirroring opportunities for clients to find themselves in the mind of the art therapist.
>
> (p. 9)

Art therapists can use their own imaginative responses in art making. Their artwork can hold meaning for others and reflect emerging themes within the group. Making art alongside patients also addresses power within the therapeutic relationship, so everyone sitting around a table using art materials provides common ground rather than the art therapist sitting watching the service user. As Marshall-Tierney (2014) suggests:

> The therapist's art making brings about equity of engagement in the struggles and rewards of the creative processes and establishes more equality under the gaze.
>
> (p. 98)

People admitted to in-patient wards may be feeling disconnected from themselves, from others, from their family members and/or from their communities. Art therapy groups can bring people together in a shared endeavour, and a reflective space at the end of the group can reinforce this. Placing images on a board and inviting reflection creates physical and psychological distance from the imagery made in the group, and this shared experience can support connection between people and is an opportunity to hear others' views and perspectives. Looking together at the physical art object with 'joint attention' (Isserow, 2008) is a distinguishing feature of art therapy and can support people to relate through their artworks. This can support increased mentalising (being curious about the other's mind, about experiences, thoughts and feelings), which can become compromised when we feel overwhelmed.

When ward staff are required to be on one-to-one observations with patients due to levels of risk, they will also need to be in groups. Staff are encouraged to use the art materials alongside others, which can enrich their therapeutic relationships with patients and offer staff reflective space. Through this, staff can build understanding about art therapy, which supports the intervention:

> The survival of art therapy itself depends upon the ability of its practitioners to survive the workplace.
>
> (Edwards, 1986, p. 11)

## Individual Art Therapy

Some patients may not feel ready or able to tolerate a group setting, or they would prefer a more private one-to-one space to explore their difficulties. Rothwell and Grandison (2016) describe the need for 'a brief period of pre – therapy to prepare the patient for therapy work'. (p. 189). The primary focus of this stage is forming a connection and beginning a therapeutic alliance, which may need to happen on an individual basis. Patients may be feeling fragile after their journey into hospital and are only able to meet with one other person in the first instance. As one service user put it

> *I found the group quite difficult as was distracted by what other people were doing and compared my artwork unfavourably with theirs. I was unable to access all the pain inside me when surrounded by others. I found the 1:1 sessions very helpful, it was much easier to reproduce what was going on inside me and then discuss the finished artwork.*

As with groups on an acute ward, individual art therapy does not exist in isolation and needs to be negotiated sensitively and collaboratively with patients who are likely to be in fluctuating emotional states. Where in other contexts, it would be usual for a service user to be in individual therapy with one psychological therapist, on a ward, there are likely to be several members of the ward team working with the same patient, 'as the nature of the work requires this level of intensity, just as a surgeon, nurse and physiotherapist might all work together with the same road accident patient'. (Rothwell & Grandison, 2016, p. 191).

It is vital then for art therapists to make explicit to patients that the confidentiality of therapy sessions sits within the ward team. The sessions are an opportunity for the individual and the art therapist to develop a shared understanding of their difficulties, which can support the views and overall treatment within the wider in-patient team. Individual art therapy on the ward may be standalone or just a few sessions, due to the pace and timing of admissions. The efficacy of such brief work has gained recognition and is explored in Hughes (2016) and Luzzatto (1997). Wood (1990) proposes that 'the single session appears to have a value that goes beyond a simple introduction' (p. 27), and Woods (2016) suggests that 'in some circumstances, brief art therapy approaches might be particularly appropriate because of the way art making can provide some protection from talking' (p. 29). Supporting a reduction of psychological distress on the acute ward is a priority. Offering individuals a space apart from the group in which art materials are explored together with the art therapist can mitigate, to some extent, the 'concrete state of mind that accompanies distress' (Springham, 2008, p. 22) and support affect regulation.

## Art Therapists Reach on the Ward – Other Roles

In contrast to Adamson's designated role as an artist who 'has no psychological training' (Cunningham Dax 1953, p. 21), art therapists working on wards today bring their psychological understanding of patients into the ward team. This can be through facilitating reflective practice, providing debriefs for staff and offering staff support: 'I find it easier to express myself through images, art therapy provides a way of visually prompting myself to understand how I am feeling'. (Staff member feedback 2025). Chapter 10 looks specifically at this growing role for art therapists. Support for patients' family members is also a helpful intervention on the ward, seeing carers as central to the individual's life, not peripheral to it. Art therapists can help to bridge communication and understanding between patients and family members, who may also have found their relative's admission traumatic and confusing. Signposting to community arts resources or to art therapy in community services can support the patients' recovery pathway and help to bridge understanding of the patient to the community team who will be supporting them after discharge.

The continuation of art therapy after discharge is included in NICE guidelines (2014, p. 37) and can enable an individual to have time to process their difficulties; *the transition from hospital was quite difficult, and continuation of the art therapy sessions helped me to work through my feelings* (Service User, 2025). During patients' admissions and in discharge planning, the art therapist can hold the bigger picture in mind: speaking about the future, instilling hope, supporting patients to restore a sense of identity and reconnecting to personal values and meaning to strengthen personal agency. These are the cornerstones of a co-produced recovery framework, given the acronym CHIME: connectedness; hope and optimism about the future; identity; meaning in life; and empowerment (Leamy et al., 2011). Rothwell and Grandison outline the benefits of art therapists holding these values in mind:

> Through innovative partnerships with outside agencies, art psychotherapy can provide a range of interventions from in-patient wards to community therapy groups that connect, for example, with mainstream culture and education sectors, for full 'social recovery', with a view to enabling an active and responsible life with the familial and cultural contexts of patients. (p. 183)

The following chapter will offer an in-depth exploration of the benefits of community arts provision through an innovative project in New South Wales, Australia.

## Conclusion

Art therapists are adapting their practice to the changing nature and pressures of an in-patient ward. This chapter has shown that art therapy offers people in disturbed and distressed states of mind a means of communicating where words alone cannot. We have described how art therapy creates a bridge: for patients to their interior lives and from art therapists to the ward team, bringing an additional lens of understanding of the patient's experience.

Art materials and art making, with the art therapist, can enable patients to engage more actively in their recovery. The relational, collaborative approach in art therapy invites patients to have a different experience of themselves and their distress. This chapter has illuminated some of the ways in which art therapists enable this and how their wider contributions within the ward team can support the individual's ongoing recovery.

As discussed in Chapter 13, there is a pressing need for art therapists' interventions to be better understood and for them to be embedded in the in-patient workforce skill mix, to ensure that patients have access to them.

> *I think so much of what you can and can't do in hospital is so regimented and decided for you that what's nice about art therapy is that it's completely within your control what you want to do, what you don't want to do, what you want to use, what you don't want to use. It kind of feels like the one thing that's actually about you and what you want, which I really, really liked about it. It was invaluable to my recovery.*
>
> (Service User, 2025)

## References

Adamson, E. (1984). *Art as Healing.* Coverture Ltd.

Allen, P. (1983). Group art therapy in short term hospital settings. *American Journal of Art Therapy*, 22: 93–95.

American Psychiatric Association. (2013). *Diagnostic and statistical manual of mental disorders.* American Psychiatric Association.

British Association of Art Therapists (2017 April 17). *Creative Cuts: Val Huet.* www.tellyjuice.co.uk (Director: Emma Baxter)

Brown, C., & Omand, H. (Eds.) (2022). *Contemporary Practice in Studio Art Therapy.* Routledge.

Cavaliero, A. (2022). Terms of engagement, Aspects of facilitating open art therapy groups for adults in a psychiatric inpatient setting. In C. Brown & H. Omand (Eds.) *Contemporary Practice in Studio Art Therapy*, pp. 155–164. Routledge.

Colley. A. (2024). *In-Patient Mental Health Care from the Asylum System to the Present Day: A Lived Experience of Policy and Practice.* Routledge.

Cutler, D (2020). *Creatively Minded. An Initial Mapping Study of Participatory Arts and Mental Health Activity in the United Kingdom.* Baring Foundation.

Dax, E. C. (1953). *Experimental Studies in Psychiatric Art.* London: Faber & Faber.

Deco, S. (1998). Return to the open studio group. In S. Skaife & V. Huet (Eds.) *Art Psychotherapy Groups, Between Pictures and Words*, pp. 89–108. Routledge.

Dissanayake, E. (2003). *Homo Aestheticus: Where Art Came from and Why.* Macmillan, Inc.

Edwards, D. (1986). Three years on: Surviving the institution. *Inscape.*

Eno, B., & Bette, A. (2025). *What Art Does: An Unfinished Theory.* Faber.

Huet, V. (2012). Creativity in a cold climate: Art therapy-based organisational consultancy within public healthcare. *International Journal of Art Therapy*, 17(1), 25–33.

Hughes, R. (2016). *Time limited art psychotherapy*. pp. 118–193. Oxford: Routledge.

Isserow, J. (2008). Looking together: Joint attention in art therapy. *International Journal of Art Therapy*, 13(1), pp. 34–42. https://doi.org/10.1080/17454830802002894

Jackson, B. (2025). *Fragile Minds, Stories from an NHS Mental Health Ward*. Doubleday.

Jarrold, K. (2018). *Other People's Shoes: 40 Questions for Leaders and Managers*. Other People's Shoes.

Johnstone, L. (2018). Diagnostic alternatives; Psychological formulation as an alternative to psychiatric diagnosis. *Journal of Humanistic Psychology*, 57(6), pp. 30–46.

Leamy, M., Bird, V., Le Boutillier, C., Williams, J., & Slade, M. (2011). Conceptual framework for personal recovery in mental health: Systematic review and narrative synthesis *The British Journal of Psychiatry*, 199, pp. 445–452. https://doi.org/10.1192/bjp.bp.110.083733

Learmonth, M. (2005). Changing our minds. *Open Mind*, 134, 18–19.

Luzzatto, P. (1997). Short term art therapy on the acute psychiatric ward: The open session as a psychodynamic development of the studio-based approach. *International Journal of Art Therapy: Inscape*, 2(1), pp. 2–10.

Malchiodi, C. A. (2020). *Trauma and Expressive Arts Therapy Brain, Body & Imagination in the Healing Process*. The Guilford Press.

Marshall-Tierney, A. (2014). Making art with and without patients in acute settings. *International Journal of Art Therapy*, 19(3), 96–106. https://doi.org/10.1080/17454832.2014.913256

Mithen, S. (1996). The early prehistory of human social behaviour: Issues of archaeological inference and cognitive evolution. *Proceedings of the British Academy*, 88, pp. 145–177.

NICE (2014). *Guidelines for Psychosis and Schizophrenia in Adults: Prevention and Management*.

Noble, J., & Hackett, S. (2023). Art therapy in acute inpatient care. *International Journal of Art Therapy*, 28(4), pp. 196–203.

Rothwell, K., & Grandison, S. (2016). Notes on service design for art psychotherapists working in time – limited group programmes on adult mental health inpatient wards In R. Hughes (Ed.) *Time Limited Art Psychotherapy*, pp. 118–193. Routledge.

Shevlin, M., Houston, J. E., Dorahy, M. J., & Adamson, G. (2008). Cumulative traumas and psychosis: An analysis of the national comorbidity survey and the British Psychiatric Morbidity Survey. *Schizophrenia Bulletin*, 34(1), pp. 193–199. https://doi.org/10.1093/schbul/sbm069

Springham, N. (2008). Through the eyes of the law: what is it that can harm people about art. *International Journal of Art Therapy: Inscape*, 13(2), pp. 40–47.

Springham, N., & Huet, V. (2018). Art as relational encounter: An ostensive communication theory of art therapy. *Journal of the American Art Therapy Association, Art Therapy*, 35(1), pp. 4–10. https://doi.org/10.1080/07421656.2018.1460103.

Timlin, J. (2001 July 9). Unreleased video interview with Ed Lawrenson & Pia Borg.

Winnicott, D. W. (1958). The capacity to be alone. *The International Journal of Psycho-Analysis*, 39, 416.

Wood, C. (2016). Quick sketches and snapshots for brief art therapy: As a time-limited approach. In *Time-Limited Art Psychotherapy* (pp. 27–43). Routledge.

Wood, M. (1990) Art Therapy in one session: working with people with aids, *Inscape: The Journal of the British Association of Art Therapists. Winter* 1990: 27–33

Woods, A., & Springham, N. (2011). On learning from being the in – patient, *International Journal of Art Therapy*, 16(2), pp. 60–68.

World Health Organization. (2022). *International Classification of Diseases: [11th] Eleventh Revision, Basic Tabulation List with Alphabetic Index*. World Health Organization.

Wright, T., & Holttum, S. (2020). *BAAT Guidelines on Art Therapy for People with a Psychosis-Related Diagnosis*. British Association of Art Therapists.

Yalom, I. D. (1995). *The Theory and Practice of Group Psychotherapy* (4th ed.). Basic Books.

# 6 Arts in Recovery

## Narrative Case Studies Exploring Artmaking as a Pathway to Becoming and Belonging

*Alan Johnson and Tess Rendoth*

Creative therapy has never claimed to be a sole or independent cure for mental illness…It should be used alongside all the other medical and therapeutic aids available in a modern psychiatric hospital; it is complementary rather than competitive (Adamson, 1970, p. 158)

### Introduction

This chapter will profile Arts in Recovery (AiR), a programme that has been running for 15 years in New South Wales, Australia. Most participants are current in-patients in long- and short-stay units or are engaged in clinical mental health service provision either in the community or in other hospital environments, such as forensic placements.

The chapter begins with a contextual introduction to the arts health landscape in Australia and an introduction to the programme and its principles of practice. Though existing outside a formal hospital environment, AiR closely adheres to many of Adamson's philosophical intents and approaches. It is overseen by artists, and its brief extends from workshop logistics and facilitation to facilitators' intentional approach towards art and mental health recovery. Its open-door policy and embrace of a studio environment share intentions with Adamson's own motivations and practices.

The chapter will present the life worlds of four of its participant artists through narrative-based case studies and personal contributions of writing, complemented by the reflections of the authors on each case study's journey and growth.

Written not by art therapists, but by a Lecturer in Education and an Occupational Therapist, the chapter looks forward to the concluding chapter of this book: *The Wider Context – Growth in Arts and Wellbeing Provision Nationally and Internationally.*

### The Australian Arts Health Landscape

Arts health is growing rapidly within a global context, and this is supporting the growth of arts health programmes such as *Arts in Recovery* (AiR) within

DOI: 10.4324/9781003613428-9

Australia (Dow et al., 2023). Arts health programmes in Australia have been developing since the 1990s, with an increase in programmes now possible due to the support of federal and state policy development. The development of policy has supported both hospitals and health systems to grow programmes as well as community-managed organisations (CMOs). This has allowed AiR to be co-developed by health services and the community equally.

Within Australia, Arts Health is defined by the Australian Federal Government's National Arts Health Framework as programmes and events which use arts initiatives for the purposes of treatment of health issues and health promotion (Department of Communication and the Arts, 2014). The New South Wales *Health and the Arts Framework 2024–2032* defines Arts Health as 'applying creative, participatory or receptive arts interventions to health problems and health promotion settings to foster health and wellbeing across the spectrum of health practice, from primary prevention through to tertiary treatment' (ACI-Health, 2024, p. 34).

## Arts in Recovery's Research Framework

AiR, as a community arts health programme, is facilitated by both mental health clinicians and artists alike; however, the mental health clinicians, educators and academics involved in the facilitation of the programme are all fine arts trained as well as being qualified in their professional roles. The AiR programme structure derives its motivations and framework from research that shows that arts health programmes mainly benefit participants by enhancing social well-being, engagement and support, and it is the intervention setting, often viewed as a safe and non-judgmental space, that contributes significantly to these outcomes (Davies et al., 2014; Goodman-Casanova et al., 2024; McCaffrey et al., 2021). Additionally, people with mental health needs value such environments for socialising and forming friendships, which can facilitate participation in other community activities (Colbert et al., 2013; Van Lith et al., 2011).

In addition, studies in arts health suggest that regular attendance may play a large part in developing structure and routine through regular engagement within the activities or community settings (Goodman-Casanova et al., 2024; Wilson & Kent, 2014). Within the AiR programme, some participants have continued to attend since its commencement in 2009.

## Arts in Recovery (AiR)

Based in a regional centre in NSW, Australia, AiR began in 2009 and is founded on a volunteer-led partnership structure between artists, participants, occupational therapists from the local health district and mental health workers and educators. Over the past 15 years, the programme has been managed by a core group of representatives from each of these partners as an expert working group. Since its inception, AiR has facilitated monthly art workshops and a yearly exhibition, *Bounceback*. Workshops run from February to November, between 40 and 60 people attend, and the exhibition profiles, on average, over 200 artworks per year. The AiR programme is embedded in a prominent professional arts space, *The Creator Incubator*. AiR and AiR participants are active members of this broader creative and artistic community, embedding links to professional practice and ad-hoc social connectivity, facilitating a sense of professionalism and acceptance into the arts world in the same way as Edward Adamson had looked on the people working in his studios at Netherne, not as patients but as artists.

AiR is a process-motivated, non-referral art programme prioritising experience, engagement and community through shared artmaking, distinct from clinical outcomes. Monthly workshops offer at least four semi-structured activities facilitated by skilled volunteer artists. Participants can also freely use studio resources or choose their focus. Health professionals (nurses, OTs and peer/support workers), educators and social supports (friends, family and carers) are encouraged to participate so the impact and experience of the workshop and art practices can extend beyond the environment of AiR. AiR also provides a social space, fostering socialisation through activities and environment, with engagement driven by individual choice.

Each workshop runs for 4 hours and includes a whole-group lunch. Cost is kept to a small donation to ensure that the programme can be accessible to all people, despite their financial situation. The accessibility of the programme is also reflected in the adoption and promotion of an open-door policy for attendance with no need for registration or referral. There is a balanced participation between people in the community and those who are currently in clinical settings, whose attendance is facilitated by hospital or health workers. Having this structure enables people to continue their engagement with the programme on their own terms in an ongoing way and is responsive to the fluid nature of complex and ongoing mental health service engagement, which most participants experience.

### *The AiR Community*

From 2009 to 2025, over 4500 people participated in over 100 AiR workshops thus far. The participants who attend identify as having a lived experience of mental illness and come from a range of services, including in-patient facilities from the local health district; these facilities include short stay acute units, intermediate stay units and long-term rehabilitation units, including a medium-secure unit. The participants may be civilian consumers under the Mental Health Act and forensic consumers who are under the Forensic Mental Health Act. From the community, people attend from accommodation supported by CMOs or private support services, and those who live in the community but are supported by community mental health teams, there are also those who live independently in the community and identify with mental illness.

### *Artmaking Practices*

#### *Resources*

AiR offers monthly art activities using accessible, low-cost mediums with entry-level skill requirements. This enables participants (often with limited financial capacity) and staff to continue artmaking as a therapeutic process at home or in in-patient settings. AiR reinforces ongoing engagement by lending resources, encouraging skill refinement, independent artmaking and extending social connections beyond workshops. This has the added benefit of participants being encouraged to refine and develop their skills, adopt more independent artmaking approaches and create ongoing and reciprocal social and community experiences as extensions outside of the workshop environment.

#### *Collaboration*

Collaborative artmaking practice is encouraged through the development of a yearly group artmaking project that is displayed at the annual *Bounceback* workshop. Each year, a collaborative artwork is slowly developed over the course of each workshop that everyone contributes to, including hospital and support staff in attendance. The artwork acts as a narrative of each year and celebrates the stories of each person's contribution to the programme's success.

#### *Mentoring*

AiR staff are all skilled artists, and although the open-access artmaking materials and techniques are designed to act as entry points for an individual's own artmaking expression, when a participant finds a technique or style that they wish to focus on, specific skills development and higher levels of complexity of practice are supported through direct mentoring and teaching. This mentoring and guidance are mirrored in AiR workshop facilitators' expectation that all health and support staff who attend also adopt the role of attendees, in the same way as participants: echoing the experience of Edward Adamson discussed in the previous chapter, where he was challenged to work alongside the patients in his studio. This creates a more equal hierarchy, where the health or support workers are sitting next to participants, exploring and learning in the same way as each other; often with participants adopting the role of peer teacher. Sitting together, learning, sharing and developing a new layer of relationship that can be reflected on and discussed between workshop days.

### *Bounceback*

We have discussed in Chapter 3 many of the issues around exhibiting art by service users from mental health settings. The Bounceback exhibition at the conclusion of the yearly workshops was designed to allow the participants to work towards goals such as completing work, skills development, share their narratives, exhibit their finished works and could celebrate their accomplishments. Since 2010, the artworks created during workshops have been exhibited for the public in community galleries in Newcastle. The programme estimates that to date 2,150 artworks have been shown, 1,500 people attended opening nights and, $32,500 has been returned to artists for their sold works. The artists have the choice to sell works or retain them for their collections. Some of the group artworks are sold to support the financial aspects of the programme, with this aim explained to all participants during the creation of the works. The annual exhibition aims to exhibit as many artworks as possible within the space, allowing people to choose as many artworks as they deem appropriate. Some of the participants who have identified the goal of becoming professional artists work with artist mentors to curate their work and price them accordingly.

The inclusion of an exhibition within the AiR programme is motivated through the understanding that the social context and personal reward gained by collective engagement, audience feedback and reinforcement of an individual's personal narrative through their art is important both in broader community discussions of creativity, but importantly for the individual to see value in their own creative expression and therefore the value and contribution of their life experiences and contributions to the broader social fabric to which they belong (Munro, 2019).

### *Health and Well-being*

People experiencing mental health problems may struggle with motivation and self-expression, and commonly find social interaction challenging, with increased rates of loneliness compared to the general population (Bjørlykhaug et al., 2022; Jenkins et al., 2023). These experiences can result in social isolation and fewer opportunities to participate in occupations like community-based leisure activities. Additionally, societal stigma associated with mental illness can further contribute to this isolation (Adu et al., 2022). AiR's environment fosters safety, freedom of expression, curiosity and self-efficacy. It is an open space prioritising individual choice, process and creative exploration, free from time constraints. For in-patients (Adu et al., 2022), AiR offers a unique environment of control, choice, imaginative freedom and promotes empathy through individual and collectivist experiences that cultivate connectivity and belonging (Riley et al., 2026; Thornhill-Miller et al., 2023).

### *Partnerships*

AiR is a volunteer and unfunded organisation, and having stakeholders from across different settings and services has meant that, over time, three partnerships have emerged, which are essential to its effectiveness. These are the partnership between AiR and *The Creator Incubator*, the arts venue where workshops and the exhibition are held; AiR and service providers, both in-patient and community; and most centrally, AiR and the participants. The partnerships demonstrate the ability of the programme to combine mental health support from trained staff and clinicians with art facilitation from professional artists and mental health staff, with the views of participants driving the development and focus of the programme. It means the provision of a safe and trusted space that supports art creation, but can dually support mental health and associated needs intervention if identified by participants.

## Case Studies: John, Rachel, Sam and Phoebe

To best exemplify the programme's impact, four case studies of AiR participants will be presented. Pseudonyms will be used, and identifying information will be changed to ensure anonymity. The information for these case studies was gained during research into the AiR programme as part of PhD research. Ethics approval was granted by the Hunter New England Local Health District Ethics Committee in January 2016 (HNEHREC/ReferenceNo:16/12/14/5.05/NSWHREC Reference No: LNR/1/HNE/570 SSA Reference No: LNRSSA/16/HNE/571) and registered with the University of Newcastle (H-2017-0055).

In each case study, we will learn a little about each individual, including brief descriptions of their mental health journey, but importantly, their own personal reflections and experiences of the role art and AiR have had in that journey. These verbatim accounts are presented below in *italics*, and will be accompanied by the author's own reflections on key attributes that the programme aims to cultivate: consistency, flexibility, trust and reciprocity as pathways to belonging and becoming for our participants.

### *John*

John is a man in his mid-50s who has been attending the AiR programme for 10 years. John is very private about his history but acknowledges his interactions with mental health services via hospital admission and the need for community supports. John is able to turn his hand to most activities at the workshops, but tends to prefer drawing. He experiments with computer tessellations and is also highly skilled in origami. He admits he is *very controlled or tight* in his work, but is working on freedom and loosening his drawing.

*Presentation*

John was admitted to hospital after becoming unwell and then attended the AiR workshops after a suggestion from the local community mental health team upon his discharge.

> *I was very ill and had to be hospitalised with a mental health problem and when I came out of that, I did get support from the community mental health team. They told me about this group [AiR], so I decided I'd give it a go. I was looking forward to being there. So, I came. That's how I started. And that was quite a few years ago now.*

*John's AiR Journey*

John attended the programme regularly and would always come alone. In his first year, he was very quiet and tended to remain on the edge of the group observing the activities and people, progressively becoming more engaged, and by his second year, he slowly began interacting:

> *It's been very helpful to me. It's not just in doing art or drawing but actually the social aspect has been very good.*

Gradually, he has become more comfortable with the programme and people; he has participated regularly, exhibited works in the annual exhibition many times.

> *I think I'm amazed that I can actually exhibit. You know as an amateur artist I think it's an incredible boost to your self-esteem just to know that you've got your artwork up there and people looking at it...That's a tremendous boost to your confidence.*

John has grown in confidence over the last ten years and is currently a key part of the AiR facilitation team as a participant representative, regularly facilitating activities, welcoming and greeting people, showing them around and assisting in planning the year's workshops and in the hanging of the exhibition.

> *Just being around all the other people is actually very good for you. A willingness...I mean [it's] a very good thing for me and I've really come right out of my shell; I'm probably way out of it here, and that's probably very good.*

*Consistency*

For John, the regularity of the programme, its setup, facilitation and support through consistent staff have allowed him the time to become comfortable in engaging in art creation, exhibiting works, engaging with others and then facilitating activities himself. This has been over a period of years for this confidence to be developed and slowly emerge through consistent engagement: A key aspect of the programme's overall success and John's continued attendance.

### *Rachel*

Rachel is in her mid-20s and began attending the AiR programme around 12 years ago. Rachel has a layered and fluctuating experience around her mental health, is a very creative individual and is involved in many aspects of the arts, from circus performing, poetry, performing and recording her own songs, writing books and illustrating graphic novels, as well as painting and drawing. She uses all of these mediums to communicate and share her journey and personal responses to her own mental health experience.

#### *Presentation*

Rachel became engaged in the AiR programme through the youth mental health services supporting transition from in-patient to community settings. Rachel has been attending the programme for the last 12 years and may attend for 6 months regularly and then not again for 12–18 months, with her attendance patterns mirroring her mental health wellness. Initially, Rachel came with support workers consistently, but has been attending mostly on her own for the past 8 years. She utilises the programme as she needs to, in the way she needs to.

#### *Rachel's AiR Journey*

Rachel often works near others on her own work or an activity she is interested in, often listening to music, but still feels connection and socialisation in a way that she feels comfortable with and benefits from. She enjoys the flexibility of the programme as it provides her access to materials, inspiration, connection and also an opportunity to exhibit her works.

> *I'll just kind of do my own thing. And I'm very happy with that. So I still feel like I'm making contact with people, because everyone's working on their own thing, so it feels like I'm kind of socializing without feeling the pressure or the need to talk. Coming here, I think it is helped in that I've been able to look forward every month to coming to a space where there's no expectations…(everyone is) very friendly and very like-minded…we're all creative on some level. It's a very free and safe space to come along and do your thing, and no one really needs to meet a criteria, which is awesome. So it's just the casual and freedom to express yourself and the [access to] resources to do that, like immediately.*

*Flexibility*

Rachel has participated in the programme for an extended period and expressed the freedom to attend and participate with no criteria or expectation is key to her attending in conjunction with the freedom and choice the programme affords her. She has grown in confidence within her engagement and socialisation during the programme. She has spoken at the exhibition's opening night, performed her own songs and has recently had her own solo exhibition Rachel states about the *Bounceback* exhibition:

> *it's a safe way to get your work out there because sharing your work can be very vulnerable, particularly if you use it by therapeutic means.*

She also uses her experiences and artistic ability to support her peers and often provides support to younger members of the programme.

***Sam***

Sam, a man in his late 30s, has attended the AiR programme since its 2009 trial workshop, initially as an acute unit in-patient. He has complex mental health needs and a complicated history with hospital services, impacting his understanding of his mental health journey. Sam states: *I never believed I had a mental illness. I still don't.*

*Presentation*

During hospitalisation, Sam showed interest in creating bird and dinosaur artworks, attending AiR with staff support. Initially, he hyper-fixated on negative experiences, violent interactions and real and imagined beliefs about mental health, often using fantasy and discussing visual hallucinations or 'otherworldly' influences. This made peer interaction and logical comprehension difficult, and he was unable to receive critique or questioning. It was initially very challenging to refocus Sam or move him towards more productive reflections on his own ideas and subjective experience of the world.

*Sam's AiR Journey*

Post-discharge, Sam attends AiR with support workers or independently. He has refined his skills, now favouring coloured pencils and oil pastels over a single black pen, though he still creates multiple line drawings, sometimes as a refocusing method. Sam enjoys the social aspect, noting: *Just seeing how people get along together...and enjoy each other's company. Just to see you guys. just to... um...torment you guys a bit.* He is now completely himself in workshops, interacting freely with facilitators and peers. While still discussing familiar topics, he now approaches them from a deeper philosophical perspective, open to alternative views and reflection. Sam has exhibited in every show, showcasing diverse media and selling multiple popular works; he is now a recognised artist. AiR allows him to express thoughts, ideas and frustrations, benefiting from public sharing. The creation of his fantasy worlds, though unspoken, offers him a safe space to explore identity and experiences.

#### *Trust*

AiR has provided Sam a safe, trusting environment to engage with his experiences and identity, both personally and with others. Despite his rigid actions and confronting statements like *all nurses are evil and should die*, AiR's format enables participation in a mental health programme without resisting hospital constructs or service provision. It grants him space and confidence to express concerns and subjective experiences of mental health services, free from fear of judgement or consequence.

### *Phoebe*

Phoebe is in her early 20s and attended the programme via a recommendation from her psychologist. Phoebe has multiple diagnoses, including but not limited to generalised anxiety disorder and severe depression. She also has Autism. Phoebe had a history of hospitalisation in adolescent wards and of using violent and aggressive behaviour towards herself and others. She disengaged from formal education at age 15 due to her complex needs profile and use of violence as communication. Phoebe began attending AiR two and a half years ago, initially with her family, but now does so on her own. Phoebe is an extremely creative individual who can create art from any media she chooses, be it drawing, sewing and ceramics to sculpture and collage. She creates imagined landscapes and characters, and enjoys dark humour, which influences her works, becoming an identifying artistic personality in all her work.

#### *Presentation*

Initially, Phoebe communicated via a hand-stitched rabbit worn on her chest, which was essential for any social interaction as a mediating bridge between Phoebe and the world around her. She avoided physical touch and close proximity to anyone other than her sister or father, and used noise-cancelling headphones at all times. Facilitators communicated with her through the rabbit, shaking its hand or using sign language. Over time, with AiR facilitator and peer support, Phoebe grew more comfortable. She gradually stopped wearing headphones, sat at group tables and became less reactive to others' communication. Her art, its creation and the stories within were central to her growth and confidence.

*Phoebe's AiR Journey*

Through her attendance at the programme, Phoebe began to feel more comfortable, given the support of the AiR facilitators and her peers who attend the programme. Slowly, Phoebe stopped wearing the headphones, would sit at small group tables and became less reactive to expressive communication from others. She was supported and encouraged through the focus and discussion of her art:

> *I wasn't doing that [talking] this time last year, and I'd only talk to family. And thanks to coming here and actually realizing, hey, not all people are going to hurt me...before, it was only family that could touch me without me throwing up or getting anxious and having a panic attack. It's made it a lot easier to start talking again.*

Phoebe began to communicate with facilitators in a more open way, and it was clear that her previous institutional (hospital and education) experiences were a significant factor in her underlying feelings of anxiousness and (lack of) connectedness. In the AiR workshops, Phoebe began to open up and speak with participants and staff who were active in a hospital environment, leading to Phoebe gaining admission at a local intermediate stay unit, at her own volition.

Phoebe has participated in two annual exhibitions and the majority of workshops. The combination of the programme and the admission have allowed Phoebe to have control over her recovery journey and is now comfortable freely engaging with others, no longer bringing her rabbit. Phoebe often attends independently, using public transport without assistance to get herself to the workshop, the first time independently using public services.

> *I've progressed more in this year since coming here than I have any other year of my life... I blame you guys for making me talk, if it wasn't for you the world still wouldn't need to deal with me, I could have just hid at home.*

*Reciprocity*

Phoebe has spoken to AiR facilitators that she feels comfortable being herself within the programme, showing off her scars and being free to identify with her sexuality and be herself. The way she experiences her own identity is not something to hide, but to explore, share and celebrate in the safety of the AiR studio process.

For Phoebe, the programme gives her a chance at reciprocating the help and support she feels she has received. Phoebe actively engages with her peers as an art practice mentor and in preparing and serving lunch as a form of social leadership. Phoebe has grown in confidence and her ability to engage and

*Image 6.1* Example artworks produced by John, Rachel, Sam and Phoebe during AiR workshops.

Reproduced by permission of Arts in Recovery.

interact with others to the extent that she will talk to new people and hold longer and longer interactions and expand her independent engagement with the world, despite the anxiety she feels (Image 6.1).

## Conclusion

AiR's collaborative partnership model has established it as a longstanding fixture in mental health care in its region. The stories of John, Rachel, Sam and Phoebe demonstrate the programme's integral relational and operational drivers since inception: reciprocity, trust, flexibility and consistency. These factors are essential for programme longevity, effectiveness and participants' ongoing attendance.

AiR participants value a safe, understanding environment with facilitators and peers familiar with mental illness, allowing them to *let the mask slip* (Rachel). Engaging in creative activities supports self-expression and recovery, enabling participants to communicate feelings about their mental health non-verbally and in a non-clinical environment. The studio model of delivery centralises social interaction without expectation.

AiR facilitators support participants through artmaking, enabling them to choose their preferred level of engagement without affecting their programme participation. The community arts centre, *The Creator Incubator*, offers an inclusive environment where participants can interact with professional artists in workshops designed to minimise stigma and judgment. These factors have contributed to AiR's continued success and ongoing operation. The AiR studio workshop model permits attendance without requiring a sign-in, and there is no expectation of monthly participation. This approach allows individuals to build creative practice skills, motivation and social connectivity, empowering them to decide whether to attend based on personal circumstances. Participants are confident in a supportive, inclusive environment that fosters control over their own recovery and leads them to feel a greater sense of belonging and becoming within their own identity, and within the world.

We have shown in this chapter how the arts are able to transcend different contexts, settings and situations, and so in the next chapter, the book will move from the relative freedom of a community arts programme to explore how art therapy is offered in a high-secure setting.

The authors would like to firstly thank the generosity of John, Rachel, Sam and Phoebe for allowing us to share their stories, and each and every person who has supported, participated and contributed to the AiR community in any large or small way.

## References

ACI-Health. (2024). *Health and the Arts Framework 2024–2032*. St Leonards, NSW: State of NSW Health. https://aci.health.nsw.gov.au/__data/assets/pdf_file/0017/970010/NSW-Health-and-the-Arts-Framework-2024-2032.pdf

Adamson, E. (1970). Art for mental health. In Creedy, J. (Ed.). *The Social Context of Art*. London: Tavistock Publications.

Adu, J., Oudshoorn, A., Anderson, K., Marshall, C. A., & Stuart, H. (2022). Social contact: Next steps in an effective strategy to mitigate the stigma of mental illness. *Issues in Mental Health Nursing*, 43(5), pp. 485–488. https://doi.org/10.1080/01612840.2021.1986757

Bjørlykhaug, K. I., Karlsson, B., Hesook, S. K., & Kleppe, L. C. (2022). Social support and recovery from mental health problems: A scoping review. *Nordic social Work Research*, 12(5), pp. 666–697. https://doi.org/10.1080/2156857X.2020.1868553

Colbert, S., Cooke, A., Camic, P. M., & Springham, N. (2013). The art-gallery as a resource for recovery for people who have experienced psychosis. *The Arts in Psychotherapy*, 40(2), pp. 250–256. https://doi.org/10.1016/j.aip.2013.03.003

Davies, C. R., Knuiman, M., Wright, P., & Rosenberg, M. (2014). The art of being healthy: a qualitative study to develop a thematic framework for understanding the relationship between health and the arts. *BMJ Open*, 4(4). https://doi.org/10.1136/bmjopen-2014-004790

Department of Communications and the Arts. (2014). *National arts and health framework*. Australian Government. https://www.artsandhealth.ie/policies-strategies/national-arts-and-health-framework-aus/

Dow, R., Warran, K., Letrondo, P., & Fancourt, D. (2023). The arts in public health policy: Progress and opportunities. *The Lancet Public Health*, 8(2), pp. 155–160. https://doi.org/10.1016/S2468-2667(22)00313-9

Goodman-Casanova, J. M., Guzman-Parra, J., Mayoral-Cleries, F., & Cuesta-Lozano, D. (2024). Community-based art groups in mental health recovery: A systematic review and narrative synthesis. *Journal of Psychiatric and Mental Health Nursing*, 31(2), pp. 158–173. https://doi.org/10.1111/jpm.12970

Jenkins, G. T., Janich, N., Wu, S., & Shafer, M. (2023). Social isolation and mental health: Evidence from adults with serious mental illness. *Psychiatric Rehabilitation Journal*, 46(2), p. 148. https://doi.org/10.1037/prj0000554

McCaffrey, T., Higgins, P., Morrison, H., Nelligan, S., Clancy, A., Cheung, P. S., & Moloney, S. (2021). Exploring the role and impact of visual art groups with multiple stakeholders in recovery-oriented mental health services. *The Arts in Psychotherapy*, 72, p. 101748. https://doi.org/10.1016/j.aip.2020.101748

Munro, J. (2019). *Creativity in Education: What Educators Need to Know*. State of New South Wales (Department of Education). https://education.nsw.gov.au/content/dam/main-education/teaching-and-learning/education-for-a-changing-world/media/documents/Munro_Creativity_Education.pdf

Riley, T., Meston, T., McCormack, B., Low-Choy, S., & Ballangary, J. (2026). From too afraid to speak to too afraid not to: exploring the potential of arts-integrated practices to confront teachers' apprehension towards Indigenous education. *Pedagogy, Culture & Society*, 34(1), 219–236. https://doi.org/10.1080/14681366.2025.2483696

Thornhill-Miller, B., Camarda, A., Mercier, M., Burkhardt, J. M., Morisseau, T., Bourgeois-Bougrine, S., Vinchon, F., El Hayek, S., Augereau-Landais, M., Mourey, F., Feybesse, C., Sundquist, D., & Lubart, T. (2023). Creativity, critical thinking, communication, and collaboration: Assessment, certification, and promotion of 21st century skills for the future of work and education. *Journal of Intelligence*, 11(3), p. 54. https://doi.org/10.3390/jintelligence11030054

Van Lith, T., Fenner, P., & Schofield, M. (2011). The lived experience of art making as a companion to the mental health recovery process. *Disability and Rehabilitation*, 33(8), pp. 652–660. https://doi.org/10.3109/09638288.2010.505998

Wilson, C. J. S., & Kent, I. (2014). Arts participation, mental well-being and social inclusion: Mixed methods evaluation of an Open Arts studio for people with mental health needs. *Journal of Applied Arts & Health*, 5(3), pp. 341–354 https://intellectdiscover.com/content/journals/10.1386/jaah.5.3.341_1

# 7 Art Psychotherapy with Adults in a High-Secure Setting

*Emma Allen*

## Introduction

The United Kingdom is home to three high-security hospitals: Broadmoor Hospital in Berkshire, Ashworth Hospital near Liverpool and Rampton Hospital in Nottinghamshire. As outlined in Chapter 4, *Enabling Spaces*, high-security hospitals are facilities that detain patients under the Mental Health Act (1983, amended 2007) due to behaviours that are dangerous, violent or criminal. Patients may also be identified as having a range of mental health needs or learning difficulties.

Chapter 4 included a discussion around the extent to which the quiet 'open' studio space Adamson (1984) describes in *Art is Healing* is something that can still be created on a busy ward in a high-security setting, and described what is known as 'seclusion hatch work' (Allen, 2019, p. 42). This chapter will develop that discussion in the context of a concise historical overview of forensic art psychotherapy for adults in high-security environments in the United Kingdom, as well as a research- and practice-informed dialogue around the role of forensic art psychotherapists.

The chapter will then advance the discussions initiated in Chapter 3 regarding the ethics of curating and collecting artworks produced by individuals who have committed offences, and finally, and in anticipation of the NHS's digital transformation, the chapter will introduce the recently developed secure physical and digital archive for forensic artworks classified as clinical records as well as initiatives aimed at establishing a high-security collection similar to the Adamson Collection.

## Art Psychotherapy in Secure Settings

There has been a long history of arts activities in prisons (Liebmann, 1994) with arts psychotherapists working across the prison services. Art psychotherapy has been established in high-security settings in the United Kingdom since the early 1990s, with Rampton being the first to employ an art psychotherapist in 1990 and the hiring of an inaugural art therapist at Broadmoor in 1993, followed by a second in 1996. The practice is now deeply intertwined with the

DOI: 10.4324/9781003613428-10

broader evolution of art therapy and is part of a comprehensive multidisciplinary approach to patient care.

The arts psychotherapies department at Rampton Hospital has included a team of art and music therapists as part of a wider service focused on therapy and education. Forensic art psychotherapy serves as a comprehensive assessment and treatment strategy available both individually, in long-term segregation, and in group settings for adult men and women (Hewins, 2023) considered to pose an immediate or significant risk to others. Sessions are held either in the arts psychotherapies' clinic room or on the wards, and the department now features an art psychotherapy team that offers a diverse range of individual and group treatments across the hospital's directorates and national services, with trainee placements also available. Innovative image-making methods, such as sand play, have been introduced (Allen, 2018a), and the service continuously evolves to meet the changing needs of the patient population, integrating advancements in therapeutic techniques and therapy outcome measures (Allen, 2024).

For some patients, art psychotherapy might be the central individual psychological therapy; for others, it may be supportive to offence-related work or provide a manageable way to begin therapeutic work. The vision for this service for many years was to develop a diverse and innovative range of arts psychotherapies to meet the needs of the forensic patient groups, and to promote creative, culturally sensitive treatment choices. The department fosters a culture of learning and has had regular networking events with visiting artists and clinical experts.

Adamson (1970) stated that 'the patient's work is an aspect of his own personality which meets with no disapproval' (p. 153), and in forensic settings in particular, art psychotherapy enables patients to reflect upon their incarceration, regret or guilt for offending, and explore complex emotional responses to institutionalised hospital life (Allen, 2019). Patients are able to express and reflect on themselves verbally and non-verbally, where sessions aim to understand patients' communication on both conscious and unconscious levels, facilitating long-term exploration of internal states (Geraghty et al., 2024). Forensic art psychotherapy can be beneficial for a wide range of patients, particularly those who isolate themselves or struggle with emotional connection, requiring a supportive and non-directive approach. Patients use creative mediums to access and recognise dissociated emotional aspects of their identities, aiding those with limited language or social communication skills.

Forensic art psychotherapy is a form of psychodynamic treatment, traditionally non-directive, conducted within the confines of prisons, secure units and hospitals, and the forensic art psychotherapist is witness to the creative process by which the patient's projections and expressions are contained within visual imagery, enabling safe exploration of their inner world, trauma and offence histories. This approach is rooted in trauma-informed principles (Geraghty et al., 2024), aimed at fostering a creatively attuned psychotherapeutic relationship that minimises the risk of harm to oneself or others. Forensic art psychotherapists have provided and consolidated treatment, rehabilitation and relapse prevention inputs to the United Kingdom Forensic Services for more than four decades, working on time-limited and long-term interventions that are flexible and reflective, directive or non-directive (Rothwell & Grandison, 2016).

## Art in Prisons and the Koestler Awards

During the same period that Edward Adamson pioneered art therapy for psychiatric patients at Netherne Hospital, the value of art in prisons was being advocated by the Austro-Hungarian author and journalist Arthur Koestler (1905–1983). Koestler had a profound, personal connection to and experience of the prison system, having been imprisoned in three different countries: in 1936, he faced execution for espionage in Spain under Francisco Franco, was later detained in France at the Le Vernet Internment Camp, and was subsequently incarcerated at Pentonville prison in England as a suspected illegal immigrant. These experiences compelled Koestler to seek transformative changes in the prison environment, leading to his campaign for what the British Home Secretary at the time, RA Butler (1902–1982), described in a speech to launch the Koestler Awards in 1962 as *an imaginative and exciting way to stimulate...the mind and spirit of the prisoner.*

The Koestler Awards now serve to highlight creative works in literature, arts and sciences produced by individuals in confinement (Tucker & Moore, 1997). Each year, over 3,500 participants submit their artistic creations across various mediums, including art, design, writing and music. Forensic art psychotherapists assist patients in submitting personal artwork created outside therapeutic sessions, as therapy-related images are typically not exhibited. The experience of seeing their work displayed publicly requires staff support, especially since the artists cannot physically attend the exhibitions. Staff members often attend Koestler exhibitions, photographing artworks and sharing these images with the artists.

In both prison and psychiatric in-patient settings, art therapy has played a pivotal role in redirecting antisocial behaviour towards socially acceptable forms of self-expression (Collins et al., 2023). Ripley (1994) has further argued that creativity in visual arts, music and literature offers unparalleled satisfaction, a sense of achievement, and a profound means for prisoners to articulate their emotional and social identities, stating that 'art is about taking risks, while prison is about regulations, imposed controls, and minimizing risks' (p. 13).

Teasdale (1995), addressing the history of art therapy in prison settings, observed that 'generations of men and women serving custodial sentences have utilised art making for purposeful self-expression and self-valuation, as well as for recreational and educational benefits' (p. 2), and historical studies from the Centre for Research in Social Policy at Loughborough University, including *The Arts in Prison Research* (1990) and a subsequent study for the Special Hospitals Authority in 1992, highlighted the significant impact of art education on the overall prison environment.

## The Open Studio Model in a High-Secure Setting

Implementing an open studio model presents unique challenges (Takkal et al., 2018). Open art therapy groups for hospitalised adults aim to reduce feelings of isolation and alleviate the anxieties associated with incarceration. These groups can serve as a sanctuary from the depersonalising elements of large institutions, offering a distinctive space for expressing difficult emotions (Allen, 2019). For individuals who have posed significant risks to others, creating art alongside peers presents a valuable opportunity for self-reflection regarding interpersonal and relationship challenges, offending behaviours and risk management. The visual aspects of reminiscing provide a conduit for 'life reviews' in images made, allowing participants to confront issues of loss that may evoke anger and to initiate healing in a secure context (Allen, 2019).

The objectives of these open groups can also be to facilitate contained social engagement, group skills and a positive group experience through which patients may gain confidence and subsequently engage in more intensive offence-focused psychology groups. Open groups encourage the creative process and emotional self-expression within clearly defined boundaries, enhancing choices through diverse art materials and promoting positive social interactions while safely addressing daily challenges. This approach allows patients to learn indirectly from the experiences of their peers and the therapist (Vygotsky, 1978).

In one high-security setting in the United Kingdom, an open studio model art therapy group was conducted weekly for over five years. Due to the tendencies for these men to retreat to their side rooms to rest after meals, it was important to capture some time to invite them in before they left, and patients were always advised that they would be able to come into the room for part or all of the session, according to their personal preference and physical needs. Participation was inclusive, allowing everyone to engage at their own level, and hospital staff were also encouraged to take part in the artmaking process. All participants contributed a sense of their own creativity – even if only for a brief moment or throughout the whole therapeutic hour. Many patients who entered art therapy tentatively later developed a genuine interest in art.

On wards for people with personality disorders, an open studio model session can be implemented within a closed group of patients. Here, patients have the opportunity to receive feedback on group dynamics from therapists. This approach allows therapists to present images of various topics, making it easier for patients to engage with and explore these subjects in a less intense or direct manner.

## The Forensic Art Psychotherapist

Forensic art psychotherapists adapt their methodologies to suit the forensic context of prisons and secure settings, informed by psychotherapeutic theory and their experience as artists. They cultivate unique relationships with their clients, drawing upon their expertise in the creative process. Schaverien (1989) emphasised this connection, noting that 'the art therapist's understanding of the artistic process enables them to empathise with their patients 'image-making' (p. 109). Comprehensive risk assessments are conducted for all patients, with staffing levels adjusted as necessary in response to any concerns, and resources adapted to suit levels of risk. Close attention is given to physical and non-physical aspects, verbal and non-verbal cues, and forensic art psychotherapists working in high-secure settings will also have annual, mandatory training in managing violence and aggression, and additional radio, patient escort and area search training.

The art psychotherapeutic relationship is traditionally conceptualised as a triangular model, focusing on the interactions between the artist (client), artwork and art psychotherapist. However, within the high-security context, a quadrangular relationship emerges, incorporating the element of security as a critical factor. This fourth dimension of security acts as both an observer and regulator, providing the client-artist with an awareness of examination or judgement. Such dynamics may induce feelings of vulnerability, exposure or restriction, creating anxieties regarding what may emerge in visual expressions, possibly affecting engagement and trust in the therapeutic process. In rare cases, the security dynamic could become external to the secure setting, as forensic art psychotherapists may be asked to attend court cases and discuss imagery or artistic representations.

The psychodynamic essence of the therapeutic process takes into account aspects of transference and countertransference (Prasko et al., 2022) as they manifest in the imagery created. Within this process, the art psychotherapist is most commonly a compassionate observer, although this is not necessarily a passive stance, and offering genuine responses to artworks is important for those in secure settings. This can include the therapist sharing some symbolic knowledge or insights if this is deemed beneficial. Patients are invited to say something about what they have made if they want to, which encourages some support in reflecting on the form, content, emotional expression and cognitive distortions in the artwork and can allow meaning-making to occur over time, leading to self-insight and awareness.

Forensic art psychotherapy treatments are useful in carefully promoting engagement with emotional aspects of offence-related work, such as anger, guilt, shame, unresolved grief and loss, childhood and sexual abuse, as well as self-harming behaviours, pain and sorrow. This can lead to the building of self-confidence, a stronger sense of self and the development of social functioning. The aim is towards the gradual restoration of a compassion towards self and others, and a personal sense of acceptance as insight and feelings of remorse develop. The sessions can offer a supportive and creative space in which to explore thoughts and feelings, allowing the individual to make discoveries about themselves and how they relate to others. The therapist will not be teaching or judging how the materials are used but supporting the individual through the process. Words are not primary, although the aim is that the expressive qualities of the art created lead to enhanced and meaningful verbal communication.

## Forensic Arts Therapies Advisory Group (FATAG)

The Forensic Arts Therapies Advisory Group (FATAG) was created in the early 1990s to address challenges faced by therapists in prison settings, particularly regarding lone working and health issues, and in 1998, it evolved to better represent arts therapists in various forensic environments, including secure hospitals and probation settings.

The Arts in Prisons Working Party was formed under the Home Office to enhance the use of arts within prisons, which led to regular meetings of a subgroup focused on arts therapies starting in 1993. The subgroup aimed to promote safe and effective application of arts therapies in prisons; foster dialogue with prison education and healthcare services; provide guidelines and information related to arts therapies, and advocate for the recognition of professional qualifications. FATAG's achieved milestones include organising seminars and conferences, publishing *Guidelines for Arts Therapists Working in Prisons* in 1997 and an anthology of practice in 2016 (Rothwell & Grandison, 2016), as well as securing endorsement of employment condition recommendations. Forensic art psychotherapists have also established an ongoing research presence at the International Association for Forensic Psychotherapy (IAFP).

## Curating and Archiving in a High-Secure Setting

Art created within the context of art psychotherapy must always be handled with respect, care, and confidentiality. The British Association of Art Therapists (BAAT) Guidelines are clear:

> Images left by clients after art therapy ends do not need to be stored or kept by the art therapist or the organisation. This is because images produced in art therapy do not have a definite and fixed meaning and cannot be an admissible item of evidence in court.
>
> When the art therapy ends, the artworks that clients do not wish to keep themselves can be disposed of in the same way as any confidential material (shredding, etc).
>
> (BAAT, 2025)

However, in high-security settings, these artworks are regarded as clinical records and treated as such. This means that disposal is not always permitted.

Gussak (2013) argues that using art as evidence in homicide cases can be beneficial, as artistic expressions serve as valuable assessment tools to evaluate mental health status during both the committing of the crime and subsequent legal proceedings. These expressions can humanise the defendant and help uncover and validate the truth behind their statements and information. Studies (e.g. Karaca & Eren, 2014) demonstrate that art can significantly contribute to case formulation. Furthermore, artworks created in forensic art psychotherapy can additionally serve as an effective tool for forensic risk assessment, evaluation, and case formulation, reflecting unconscious symbolic expressions that are observed and shared. For instance, artwork may include details relevant to disclosures about criminal offences, and imagery, particularly that derived from offence-focused therapy, may reveal specifics about the crime. Any new information is documented, and imagery indicating risks to self or others is communicated back to the multidisciplinary team.

## Forensic Physical Archiving

In high-security facilities, forensic art psychotherapists are responsible for dating each artwork on the reverse side, along with the patient's name, ensuring that these pieces are securely stored and archived. Typically, artworks created in both therapy rooms and ward settings are organised into patient folders and portfolios, which therapists transport back to the designated archive room secured with a check-lock key. This specialised room is dedicated to the archiving and storage of both historical and current artworks. The space can also accommodate clinical supervision where images are located and shared between the therapist and the supervisor.

The Rampton arts psychotherapies archive room features locked drawers, each equipped with a separate lock and key to meet high-security standards (NHS, 2019), and organises artworks made by patients alphabetically. This space has preserved many historical artworks from various art therapy sessions conducted by multiple therapists and trainees. In recent years, the establishment of a digital archive by the author, as described below, has further enhanced the preservation of these works.

The only time that artworks leave the archive is after they are requested by the service user for retention after discharge from the hospital, though digital records of the artworks remain in the patient's files. Upon completing art psychotherapy or upon hospital discharge, patients receive a visual consent form that allows them to express their preferences regarding their artwork. They can choose to keep their pieces or can now arrange for alternative outcomes. Patients are fully informed about the archiving system at the outset of their therapy, raising important questions about the potential impact on clients knowing that their work is stored for possible use in the criminal justice system. Additionally, clarification is needed on the distinction between an anonymous archive and one that could be utilised within the criminal justice framework. Capturing this work anonymously is significant for its historical and psychiatric relevance, as it provides insights into the motivations and commonalities underlying harmful behaviours.

## Forensic Digital Archiving

In 2009, the author initiated a digital archive, accessible only to the core team of therapists, to ensure that images were treated as clinical records and could be accessible for potential legal proceedings, and/or potential research. The current digital archive comprises hundreds of patient files, along with signed consent forms for the copying and educational use of the artworks.

## A Rampton Collection

Securing adequate space and resources for the ongoing display of sizeable 3D artworks of large paintings has proven to be a significant challenge. These works would be better preserved and protected if housed within a dedicated high-secure collection, for example, with the Wellcome Trust or other NHS archival organisations. The purpose of future exhibitions of this nature would be very much in keeping with what Adamson (1990) states:

> They break down the barricade of nervousness, or even hostility, of the 'sane' on-looker, by showing him what might so easily have been his fate. Hopefully they replace prejudice with compassion, and sympathy with positive action. They are a vital source of help for the mental health organisations.
>
> (1990, p. 70)

## Concluding Thoughts

Forensic art psychotherapy artworks are clinical records that serve a significant role in uncovering unconscious symbolic expressions, as well as offering valuable insights into criminal offences, motivations, thoughts and feelings, and behaviours. They also function as important historical documents, reflecting the experiences of patients who reside in high-security settings and contributing to the fields of psychiatric and outsider art. While the identities of the artists remain anonymous, the practice of archiving emphasises two crucial objectives: safeguarding patient privacy and preserving the integrity of the artwork itself.

As we transition into an increasingly digital future, it raises the question of what will happen to these artworks that are currently stored in cupboards, drawers, and locked rooms. It may be incumbent upon forensic art psychotherapists to proactively ensure the preservation of these artworks, along with the historical context of the incarcerated artists.

One potential solution is to encourage donations to trusted art collections, and an initiative such as this would reflect a contribution to the significant psychiatric collection of historical relevance, as well as assisting in transforming bias, fear or prejudice into understanding, and empathy and compassion into constructive initiatives that may well bring a humanistic approach to forensic psychiatry, to help us see beyond a person's criminal activity, and to help us to consider how to live safer, more creative lives.

## References

Adamson, E. (1970). Art for mental health. In J. Creedy (Ed.). *The Social Context of Art*. London: Tavistock Publications.

Adamson, E. (1984). *Art as Healing*. London: Coventure.

Adamson, E. (1990). *Art as Healing, in Association with John Timlin*. London: Coventure.

Allen, E. (2018a). Introducing forensic sand play. *British Journal of Play Therapy*, 13, pp. 50–64.

Allen, E. (2018b). The boy who cried wolf: A collaborative approach to long term segregation. In T. Colbert & C. Bent (Eds.) *Working Across Modalities in the Arts Therapies*, pp. 139–151. Oxon & New York: Routledge.

Allen, E. (2019). Killing time: The dying art therapy group in a high secure hospital. In M. Wood, B. Jacobson & H Cridford (Eds.) *The International Handbook of Art Therapy in Palliative and Bereavement Care*, pp. 303–317. London: Routledge.

Allen, E. (2024). Therapy outcome measures and forensic sand play therapy in a high security hospital. In P. Enderby & A. John (Eds.) *Therapy Outcome Measure: Theoretical Underpinning and Case Studies*, pp. 483–487. Croydon: J & R Press Ltd.

British Association of Art Therapists (BAAT). (2025). *Artworks and Clinical Notes Disposal. Artworks and Clinical Notes Disposal.* The British Association of Art Therapists.

Collins, B., Darewych, O. H., & Chiacchia, D. J. (2023). The efficacy of art therapy on hope and resilience in youth within a secure care centre. *International Journal of Art Therapy*, 28(3), pp. 97–105. DOI: 10.1080/17454832.2022.2145322.

Geraghty, K. A., Vahabzadeh, L. J., & Simonet, R. (2024). Art therapy in a multidisciplinary team with young men in prison. *International Journal of Art Therapy*, 29(1), pp. 39–44. DOI: 10.1080/17454832.2024.2303511

Gussak. (2013). *Art on Trial: Art Therapy in Capital Murder Cases.* New York: Columbia University Press.

Hewins, H. (2023). Art therapy, intersectionality and services for women in the criminal justice system. *International Journal of Art Therapy*, 28(1–2), pp. 74–83. DOI: 10.1080/17454832.2023.2175001

Karaca, S., & Eren, N. (2014). The use of creative art as a strategy for case formulation in psychotherapy: A case study, *Journal of Clinical Art Therapy*, 2(1), pp. 1–6.

Liebmann, M. (Ed.) (1994). *Art Therapy with Offenders.* London: Jessica Kingsley Publishers.

NHS England. (2019). *The High Security Psychiatric Services (Arrangements for Safety and Security) Directions.* https://www.gov.uk/government/publications/high-security-psychiatric-services-directions-2019-arrangements-for-safety-and-security

Prasko, J., Ociskova, M., Vanek, J., Burkauskas, J., Slepecky, M., Bite, I., Krone, I., Sollar, T., & Juskiene, A. (2022). Managing transference and counter transference in cognitive behavioural supervision: Theoretical framework and clinical application. *Psychology Research and Behavior Management*, 11(15), pp. 2129–2155. Doi: 10.2147/PRBM.S369294.

Ripley, P. (1994). *Managing the Curriculum in Prisons Prison Education in England and Wales* (2nd Revised Edition). Mendip Papers MP 022. https://eric.ed.gov/?id=ED388842.

Rothwell, K., & Grandison, S. (2016). Notes on service design for Art Psychotherapists working in time – limited group programmes on adult mental health in-patient wards. In R. Hughes (Ed.) *Time Limited Art Psychotherapy*, pp. 118–193. London: Routledge.
Schaverien, J. (1989). The picture within the frame, in pictures at an exhibition. In A. Gilroy and T. Dalley (Eds.) *Pictures at an Exhibition Selected Essays on Art and Art Therapy*, pp. 147–155. London: Routledge.
Takkal, A., Horrox, K., & Rubio-Garrido, A., (2018). The issue of space in a prison art therapy group: A reflection through Martin Heidegger's conceptual frame. *International Journal of Art Therapy*, 23(3), pp. 136–142. DOI: 10.1080/17454832.2017.1384031
Teasdale, C. (1995). Art therapy as a shared forensic investigation. *Inscape: Journal of the British Association of Art Therapists*, 2(2), pp.32–40.
Tucker, A., & Moore, J. E. (1997). Inclusion of Women in the Randolph-Sheppard Program. *Journal of Visual Impairment & Blindness*, January 1999.
Vygotsky, L. S. (1978). *Mind in Society: The Development of Higher Psychological Processes*. Harvard University Press.

# 8 Working Collaboratively with Patients and Staff

*Fiona Grainger*

## Introduction

As we have heard in previous chapters, art therapy within acute mental health in-patient settings presents both significant challenges and powerful opportunities. This chapter explores the role of collaboration in therapeutic practice, with a particular focus on joint working between patients and staff. Underpinned by research in the field, it examines the development and impact of a weekly art therapy group established in a 12-bed male Psychiatric Intensive Care Unit (PICU) in a busy London NHS hospital, and how a collaborative ethos has underpinned both its emergence and sustainability.

Central to this discussion is the evolving role of the art therapist within contemporary in-patient teams. In high-risk, high-stress environments where clinical priorities often centre on safety, containment and pharmacological intervention, the presence of counterbalancing creative, relational approaches becomes vital. This chapter extends a discussion started in Chapter 5 around how art therapy can offer more than emotional expression: it can create space for shared experience, relational repair and self-regulation amongst staff as well. Working alongside patients and staff, the art therapist is positioned not as an isolated clinician but as a co-facilitator of a more compassionate and inclusive culture, one grounded in co-production and mutual respect.

The group, co-led by an art psychotherapist and the ward's full-time Activities Coordinator, offers a flexible environment for creativity. Open to both patients and staff, it provides a rare opportunity for connection in a setting often shaped by risk, volatility and emotional intensity. Over time, the group has become embedded in the rhythm of the ward, offering consistency and relational trust. Artworks created in the group are displayed throughout the ward, transforming the clinical space into a communal gallery. Murals co-designed and painted by patients and staff serve as a visible symbol of this ethos. For new arrivals, it communicates a clear message: That creativity, contribution and belonging are possible here.

At the heart of this group's success is its collaborative foundation. Patients are not passive recipients of care but active participants in shaping the therapeutic environment. Creativity enables positive change – supporting not only

DOI: 10.4324/9781003613428-11

individual expression but also the co-creation of a more humane and inclusive ward culture.

The legacy of Edward Adamson resonates throughout this work. Adamson's commitment to providing therapeutic spaces grounded in respect, non-judgement and creative freedom remains profoundly relevant. This chapter will explore both the parallels and differences from Adamson's approach, considering how his pioneering ethos has been adapted to meet the complexities of modern psychiatric in-patient care.

## The Purpose of the Group

The group was established in 2023 as a weekly, rolling art therapy group within a secure 12-bed male PICU. It takes place at a fixed time each week in the ward's multi-purpose activities room, providing a consistent and welcoming environment for creative therapeutic engagement. Although the ward is locked, the group operates as an open format, allowing patients to join when able. Sessions last for ninety minutes and are designed to offer a psychologically safe space in which participants can explore emotional experiences, build interpersonal connections and develop adaptive coping strategies through art-making.

This aligns closely with Yalom's (1995) six therapeutic factors of in-patient settings: engagement, normalisation, interpersonal learning, reduced isolation, altruism and a reduction in hospital-related anxiety. On the PICU, engagement might begin as simply as stepping into the room or picking up a pencil, small acts that signal readiness to connect. Normalisation is particularly powerful in this context. Many patients arrive feeling their struggles are shameful or unique; seeing others express similar emotions through art can provide a deep sense of relief. Interpersonal learning often emerges through subtle exchanges – patients notice similarities in each other's images and offer encouragement. Isolation is eased not just by proximity but by participating in a shared task.

Altruism surfaces when one patient praises another's work or helps tidy up – small but meaningful kind gestures that challenge internal narratives of worthlessness. Even without verbal disclosure, these interactions carry significant therapeutic value. Some patients are young and disorientated, often it is their first admission, which can feel shameful. Sometimes behaviour of other patients can be bizarre or frightening. The side effects of medication can be distressing. The group can offer something grounding, especially when these worries are named and shared. It helps people feel less alone.

Robb (2022) builds on Yalom's framework, identifying four art therapy-specific aims: self-expression, self-awareness, interpersonal connection and creativity as a force for change. She states, 'art making is active self-expression' (p. 76), enabling participants to externalise thoughts and feelings that may otherwise remain unspoken. Self-awareness then follows, not only in terms of personal insight, but in recognising one's impact on the group (Robb, 2022).

Often, this unfolds quietly: through mirroring and resonance in mark-making. Interpersonal connection develops not just from sharing, but through the collective process of making. Sitting side by side, people connect without necessarily needing to speak. The lack of pressure can be freeing, especially for those who find emotional expression triggering or unsafe.

Waller (1991) notes of Edward Adamson that he 'provided a very powerful receptive container for many of the patients who worked with him' (p. 27). His quiet, non-directive approach allowed patients to explore their inner worlds through art, without the pressure of verbal explanation or interpretation. This is what I, as an art therapist, try to hold in the room – a space where making, not explaining, does the work. Creativity is both the process and the product of therapeutic engagement, allowing individuals to experiment, play and reimagine themselves outside of illness or diagnosis.

These sessions also have an important relational impact on the wider ward environment. By engaging in collaborative experiences – be it art, music or simply sharing space, staff and patients are reminded of their humanity. Often, what emerges is a warm, conversational atmosphere, filled with everyday humour, gentle interaction and sometimes boisterous fun. The experience feels less clinical and more like a 'kitchen table' moment that is ordinary and quietly reparative.

## Collaboration

> *Collaboration with ward staff is essential, bringing together diverse perspectives and expertise to engage with patients, assess needs, and evaluate care in a person-centred, co-produced manner that prioritises the interests and dignity of each individual.*
>
> (The Ward Manager)

From the outset, I approached the group with a collaborative mindset, recognising that it could not function in isolation. As Yalom (1995) observes, the therapy group is 'always in complex relationship to the larger group: the in-patient ward in which it is ensconced' (p. 512). On a busy psychiatric ward, staff are not only key to supporting patient engagement but also to shaping the emotional climate in which the group takes place.

I wanted the art therapy group to slot naturally into ward life and to offer something harmonious without disrupting existing routines or creating added pressure for the staff. With limited time each week, my aim was to offer something meaningful while respecting the structure and expertise already in place. I was also mindful of working in a way that felt emotionally safe for patients, avoiding any interventions that might overwhelm or destabilise. As Yalom (1995) reminds us, it is always more therapeutic to contain distress than to provoke it. Exploring trauma at a patient's most vulnerable point without sufficient time for emotional containment can lead to overwhelm for both patient and staff.

The ward is well-staffed with a diverse team of male and female healthcare professionals, led by a strong, compassionate and highly respected ward manager. Her leadership sets the tone for the multidisciplinary team, creating a culture of collaboration, integrity and care. The staff work long, often demanding shifts in a high-pressure environment. They routinely manage complex needs, unpredictable behaviours and incidents of violence and aggression, all while striving to maintain safety and compassion. As Bowers et al. (2011) highlight, these challenges are a daily reality of psychiatric in-patient care, yet this team continues to show up with professionalism, empathy and a deep commitment to those they support.

At times, the ward feels like an intense family, diverse in race, culture and belief systems, yet all contained within a locked space. With limited autonomy and few familiar coping strategies available, tensions can escalate quickly. Resistance and emotional withdrawal in the patients and signs of staff burnout are not uncommon (Maslach & Leiter, 2016). The art therapy group helps to ease some of this pressure, offering a space that feels calmer, more open and where emotions can be contained in the room. Creative engagement has been shown to support emotional regulation and staff-patient connection in challenging environments (Malchiodi, 2013; Stickley & Freshwater, 2006).

The Activities Coordinator plays a key role in supporting the group. As a full-time member of staff, she knows the patients well and understands the rhythms of the ward. She often shares helpful feedback and offers valuable insight into who might be ready to engage. She actively promotes the group, walking around the ward beforehand to encourage participation and framing the session as something fun, accessible and worth trying. Her involvement helps bridge the gap between patients and the group, making it easier for people to take that first step.

Patients may be under enhanced observation, in which case staff presence in the group is necessary. Over time, inviting staff to participate makes a difference. When they join in the creative activity, it softens hierarchies and helps reframe their roles. Shared art-making shifts the dynamic from surveillance to solidarity. Patients often seem surprised and moved to see staff draw, paint or play music alongside them. There is no expectation of interpretation or judgement in the group, which allows people to create without fear. This helps to build trust and mutual recognition.

Edward Adamson understood the power of this kind of presence. His work at Netherne Hospital was defined not by interpretation, but by trust in the art-making process and in the individuals creating it. He avoided pathologising what was being expressed and instead held space for patients to relate to him and the materials on their own terms (Adamson, 1984). Similarly, our group is not about deep analysis or emotional excavation. For many of the men on the ward, the aim is simple: relief, not growth. Just having a space to make something without pressure can be enough. A positive experience in art therapy during admission can increase openness to ongoing support post-discharge, and I have sometimes continued working one-to-one with men who previously attended the group on the PICU.

Therapeutic love, as described by McNeilly (2025), underpins the group, meeting both staff and patients with warmth, presence and unconditional regard. Everyone on the ward – patient or staff – is carrying something: emotional burdens or unspoken troubles. Offering a steady, respectful presence becomes its own form of care. As van der Kolk (2015) states, 'being able to feel safe with other people is probably the single most important aspect of mental health' (p. 81).

With the mutual trust and containment offered by staff, the therapist can practise what Zinker (1977) described as the 'I-Thou' relationship, which is a way of meeting others in the present, without judgement or agenda. As Mann (2010) describes, this requires a stance of 'creative indifference' – staying curious and responsive, rather than rigid or reactive, creating the conditions that allow me to work flexibly and authentically within it.

When I sit at the table and make art too, it is not only about modelling possibilities, but also about saying: we are in this together. McNiff (1992) wrote that 'attending to others does not require me to stop expressing myself' (p. 39). His phrase, 'soul communicates with soul through the process of painting' (p. 40), captures something of what happens in the group, and the group in turn contributes to the overall emotional tone of the ward. Insights from interpersonal neurobiology (Siegel, 2010) show that regulation can be contagious: a calm, grounded person can help a distressed individual settle simply through their presence. When staff participate, they offer opportunities for co-regulation – nervous systems attuning to one another until both move towards balance.

## Meeting Challenges with Creative Adjustments

The PICU supports a diverse population, though a high proportion of patients are young men from Black ethnic backgrounds, many of whom are also involved in the criminal justice system. The ward reflects a wide range of socioeconomic, cultural and neurodiverse experiences, alongside a spectrum of gender and sexual identities.

To meet the demands of a modern psychiatric setting, the group has to be flexible, creative and often unconventional. In a system where medical models and treatment pathways tend to dominate, people can easily be reduced to a diagnosis and strong emotions can be pathologised and quickly managed with medication. The group offers some space to feel something, to express it and find it met with curiosity rather than correction.

In contrast to Adamson's long-term work at Netherne Hospital, where extended admissions allowed for the development of deep, sustained therapeutic relationships (Adamson, 1984), contemporary in-patient settings are marked by time-limited admissions, high levels of risk management and rapid patient turnover. In this context, art therapists must work without knowing how much time they have with a patient. The challenge becomes creating moments of meaning and connection in brief encounters. As Robb (2022) notes, even short interactions can offer therapeutic value when approached with presence and intention. Yalom (1995) echoes this, suggesting that 'the in-patient group therapist must consider the life of the group to be only a single session' (p. 484), highlighting the need to treat each meeting as potentially complete in itself.

Engagement can be particularly challenging when patients are heavily medicated. Common side effects – such as avolition, sedation, hyper-salivation, gastrointestinal discomfort and impaired cognition – can severely limit patients' ability to participate in therapeutic activity, even when they genuinely want to (Lieberman et al., 2005). What may look like disengagement is often a physiological response. Recognising this helps the art therapist stay patient and attuned, offering flexibility and gentle encouragement without adding pressure.

Confidentiality also presents challenges. Patients are in close proximity to each other, which makes privacy difficult. Sometimes, participating in a group can feel emotionally risky, as personal disclosures can be misinterpreted. Trauma-informed practice asks us to acknowledge how this environment can replicate earlier experiences of exposure, silencing or loss of control (Fallot & Harris, 2009). For many trauma survivors, trust is already fragile and emotional safety is easily compromised. I am often moved by the group's ability to show care and empathy for one another, demonstrating a kind of brotherhood. In a setting full of chaos and challenge, their instinct to look out for each other feels both unexpected and deeply moving.

The door to the activities room is left open, allowing patients to enter and leave freely. The goal is not to confine, but to create a space that feels safe enough to remain. Some patients hover at the threshold for weeks before joining fully; others stay for the whole session and offer to tidy up at the end, which is a small but powerful marker of belonging and recovery.

Cultural and gender norms can also influence how safe patients feel participating. For some, especially those from backgrounds where emotional expression is discouraged, making art may feel unfamiliar or uncomfortable (Cooper, 2020). This is sometimes the first time they have encountered creativity in a therapeutic context. Choosing to engage at all can require significant courage. Older Black male staff are often instrumental in encouraging participation among younger Black male patients, acting as cultural bridges, trusted figures and positive role models within the therapeutic space.

My approach is simple but deliberate. I sit alongside patients and work with them, sharing the experience. This co-creation helps ease anxiety, reduce shame and break down the power dynamics that so often define in-patient care. In these moments, we meet each other not as patient and professional, but as people making something together. Edward Adamson (1984) championed this quiet, non-directive presence, trusting in the therapeutic potential of art made in safety and freedom. It offers a quiet reminder: you are more than your diagnosis. You are seen.

My therapeutic approach to working with his group involves blending a range of art forms and theoretical models within a humanistic, person-centred framework. I draw on Rogerian principles of empathy, congruence and unconditional positive regard to create a therapeutic environment rooted in psychological safety (Rogers, 1957). Holding the group at the same time and place each week establishes consistency and predictability – what Winnicott (1965) would describe as a 'reliable holding environment' (p. 44). This dependable structure forms the container within which creative risk-taking and emotional exploration can occur.

Themes and art activities are selected to balance clinical risk with opportunities for emotional expression and music helps to create a contained atmosphere, masking the background noise of alarms or distress outside the room. Spontaneous singing and dancing often emerge, bringing moments of joy and connection that can lift the mood and ease the emotional weight of the ward. Throughout each session, I track the group's emotional tone to help keep participants within their 'window of tolerance' – that space where feelings can be accessed without overwhelm (Siegel, 1999). I scan for subtle shifts in affect and engagement, adjusting my stance accordingly. Zinker (1977) compares this to operating a 'complex radar machine' (p. 47), requiring constant responsiveness to the group's needs. He also speaks of a 'healthy capacity for wonderment' (p. 5) which manifests as the ability to take genuine pleasure in another's unique experience. This mindset grounds participants as individuals in the here and now. This approach only works because of the support of the staff team. It is a shared endeavour, and when it works well, you can feel the group settle into something steady and quietly powerful.

When the ward feels sufficiently stable, I incorporate percussion instruments into the sessions. Making music together offers a multi-sensory and embodied form of connection that transcends the limitations of language. Rhythmic activity can support regulation by influencing the autonomic nervous system, up-regulating those in depressive or shut-down states and down-regulating those who are hyper-aroused or manic (Porges, 2011; van der Kolk, 2015). Group drumming encourages synchrony, shared attention and a sense of social cohesion. McFerran and Hunt (2008) emphasise the value of music-making in psychiatric contexts, noting its capacity to strengthen group bonds, facilitate emotional release and engage individuals for whom verbal therapy may feel difficult. In this setting, rhythm becomes a parallel therapeutic modality, offering an embodied, expressive channel alongside visual art. Patients and staff often join in together, and the room fills with rhythm, singing, dancing and laughter.

The spirit of curiosity, acceptance and respect informs the relational core of the work. Rather than applying a fixed model, the therapeutic stance is adaptive and personalised. In a setting that can often feel impersonal or overly medicalised, the act of witnessing creative expression, without judgement or agenda, becomes a radical form of care.

I often bring in work by artists such as Matisse, Haring, Basquiat and Mondrian, along with the resources for participants to respond in the style of these artists. In his article *The Madness of Van Gogh* (1968), Adamson notes poignantly that 'sensitivity carries a toll of suffering as well as ecstasy' (p. 29), and so sharing stories from these artists' lives, many of whom experienced mental health struggles, helps to normalise creativity as a valid and powerful outlet for emotional processing (Malchiodi, 2012; Robb, 2022). The tasks are structured to be achievable and non-threatening, building confidence without infantilising. As Robb (2022) suggests, completing a creative task can play a vital role in rebuilding agency and strengthening self-worth.

Participants are invited to title and sign their work, offering a subtle bridge between non-verbal and verbal expression. This small act often reveals emotional nuance, reinforcing pride, autonomy and ownership. Over time, a supportive culture has developed within the group, where participants notice and affirm one another's contributions, even without words.

## Displaying the Artwork

> Every picture that is created is a reflection of a human being. It must be treated with care and respect.
>
> Adamson (1984, p. 6)

Edward Adamson believed that displaying artwork made by patients was a way to honour their humanity and to move beyond diagnosis and see the person. He used exhibitions to challenge stigma and make space for a different kind of conversation about mental health, one rooted in creativity, sensitivity and dignity (Maclagan, 2009).

This spirit also shapes how artworks from the group are shared. With patient consent and managerial approval, artworks are printed on wipeable vinyl paper while also preserving the original works. Displaying the art throughout the ward has transformed the once bare, institutional walls into a space that feels more colourful and alive. Patients take pride in seeing their work on display; it becomes something they can celebrate, and it sends a clear message: what they have created matters. As Killick (2017) notes, displaying patient artwork in clinical environments not only enhances the aesthetic of the space but also supports identity, agency and relational connection.

Framed original artworks and poems created in the group are also displayed in the corridor leading into the ward, transforming this transitional space into a visual threshold of creativity. There is no distinction made between patient and staff contributions, reflecting the equal value of each piece and reinforcing a non-hierarchical ethos. The display invites viewers to look beyond diagnostic labels and behavioural histories, offering an alternative narrative, one that highlights expression, agency and potential. In doing so, the installation quietly resists institutional discourses of pathology, reframing the patients not as passive recipients of care, but as creative, resilient individuals with something meaningful to communicate.

## *Behind the Mask*: Mural Project

The *Behind the Mask* mural grew out of a simple but powerful idea: to bring colour and life to the ward's communal dining area. It began with a request from the ward manager, who asked the art therapy group to create something visual that would brighten the space. From there, the project evolved into something far more meaningful.

Over several weeks, patients were invited to reflect on their experiences of being on the ward and explore how these could be expressed visually. A recurring theme in early group discussions was the difficulty of maintaining a sense of authentic self within the institutional context. Many of the patients had been admitted under distressing circumstances, often through forced detainment by the police. These experiences, often initiated by people they had previously trusted, like family, friends or partners, were characterised as deeply traumatic, marked by feelings of betrayal and shame. The sense of being 'handed over' by loved ones reinforced the stigma already associated with psychiatric diagnosis. As van der Kolk (2015) has shown, the loss of control and agency associated with trauma can deeply fragment one's sense of identity and safety.

As the group gave voice to these complex emotions, a powerful metaphor began to surface. Participants spoke of needing to wear a mask – a psychological defence mechanism to hide pain, confusion or fear. The metaphor of the mask captured the tension between external presentation and internal experience. However, the men were also keen to emphasise that these masks concealed more than just vulnerability: behind each one was a narrative, a personal truth that often went unseen. This metaphor became the conceptual foundation of what would later be titled *Behind the Mask*.

Participants also expressed a strong desire to celebrate the ward's cultural richness. Staff and patients represented a wide range of nationalities, ethnicities and faiths, and the group saw the mural as an opportunity to reflect that diversity. Drawing inspiration from British Nigerian artist Yinka Shonibare's *Modern Magic* series, particularly his work *Studies of African Art from Picasso's Collection V* (2020–2021) – participants began developing a plan to create a mask-themed mural that honoured their international heritage while also communicating their personal stories.

Each group member selected a mask template from a range of traditional masks from around the world and was invited to reflect on what lay behind it. As they worked, many began sharing autobiographical narratives and emotional insights, telling stories of survival, displacement, trauma and hope.

Some participants composed poetry or lyrics to accompany their masks, which were later incorporated into the final composition.

The artwork created by the participants was not analysed or interpreted; instead, each mask was treated as a personal expression deserving of respect on its own terms. Adamson believed that art could serve as a medium for healing when free from clinical scrutiny, allowing individuals to retain ownership over their symbolic language. In this sense, the *Behind the Mask* mural functioned as more than a creative exercise; it became a collective archive of voice, experience and identity.

The group decided to use vibrant but non-overstimulating paint for the background of the mural, aware that certain colours and patterns can be triggering for individuals with sensory sensitivities or psychotic symptoms. Patients and staff alike coloured designated sections. The atmosphere during this period was notably buoyant, sunlight poured into the room, music played in the background and the space was filled with a palpable sense of joy and engagement. Patients and staff worked side by side, holding ladders for each other and sharing paint pots, the usual institutional roles temporarily suspended in favour of shared creative focus. Once the painted elements were completed, participants were able to carefully position their contributions on the mural wall. This act of placement was an important moment of ownership and pride (Image 8.1).

A week later, the ward hosted a celebratory event to unveil the finished work. The occasion included rap performances, spoken word poetry, music, food and dancing. Staff, patients and even members of the Trust's senior

*Image 8.1 Behind the Mask* Mural.

Photo: Fiona Grainger.

management team attended. For many of the participants, this public recognition was deeply affirming. In a setting where people are often reduced to diagnoses or risk profiles, being seen as artists and contributors, capable of insight and creativity, was profoundly empowering. As Brown (2006) notes, shame is mitigated not by silence or correction, but by empathic connection and visibility. Recognition of participants' creative agency helped restore a sense of worth and dignity.

The emotional impact of the project was reflected in the broader ward environment. During the weeks of the mural's development and directly following its completion, a significant decrease in incidents of aggression and violence was recorded. While this correlation may not be solely attributable to the mural, it highlights the potential of creative engagement to shift ward culture, strengthen community bonds and offer meaningful outlets for emotional expression. Kapitan (2008) underscores this in her work on trauma and community art, noting that collective creative practices can foster a sense of continuity, trust and shared identity in institutional spaces.

The *Behind the Mask* mural stood for a year as a living installation; a visual artefact that continued to evolve. New patients arriving on the ward were invited to create and add their own masks, contributing to a shared narrative that is both personal and communal. It not only transformed the physical space of the dining area but also served as a lasting reminder of the importance of looking beyond surface behaviour to the stories and emotions that lay beneath. It challenged the viewer to reconsider what was visible, to honour what was hidden and to embrace the complexity and dignity of each person behind the mask.

## Conclusion

This chapter has illustrated how collaboration forms the cornerstone of effective art therapy practice within a contemporary psychiatric in-patient setting. By co-creating with both patients and staff, the art therapy group encourages a relational culture that contrasts with the often hierarchical and risk-averse nature of acute mental healthcare. The group does not function in isolation but is embedded within the wider ward, relying on strong interdisciplinary partnerships and a shared commitment to co-production.

Staff involvement enhances emotional safety, supports continuity and models relational engagement. Patients are not passive recipients of care but are positioned as creative agents, shaping both the therapeutic space and the wider ward environment. Initiatives such as the *Behind the Mask* mural exemplify how collective artistic practice can promote ownership, visibility and dignity within institutional contexts.

This chapter has focused on collaboration between patients and staff. The following chapter looks at how art therapy can be used specifically to support the wellbeing of staff on in-patient wards.

## References

Adamson, E. (1968). The madness of Vincent Van Gogh. *Art and Artists*, 3(9), pp. 27–31.
Adamson, E. (1984). *Art as Healing*. Coventure.
Bowers, L., James, K., Quirk, A., Simpson, A., Stewart, D., & Hodsoll, J. (2011). Reducing conflict and containment rates on acute psychiatric wards: The safewards cluster randomised controlled trial. *International Journal of Nursing Studies*, 48(10), pp. 1274–1283.
Brown, B. (2006). Shame resilience theory: A grounded theory study on women and shame. Families in society. *The Journal of Contemporary Social Services*, 87(1), pp. 43–52. https://doi.org/10.1606/1044-3894.3483
Cooper, L. (2020). *Boys do Not Cry: Rethinking Masculinity and Mental Health*. Penguin Life.
Fallot, R. D., & Harris, M. (2009). *Creating Cultures of Trauma-Informed Care (CCTIC): A Self-Assessment and Planning Protocol*. Community Connections.
Kapitan, L. (2008). The art of healing trauma: Creative expression in the work of Judith Rubin. *Art Therapy: Journal of the American Art Therapy Association*, 25(4), pp. 169–175. https://doi.org/10.1080/07421656.2008.10129550
Killick, K. (2017). *Art Therapy for Psychosis: Theory and Practice*. Routledge.
Lieberman, J. A., Stroup, T. S., McEvoy, J. P., Swartz, M. S., Rosenheck, R. A., Perkins, D. O., & Hsiao, J. K. (2005). Effectiveness of antipsychotic drugs in patients with chronic schizophrenia. *New England Journal of Medicine*, 353(12), pp. 1209–1223. https://doi.org/10.1056/NEJMoa051688
Maclagan, D. (2009). *Outsider Art: From the Margins to the Marketplace*. Reaktion Books.
Malchiodi, C. A. (2012). *Handbook of Art Therapy* (2nd ed.). Guilford Press.
Malchiodi, C. A. (2013). *Art Therapy and Health Care*. Guilford Press.
Mann, D. (2010). *Gestalt Therapy: 100 Key Points and Techniques*. Routledge.
Maslach, C., & Leiter, M. P. (2016). Burnout: A multidimensional perspective. In M. P. Leiter, A. B. Bakker, & C. Maslach (Eds.). *Burnout at Work: A Psychological Perspective*, pp. 15–32. Psychology Press.
McFerran, K. S., & Hunt, M. (2008). Learning from experiences in practice: An exploratory study of music therapy student placements in psychiatry. *The Arts in Psychotherapy*, 35(3), pp. 190–200. https://doi.org/10.1016/j.aip.2008.02.002
McNeilly, G. (2025). *Therapeutic Love: The Healing Power of Relational Depth in Mental Health* [In preparation].
McNiff, S. (1992). *Art as Medicine: Creating a Therapy of the Imagination*. Shambhala.
Porges, S. W. (2011). *The Polyvagal Theory: Neurophysiological Foundations of Emotions, Attachment, Communication, and Self-Regulation*. W. W. Norton & Company.
Robb, M. (2022). *Group Art Therapy: An Illustrated Guide*. Jessica Kingsley Publishers.
Rogers, C. R. (1957). The necessary and sufficient conditions of therapeutic personality change. *Journal of Consulting Psychology*, 21(2), pp. 95–103.
Siegel, D. J. (1999). *The Developing Mind: Toward a Neurobiology of Interpersonal Experience*. Guilford Press.
Siegel, D. J. (2010). The mindful therapist: A clinician's guide to mindsight and neural integration. In *Norton Series on Interpersonal Neurobiology*. WW Norton & Company.
Stickley, T., & Freshwater, D. (2006). The art of caring: An aesthetic approach to health and social care education. *Journal of Psychiatric and Mental Health Nursing*, 13(6), pp. 687–693.
Van der Kolk, B. A. (2015). *The Body Keeps the Score: Brain, Mind, and Body in the Healing of Trauma*. Penguin Books.
Waller, D. (1991). *Becoming a Profession: The History of Art Therapy in Britain 1940–82*. Routledge.

Winnicott, D. W. (1965). *The Maturational Processes and the Facilitating Environment: Studies in the Theory of Emotional Development*. Hogarth Press.
Yalom, I. D. (1995). *The Theory and Practice of Group Psychotherapy* (4th ed.). Basic Books.
Zinker, J. (1977). *Creative Process in Gestalt Therapy*. Vintage.

# 9 Art Therapy and Staff Wellbeing

*Fiona Williams*

## Introduction

Working with people who have come to a crisis point in their lives has many rewards but also many challenges for healthcare staff. There is a growing awareness of how caring for people who experience acute mental health problems, thoughts about ending their own life and intense psychological pain can generate feelings of distress and disturbance within the staff themselves. There is an unconscious aspect to this type of work, which is driven by strong emotions, and these can undermine the effectiveness of that work. Bion (1961) called this the *basic assumption*: an avoidance or defence against the anxiety of managing the allotted task of care and treatment.

Working in multi-disciplinary teams and paying close attention to our own need for care and the shared humanity of our emotional wellbeing (Bion, 1961) has now become an increasingly important area of art psychotherapy practice. This chapter will initially examine the impact of the work of Edward Adamson and some of his contemporaries on the use of art psychotherapy today for the wellbeing of staff working on in-patient wards. The chapter will then go on to discuss how wellbeing creative reflective practice groups can help staff cope with the strong emotions engendered by their work and support each other with increased connection, courage and kindness.

## The Historical Background

Adamson lived through a period of war and conflict; however, this was also the period of a growing reservoir of knowledge and understanding about groups (Balint, 1957; Main, 1957), interrelationships (Laing, 1972) and attachment theory (Bowlby, 1988). Adamson brought this knowledge to his studio environments, and they became containing vessels for stimulating the creative process and enabling the transformative power of the arts to enhance well-being and understanding (Magsamen & Ross, 2023).

We saw in Chapter 2 that one of the earliest influences on Adamson was the work of his friend Adrian Hill (1945), who drew on his own experience of serious physical illness to use art making and appreciation to help in the

DOI: 10.4324/9781003613428-12

recovery of returning soldiers from both world wars. This could be seen as an early example of using lived experience and what is now known as an 'expert by experience' (Care Quality Commission, 2025), using his knowledge of being in a vulnerable situation to help others. More recently, Dartington (2019) writes of this internal need to digest and make sense of our experiences when working in challenging healthcare environments:

> Many people are drawn to working in the caring professions because they have a need to put something right... to heal emotional wounds: one's own and those of the damaged figures of one's internal world. It can be expressed in a socially acceptable way by helping others.
>
> (p. 104)

Another contemporary of Adamson was the South African-born psychiatrist Thomas Main (1911–1990). Eric Cunningham Dax, the medical superintendent at Netherne Hospital who appointed Adamson in 1946, had visited Main in Northfield Military Hospital, where he had witnessed artists at work alongside service users and was impressed by the socially orientated therapies for the rehabilitation of service personnel (Waller, 1991).

Main's *The Ailment* (1957) remains very relevant to healthcare practice today. He became interested in staff responses in relation to service users not getting better quickly despite attentive care, and noticed a pattern to these responses: it became apparent that when staff reached the limits of their resources of what was bearable for them, strong emotions including anger, fear, worry, guilt and even hatred could be experienced and disrupt their ability to offer helpful care, treatment and relationships. In these often-unconscious states of mind, Main noted, the healthcare staff gave sedative medication to service users when they, the staff, could not cope any more.

Main's response was to develop an active group discussion model and encourage healthcare staff to take part in this twice a week. A regular group developed a sense of trust, safety and connectedness between participants and enabled a growing openness to be able to share strong emotions as an essential part of being able to work well together. This helped the staff to understand, make sense of and ultimately bear the distress of the work and enabled them to feel more confident in their relationships and in their clinical decision-making.

Another contemporary of Adamson, Hungarian psychoanalyst Michael Balint (1896–1970), trained with Main and developed a further relational regular group model which had a similar purpose to Main's work and which he described in his book *The Doctor, His Patient and the Illness* (1957). Balint was clear that self-knowledge was an important aspect of being able to care for others safely and with compassion. A key aim of his group model is to help healthcare staff value their own emotional responses and develop understanding to create meaningful therapeutic relationships between themselves and service users (Salinsky, 2009). This work helps healthcare staff by having a safe place to share the interpersonal aspects of the clinical work and to support a sense of authentic connection with each other. It also supports them to relate with service users as rich and multi-faceted and to realise that 'certain patients or their emotions may resonate with what is going on in their own lives' (Salinsky, 2009).

These formative influences, alongside his training as an artist, enabled Adamson to understand that an important feature of art making is externalising internal experiences in art form. He understood that his own artist insights from drawing on an inner world enabled self-understanding and knowledge that could be harnessed for healing. Timlin in *Art as Healing* (1984) reflected that Adamson 'intuitively realised that no-one can hope to help others effectively without a certain degree of self-knowledge'. (p. 64), and there is a clear contemporary echo of this in the *NHS People Plan* (2020): 'If we do not look after ourselves, and each other, we cannot deliver safe, high-quality care'.

## The Importance of Self-Knowledge

To 'know thyself' is the philosophical principle inscribed on the pediment of the Temple of Apollo in ancient Greece. Plato's invitation is to examine what it is like to be in our minds and understand how our minds work. This is achieved by paying close attention to what is happening internally in our thoughts, feelings, intentions and beliefs. As well as through experiencing the external physical world via information coming into our bodies and minds through our senses. We are in a constant dynamic feedback process, alongside the important influence that others' minds have on our experiences and understanding of ourselves. The term Mentalisation (Bateman et al., 2023) describes self-knowledge and why it is vital for us individually and socially. It is a multi-faceted explanation of how we understand our own and others' mental states and intentions. This can lead to improved relationships with fewer misunderstandings. However, our natural and ordinary ability to mentalise can be disrupted quickly when we experience strong emotions. Our minds may respond to a possible threat by turning to a survival response, leaving the primitive part of our brain that is closest to our brain stem in charge of our actions until we can regain the relatively stable internal balance known as homeostasis (Van Der Kolk, 2014). Mentalising can come back online again once the threat is over, and we have all of our minds available to enable clear thinking. This knowledge is important as strong emotions can be generated constantly in the in-patient hospital environment. The ability to think clearly and mentalise is a core skill in holding onto a compassionate and open-minded clinical stance. It helps us to take the time to respond to others and not act in the heat of the moment.

## Contemporary Perspectives on Staff Wellbeing

Edmondson (2019), who cites Main's concern about the emotionally reactive use of medication by staff, describes psychological safety as an aspect of quality team working and notes that the strong emotion of fear in the inter-relationships between healthcare staff teams can lead to mistakes not being reported, or being reported but with limited discussion or learning. Edmondson identified that teams that were able to discuss openly with each other and work together well with the challenges in the workplace and learn from them were more successful. From this study, she defined *psychological safety* as:

> A climate in which people are comfortable expressing and being themselves. sharing concerns and mistakes without fear of embarrassment or retribution. They know they can ask questions if they are unsure about something.
>
> (p. xv)

Echoing Main and Balint, Edmondson also notes that healthcare teams who had a trusting, open culture and were able to be vulnerable with each other, rather than disengaging or defending themselves through fear, had a higher sense of wellbeing and confidence. Working towards a sense of psychological safety and inclusion is a multi-layered dynamic that changes over time, especially in the fast-paced environments of in-patient wards. It takes time to establish an enabling environment to allow team members to create a culture of trust and safety, and it is an aspirational and ongoing process for healthcare staff and leaders. It is also important here to consider the rich diversity and intersectionality in the NHS healthcare workforce, and to offer a range of ways and models to make the most helpful fit for staff wellbeing needs. A single model may not be suitable or helpful for everyone.

Another more recent model introduced into healthcare environments is Schwartz Rounds (Point of Care Foundation, 2025), named after Ken Schwartz, who in 1994 was diagnosed with terminal cancer and during his treatment found that what mattered to him most as a service user was the simple acts of kindness from his caregivers, which he said made 'the unbearable bearable'.

The aims of Schwartz Rounds are to:

> Humanise health and social care by working to enable health and care staff to provide high-quality, person-centred care, through support for their wellbeing and the organisational cultures within which they work.
>
> (Point of Care Foundation, 2025)

The Schwartz Rounds model is now available across many NHS services.

Other new initiatives in healthcare settings, such as arts-based staff wellbeing reflective practice groups, draw more widely on trauma-informed practice (Van der Kolk, 2014) and epistemic trust (Bateman et al., 2023) to inform a culture of understanding. This can provide a creative and compassionate approach to supporting staff in contemporary healthcare practice (Huet & Holttum, 2016; Tjasink & Stevens, 2022)

## The Arts as a Vehicle for Understanding Others' Experiences

Edward Adamson was aware of the power of viewing artworks as a link to being able to see and think about other people's mental states and perspectives, and in turn, the possibility of generating empathy and compassion. The permanent exhibition space he created at Netherne Hospital was an opportunity for healthcare staff to see and view the artwork created and to stimulate compassion and understanding about what it might feel like to experience mental health problems and understand the service user's point of view.

As we have seen in Chapter 4, there are now many programmes introducing the arts into healthcare training to help stimulate and increase empathy, compassion and wellbeing resources. In Magsamen and Ross (2023), American Professor of Psychiatry, Dr Meg Chisolm, explores what it means to be human through a lens of the arts and humanities:

> because it's a non-threatening way into having important conversations.... It's a prompt for reflection where people gain personal insights and get to appreciate other people's perspectives.
>
> (p. 173)

Levett-Jones et al. (2024) also find that the arts can be of benefit for learning and generating empathy as they have unique qualities that foster empathic responses, engagement, creativity and new understandings (p. 12).

They find that the active element in the arts seems to be their subjective nature, which can enable a less fixed or concrete thinking style, enhancing tolerance and sharing meaning, transcending cultural and language barriers, connecting with people from a wide range of backgrounds, and valuing diversity and inclusion of all voices in the workplace. Winnicott (1971) put it succinctly when he said that 'creativity makes the individual feel that life is worth living'. (p. 65)

## A Creative Staff Wellbeing Reflective Practice Group on an In-patient Ward

### *Introduction*

The acute role of healthcare staff in hospitals is now a focus for the NHS, as staff regularly put themselves in harm's way and face threats to themselves and to their wellbeing. They regularly experience stress, anxiety and burnout at work as a result of high demands and caseloads. In the 2021 NHS publication *Health and Wellbeing Framework*, Prerana Issar, Chief People Officer, stated that:

> Our NHS People Plan and People Promise places the wellbeing of our NHS people at the heart of what we do. Caring for the wellbeing of our

> NHS people enables them to care for the wellbeing of our patients. This framework flexibly supports NHS organisations to create a culture of wellbeing for our NHS people to thrive.
>
> (p. 5)

NHS England and the Royal College of Psychiatrists (2024) created the *Culture of Care Standards*, a vision for re-imagining in-patient care for the whole organisation as well as frontline staff. Training offered to in-patient staff raised awareness of working alongside service users through a trauma-informed lens: understanding mental health problems created from the multiple layers of childhood, societal and other adversity experiences.

The following reflections are from the author's own experience of facilitating a creative staff wellbeing reflective practice group for in-patient staff within a large NHS Trust in response to the issues and concerns around staff wellbeing discussed above, and concerns being raised by the service director about the staff team, particularly after a period of external inspection.

### *Format and Structure of the Group*

There was an initial period of liaison with senior staff and discussion about the wellbeing aims of the group, and whether this style of arts-based reflective practice group would be beneficial. The group then met on the ward weekly for a period of 18 months. It took place directly after the clinical handover in the middle of the day to enable a wider group of staff from the morning and afternoon shifts to attend, within a protected timeframe of 30 minutes agreed for the work. The reliability and consistency of the art psychotherapist and the artwork created a regular rhythm that some of the staff team socialised into and became regular attenders when their shift patterns allowed. However, not all staff attended or welcomed the arts-based group as useful for them, and some avoided the group. There was some brief hostility at the beginning, which had to be sensitively handled, with the validation that one model will not suit all staff needs. Using art psychotherapy approaches and arts materials with NHS clinicians, Tjasink and Stevens (2022) state the importance of feelings of safety for healthcare staff to try something new, using helpful aspects of the Compassionate Focused Therapy approach drawn from the work of the clinical psychologist Paul Gilbert (b. 1951)

The flexible, threefold structure for the group was adapted from Kurtz and Levene's (2022) *Heads and Hearts model* and involved:

> creation of a space for sharing lived experience of practice with colleagues, an opening-up space for the group to respond in a free and human way, and a gathering together space for more concerted meaning-making.
>
> (p. 251)

A small 'magic carpet' was the frame for the group: A jewelled velvet blanket fringed in gold, laid on the floor. It was the vessel, or what Anthony Stevens in his foreword to *Art as Healing* called the *temenos*, a safe and protected space, to support joint attention (Springham & Huet, 2018) into the centre of the room, where the arts materials and relationships between staff became our focus. The group circle we created enabled easy eye contact with each other, a sense of physical proximity and connectedness, as well as facilitating the articulation of thoughts and feelings about the work.

The arts materials consisted of images of artworks on postcards and a box of small playful and tactile objects, including natural, comforting and symbolic pieces, carefully selected colourful shells, animals, gems, houses, keys, birdcages, shoes, a purse, masks, cars, marbles and butterflies. This allowed a sense of playfulness and visual stimulation to support a connection with memories and work relationships (Image 9.1).

The model followed a consistent weekly structure of opening up the space with the magic carpet and inviting the staff to choose and share an object and/

*Image 9.1* Tactile objects to encourage and enrich opportunities for self-reflection and being in touch.

Photo: Fiona Williams.

or an artist's postcard that resonated with their experiences of their work that day or week. Curiosity about how the postcard or object chosen resonated with the group created a network of connections. The material discussed gave rise to a range of regular wellbeing themes: time away from work, taking holidays and self-care, recharging batteries and other ways to look after both physical and mental health.

### *Participant Feedback*

Anger and frustrations about the organisational dynamics appeared at times, as well as concern and compassion for service users and each other. The team worked hard relationally, welcoming new staff members, explaining the purpose of the group and taking time to share goodbyes. There was much wisdom and kindness expressed, as well as real passion for their client group. One member wrote *I would like to be able to be the key to open a better quality of life for in-patients* and another said *it makes me come to terms with what I am feeling rather than brushing it off*. The reflective work also had an impact on general wellbeing away from work: *I spend more time away from work reflecting, than I have done previously*.

The art psychotherapist who facilitated the wellbeing group was from an external team within the Trust. Adamson (1984) wrote about his identity as an artist in the hospital setting as being 'in between' the staff and residents, perhaps a liminal space. As such, he was beneficial as a safe container for each person's voice, thoughts and feelings:

> although I was part of the medical staff, I was also separate from them. I was therefore someone in-between, to whom the residents and staff could appeal as an independent artist.
>
> (p. 4)

The outsider role of the art psychotherapist was an aspect included in the staff satisfaction questionnaire, where comments noticed a helpful aspect to this: *Very, very important for staff to be able to speak honestly*. In addition, *I feel I can say a bit more to someone different*.

The use of the two-page questionnaire developed by the art psychotherapist, with scaling questions and space for narrative reflections, was offered to the staff to complete by choice and anonymously on a regular basis to gather information about satisfaction and the value of using the arts to support wellbeing. Regular reviews held with the modern matron reported on attendance and broad themes, without identifying any individual staff. This enabled a sense of trust and agency in the process. The focus was to facilitate a sense of connection with the organisational aims of increased wellbeing and attuned quality care.

## Reflections and Conclusion

Important themes developed by Adamson with service users and an awareness of the significance of knowing thyself are evident in the work of his contemporaries. Bion, Main and Balint each shed light on establishing a regular wellbeing group for staff as an essential space to work with psychological safety and to communicate openly about concerns and challenges. It seems that without this vital regular space, unprocessed distress and disturbance can lead to healthcare staff becoming stressed, and thus iatrogenic harm can be a real possibility. This can impact the organisation, not just the ward and its service users.

The arts can have a significant role to play in this wellbeing work: they can transcend cultural and language barriers, and their subjective, playful and accessible material qualities allow perspective taking, flexibility of thinking and tolerance. The arts have an ability to stimulate and amplify learning, create a community and enhance empathy and compassion.

So far, this book has focused largely on art psychotherapy. In the next chapter, we broaden the discussion to include the other arts therapy modalities of dramatherapy, music therapy and dance movement psychotherapy.

## References


Adamson, E. (1984). *Art as Healing.* London: Coventure Ltd.

Balint, M. (1957). *The Doctor, His Patient and the Illness.* London: Churchill Livingstone.

Bateman, A., Fonagy, P., Campbell, C., Luyten, P., & Debbane, M. (2023). *Cambridge Guide to Mentalization-Based Treatment (MBT).* Cambridge: Cambridge University Press.

Bion, W. R. (1961). *Experiences in Groups.* London: Tavistock.

Bowlby, J. (1988). *A Secure Base.* Abingdon: Routledge.

Care Quality Commission. (2025 February 10). *What Do Experts by Experience Do?* https://www.cqc.org.uk/about-us/jobs/experts-experience

Dartington, A. (2019). Where Angels Fear to Tread: Idealism, despondency and inhibition of thought in hospital nursing. In A. Obholzer & V. Roberts (Eds.). *The Unconscious at Work*, pp. 99–108. London: Routledge.

Edmondson, A. (2019). *The Fearless Organization: Creating Psychological Safety in the Workplace for Learning, Innovation, and Growth.* New Jersey: Wiley.

Hill, A. (1945). *Art Versus Illness.* London: George Allen & Unwin.

Huet, V. & Holttum, S. (2016). Art therapy-based groups for work-related stress with staff in health and social care: An exploratory study. *The Arts in Psychotherapy*, 50, pp. 46–57.

Kurtz, A. & Levene, J. (2022). The Heads and Hearts Model of Reflective Practice. In Conniff (Ed) *Psychological Staff Support in Healthcare: Thinking & Practice.* (pp. 247–267). UK: Sequoia Books..

Laing, R.D. (1972). *Knots.* London: Penguin.

Levett-Jones. T., Brogan, E., Debono, D., Goodhew, M., Govind, N., Pich, J., River, J., Smith, J., Sheppard-Law, S., & Cant, R. (2024). Use and effectiveness of the arts for enhancing healthcare students' empathy skills: A mixed methods systematic review. *Nurse Education Today*, 138, 106185, https://doi.org/10.1016/j.nedt.2024.106185

Magsamen, S. & Ross, I. (2023). *Your Brain on Art – How the Arts Transform Us.* Edinburgh: Canongate Books.

Main, T. (1957). The Ailment. *British Journal of Medical Psychology*, 30, pp. 129–145.

NHS England. (2020, July 30). *We Are the NHS: People Plan for 2020/21 – Action for us all.* https://www.england.nhs.uk/publication/we-are-the-nhs-people-plan-for-2020-21-action-for-us-all/

NHS England. (2021, February 24). *Health and Wellbeing Framework Strategic Overview.* https://www.england.nhs.uk/publication/nhs-health-and-wellbeing-framework/

NHS England. (2024, June 3). *Culture of Care Standards for Mental Health Inpatient Services.* https://www.england.nhs.uk/publication/culture-of-care-standards-for-mental-health-inpatient-services/

Point of Care Foundation. (2025). *Schwartz Rounds.* https://www.pointofcarefoundation.org.uk/our-programmes/schwartz-rounds/

Salinsky, J. (2009). *A Very Short Introduction to Balint Groups.* https://balintsociety.org.uk/very-short-introduction-balint-groups

Springham, N. & Huet, V. (2018). Art as relational encounter: An ostensive communication theory of art therapy. *Art Therapy*, 35(1), pp. 4–10. https://doi.org/10.1080/07421656.2018.1460103

Tjasink, T. & Stevens, P. (2022). The innovative use of art psychotherapy with NHS clinicians. In H. Jury & A. Coles (Eds.). *Art Psychotherapy and Innovation* London: Jessica Kingsley Publishers, pp. 83–103.

Van Der Kolk, B. (2014). *The Body Keeps the Score.* London: Penguin Books.

Waller, D. (1991). *Becoming a Profession: The History of Art Therapy in Britain, 1940–82.* London: Routledge.

Winnicott, D. W. (1971). *Playing and Reality.* London: Routledge.

# 10 The Common Language of Arts Psychotherapies

*Jackie Edwards and Estelle Kane*

## Introduction

Adamson himself acknowledged that art was only one of the creative therapy modalities. It stood equally alongside drama, music, dance and movement, and these four arts psychotherapies are now recognised within the UK NHS mental health in-patient care settings (NHS England, 2022). In the previous chapters, Adamson's perspective on the therapeutic nature of art and the role of the artist has been discussed, and this aligns with the other arts modalities, with pioneering dance movement psychotherapist Marian Chace maintaining that

> one needed to have the art form well integrated within oneself in order to then make use of it as a therapeutic modality.
>
> (Chaiklin, 2020)

Written by practitioners across these modalities, this chapter will begin by discussing this common human need for artistic expression. It will then give an overview of how these arts psychotherapies have developed in the UK since Adamson's work in the post-war period and discuss the values and language of the modalities as expressed in in-patient settings. The chapter concludes with the perspectives of therapists drawn from all four modalities, giving examples of how changes over the past 45 years are reflected in their clinical practice, training standards and statutory regulation.

## Artistic Expression as Fundamental Human Need

There is a fundamental human need to communicate: In developmental terms, communication is vital to survival. The infant vocalises, gestures, begins to symbolise and explore their world, enabled by their primary caregiver, who, optimally, receives these communications in an attuned and relational stance:

> When an infant is able to have his or her needs met (e.g., the needs for physiological regulation or attachment), he or she experiences both a

DOI: 10.4324/9781003613428-13

> sense of efficacy and achieves satisfaction of the original need and an intrinsic pleasurable feeling.
>
> (Ammaniti & Ferrari, 2013, p. 368)

The arts forms used in the arts therapies harness this basic need to be heard and understood in ways that are not primarily reliant on verbal language, and as Stern (2010) describes:

> implicit relational knowing forges intimate interactions which are not language-based and are not translated into semantic form.
>
> (p. 111)

Cathy Malchiodi, a US research psychologist, clinical mental health counsellor, expressive arts therapist and visual artist, states that from an evolutionary perspective,

> humans turned to arts-based expression as a way of transforming difficulties when confronted by crisis, tragedy, or loss. As a species we have been turning to…the arts to confront and resolve distress for thousands of years.
>
> (Malchiodi, 2020, p. x)

Arts psychotherapies bring together a range of expressive arts approaches, which she proposes are powerful means of communication that 'capture not only the brain's explicit imprint of traumatic stress, but also the body's implicit experience that does not translate easily through words alone'. (Malchiodi, 2020, p. xi). She calls this a 'brain-wise as well as a body-based' (p. 86) approach, which is a commonality between all the arts psychotherapies.

There is increasing evidence supporting the understanding that responses to stress and trauma are held somatically, as explored in Bessel van der Kolk's *The Body Keeps the Score* (2015), where he states that

> The capacity of art, music, and dance to circumvent the speechlessness that comes with terror may be one reason they are used as trauma treatments in cultures around the world.
>
> (p. 243)

People admitted to in-patient wards are likely to be in heightened states of distress, where using words to describe how they are feeling may, initially at least, not be possible, and all the arts therapies can provide an intermediate space, using the arts, to both alleviate some of the intensity of distress and to help people find form for their feelings.

Malchiodi cites Paolo Knill (1932–2020), a Swiss scientist, artist and therapist, who coined the term *inter-modal expressive therapy* to describe the interplay between arts modalities. She also references the UK art therapist and art therapy educator, Shaun McNiff, explaining that he proposes that 'the connectedness of the arts in psychotherapy provided the necessary dynamics for personal growth and wellbeing' and that this 'addresses the totality of the senses – gesture, body movement, imagery, sounds, word and enactment' (p. 20), which can be drawn upon in arts therapies practice.

Malchiodi acknowledges that the arts therapies have tended to develop in some isolation from one another over decades, with 'relatively little cross-fertilization between creative arts therapies approaches in terms of practice, education, and research' (p. 18), but that there are 'many important commonalities across these approaches that complement each other' (Malchiodi, 2020). She goes on to say that '...expressive arts therapy is a humanistic experience that capitalizes on both the imagination and the integrative possibilities inherent to the arts' (p. 19). This approach, Malchiodi proposes, harnesses the 'sensory-based qualities of movement, music and sound, visual arts, dramatic enactment and other forms of creative communication' (2020, p. xi).

Arts psychotherapies, then, are based on developmental, humanistic, as well as psychoanalytic and psychodynamic theories and, as such, require a very broad and in-depth knowledge base and rigorous training. We will now explore how the professional standing of the arts psychotherapies has developed since Adamson's first tentative steps to formalise training in the 1960s.

## The Development of the Arts Psychotherapies in the UK

Karkou and Sanderson (2006) offer a research map of the field leading up to the formation of the four arts psychotherapies accepted by the NHS under the *Agenda for Change* framework established in 2004 (Table 10.1).

*Table 10.1* Recognised Arts Psychotherapies. NHS Agenda for Change Framework

| | |
|---|---|
| Art therapy/ psychotherapy | Art therapy, also known as art psychotherapy, aims to support people to express their psychological needs through the medium of art making and reflecting with a trained therapist. The British Association for Art Therapists is known as BAAT. |
| Music therapy | Music therapy aims to support people to express their psychological needs through the medium of music with a trained therapist. The British Music Therapy Association is known as BAMT. |
| Dramatherapy | Trained drama therapists aim to support people to express their psychological needs through the medium of drama, including story-making, music, movement and art. The British Association of Dramatherapy is known as BADth. |
| Dance movement psychotherapy | Trained dance movement psychotherapists aim to support people to express their psychological needs through the medium of movement, including dance, the use of music and sometimes other creative art forms. The Association for Dance Movement Psychotherapy is known as ADMP UK Ltd. |

There is a requirement in the UK for all arts psychotherapists to be registered with the Health Care Professions Council (HCPC) or the UK Council for Psychotherapy (UKCP), though Dance Movement Psychotherapists registered with the ADMP are required to register with UKCP via ADMP UK as an organisational member of UKCP, and registered therapists are also regulated as adult psychotherapists.

The development of art therapy in in-patient settings is the focus of this book, but it is important in the chapter to summarise briefly here the development over time of the other modalities:

### *Music Therapy*

Music therapy as a profession in the UK has evolved in a similar way to art therapy. The use of music as a therapeutic intervention to boost morale (Karkou & Sanderson, 2006) has been established within hospital environments since the end of the Second World War, and by the 1980s, both art therapy and music therapy were recognised by the NHS (Karkou & Sanderson, 2006). Hayman (2016) gives an account of the development of different concepts and models of music therapy, as a practicing music therapist working within in-patient services for over 20 years. Music is considered a core attribute (Carr et al., 2013), with the key pioneers themselves being professional musicians (Millard & Carr, 2021).

### *Dramatherapy*

Dramatherapy also evolved from professional artists applying theatrical and drama techniques and processes within mental health and educational contexts since the 1970s. The early modern Dramatherapy pioneers evolved within a humanistic context, in particular the Swiss-American psychiatrist Jacob Moreno (1889–1974), in developing psychodrama, a specific group therapy (Karkou & Sanderson, 2006), and a pioneer of dramatherapy within psychiatric settings (Goodwin, 2016; Mitchell, 1987) was the psychotherapist Sue Jennings (b. 1938). Dramatherapy was recognised by the NHS in 1989, and the proportion of dramatherapists working in the NHS is less established (Karkou & Sanderson, 2006) than compared to art therapy and music therapy.

### *Dance Movement Psychotherapy/Therapy*

Payne (1993) gives an account of the development of dance movement therapy within in-patient settings from the 1970s. It developed in the UK and the US from the 1940s in a similar way to the other arts therapies, but changed its name to Dance Movement Psychotherapy in 2009. Dance movement psychotherapy and dramatherapy are still considered to be smaller professions when compared to art therapy and music therapy (Karkou & Sanderson, 2006) and are less established within the NHS (Carr et al., 2021).

## The Introduction of Regulation, Standards of Education and Evidence-Based Research

Since 2009, art, drama and music therapists have all been regulated under the HCPC and are allied health professionals. HCPC is included within the Professional Standards Authority (PSA) introduced by the government in 2013. The PSA is an independent regulatory body for all approved health and social care professionals in the UK. The PSA was created to ensure public safety and a high standard of practice could be established within each profession. NHS England, in association with the associations representing drama, art and music therapists, also publishes a *Clinical Career Development Framework for Art, Drama and Music Therapists.*

In response to the increased need for the public as well as the employing authority to have confidence in the arts psychotherapies, training standards have continued to develop since the 1980s. There is now a range of courses available across the UK, each having psychotherapeutic understanding in addition to art forms (Karkou & Sanderson, 2006; Payne, 1993). Postgraduate diplomas, leading to the development across all four modalities of a master's level degree, became the minimum standard for all four modalities by 2009. The trainings continue to be either specific to each art modality or as an integrative master's level degree. An integrative arts approach where modalities in art, drama/puppetry, sculpture/clay, poetry, sand play, music and bodywork/movement are included in one psychotherapy training is at the heart of the training at the Institute of the Arts in Therapy and Education (IATE) based in London. It is also central to the recent NHS England Commission to support and develop art, drama and music therapy for the future, which indicates a movement towards embracing the commonalities of these professions.

### *Evidence-Based Practice Within the Arts Psychotherapies*

While most arts psychotherapists are trained with a focus on one modality, many arts psychotherapists working within in-patient settings are integrating with each other to form combinations of arts-based interventions (Hackett, 2016), for example, the use of art-making in dance movement psychotherapy, movement in music therapy, storytelling in art therapy and visual imagery in dramatherapy. In practice in in-patient settings, we also now see multi-modality working, with groups facilitated by practitioners from different backgrounds (Colbert & Bent, 2017).

Research into the arts psychotherapies has also been developing since the 1970s up to the present time. Payne (1993) describes three stages of research development:

- Stage 1 (1977–1980) is based on the researchers and practitioners as separate. Research adopts an objective view from a distance.

- Stage 2 (1980–1987) is illustrated as the researcher and practitioner becoming more closely aligned with a range of methodologies being explored.
- Stage 3 (1988–1992) is illustrated as a collaborative approach to research where practitioners and their clients are included in co-creating an understanding of the process and in-therapy lived experience.

Arts psychotherapies are still considered to be a complex intervention to research within an evidence-based NHS structure, and Chapter 11 of this book is dedicated to gathering data and outcomes from art therapy interventions in in-patient settings. There is a growing body of evidence looking at the arts psychotherapies all together (Hackett, 2016), identifying their similarities and understanding their differences (Carr et al., 2021; de Witte et al., 2021; Koch, 2017) and other research (de Witte et al., 2021; Koch, 2017) has adopted a variety of specific and general factors that support change to be evidenced in an appropriate way across all modalities.

Carr et al. (2023) looked at the effectiveness of group arts therapies compared to group counselling for diagnostically heterogeneous psychiatry community patients. The trial protocol acknowledges the art-making process as a common factor and focuses on developing principles of practice for the group intervention, rather than a detailed rules and steps approach.

Similarly, *Arts for the Blues* (Omylinska-Thurston et al., 2021) is an evidence-based intervention for depression and anxiety that integrates different arts forms including dance, drama, music, creative writing and visual arts. This model has been used in in-patient services when offering reflective practice sessions to staff.

## Practitioner Reflections from Working Within In-patient Services

In researching this chapter, the authors held two in-person focus groups with practitioners who had worked within the NHS from the 1970s up to the present time. The focus groups lasted between one and two hours and were held in March and April 2025.

A total of 14 qualified and registered arts psychotherapists with experience of working within in-patient services between 1980 and 2025 participated in these focus groups: seven art therapists; four dance movement psychotherapists; two music therapists; and one integrative arts psychotherapist. Three senior art therapists who had retired were able to reflect on the period between 1977 and 2000, alongside two art therapists and one music therapist who had qualified under the PGDip training standards.

The art therapists in the focus groups were all aware of Adamson's work. They confirmed that the open studio model of supporting people to exercise choice and agency in relation to these spaces remains a core feature of art therapy offered on the wards as current practice. Representatives of the other modalities were less aware of Adamson's work, though the concept of allowing people to come in and out of the space freely is something all 14 therapists felt reflected their current practice while working on wards within an in-patient service.

As we heard in Chapter 4 of this book, the main area that has changed from the 1980s up to the present time is the space available to offer the arts psychotherapies: modern hospitals have been built to replace the older large hospitals, which had spacious gardens and quiet areas for people to retreat to, as well as space for art studios. Some modern hospitals did include art rooms, but all 14 therapists reflected that being able to retain the art room was becoming more and more difficult, as rooms were shared spaces or even office spaces rather than specific therapy rooms. The challenges of a lack of access to a dedicated therapy space on wards are also considered in Chapter 4, which discusses the benefits of offering other spaces for arts therapies.

The number of arts psychotherapists – 2000 – employed within the NHS now, compared to the 1980s, has increased significantly and arts psychotherapists are now more understood to have dual identity as psychological therapists and Allied Health Professionals (AHPs) and these alliances are discussed in more detail in Chapter 13. Arts psychotherapists within the focus group expressed the need to work with other multi-disciplinary teams if possible, without losing the essence of the fundamental values and beliefs shared by all four arts psychotherapy modalities.

## Theoretical Influences Reflected Within the Focus Groups

The art therapists working from the 1980s spoke less about psychological therapies informing their practice than those who qualified at a Master's degree level. The focus in the 1980s was more on art as a therapeutic process to support people in expressing their psychological needs without words. This aligns with Adamson's approach of allowing people to paint freely without direction or any need to theorise the experience.

Since the introduction of regulation and an increase in the need for an evidence-based practice, training standards now include a research module. Therefore, it is understandable that the therapists included in the focus groups who trained between 2005 and 2025 spoke more about their theoretical influences, such as psychoanalytic, psychodynamic and humanistic theories. Attachment theory and a person-centred approach were discussed, although not all the therapists identified as being influenced by person-centred theory.

Interestingly, for those currently working within in-patient services, person-centred and co-produced concepts are now being introduced through *Personal Wellbeing Plans* that are being used to replace the older *Care Plans* in an attempt to ensure patients are receiving individually developed plans that meet their specific needs.

Some therapists spoke about the impact of other psychological theories, such as empowerment theories (Zimmerman, 2000) and psychotherapy theories such as Gestalt Therapy (Perls, 1951). As larger teams of arts psychotherapies are now working within in-patient settings that include all four modalities, a more integrative practice was discussed where therapists confirmed they continue to develop their knowledge and understanding from working together as a team that covers a wide range of psychological and arts-based understanding.

The therapists interviewed offered views about the changes in available spaces in contemporary in-patient settings, which is echoed by many art therapists throughout the book. Those currently working on the wards reflected on how difficult it can be to take people off the ward compared to before the COVID-19 pandemic. The rooms that were available in the past have been changed to multidisciplinary team rooms where arts psychotherapies are offered in a room that may also be used for other interventions. There was a discussion around the use of space, including how the provision of 'same time, same place, same materials' offered security and consistency in a chaotic ward environment, which may also be reflected as a chaotic internal world. The therapists spoke about allowing people to express themselves as they need to, through the art medium, from one session to the next.

The music therapists within the focus group spoke about not having a designated music therapy room. They were having to use spaces that were not designed for music therapy. This can be understood in terms of attachment theory and the need for a secure base (Bowlby, 1988) for arts therapy practitioners and their clients.

Within NHS mental health services, the trauma-informed approach discussed in Chapter 5 and elsewhere is now considered to be a core part of arts psychotherapies (Office for Health Improvement and Disparities, 2022). The therapists currently working on the wards from all four modalities acknowledge the need to be aware of trauma, including the experience of being sectioned and held involuntarily as a patient on a ward, and the retired arts psychotherapists referenced trauma-informed theory and language around trauma evolving over time since the 1980s, noting:

> *But it wasn't [until] so much later, was it, to the research being done around all illness potentially being an expression of some form of trauma as defined by the person who'd had the trauma rather than, you know, category of diagnosis again.*
>
> (Retired Art Therapist)

The focus groups reflected on how the arts psychotherapies operate in a different way than what they felt was a medical model of understanding. They felt the influence of an evidence-based model of understanding, which prioritises 'what can be measured' rather than allowing for an individualised person-centred approach. The therapists spoke about their perception that this could be experienced by some service users as the arts psychotherapies being separate from the rules and restrictions of the day-to-day ward environment.

## Clinical Approaches Adopted by the Therapists in the Focus Groups

The current therapists working in in-patient services discussed clinical approaches such as mirroring and attuning as a relational two-way non-verbal form of communication used to connect with others in a group or individual dyad. Mirroring and attuning are well-established psychotherapy approaches used by music therapists, drama therapists and dance movement psychotherapists, and though the art therapists in the focus groups did not specifically mention mirroring and attuning, this relational stance also underpins art therapists' approach and theoretical framework. A music therapist within the focus group explained this as follows.

> *First of all, I want to let them know that I'm understanding them and hearing them. So I want to find a way into their world rather than expecting them to come into my therapy or even the ward, and part of that will sort of be observations and how they are physically: how they move, how they breathe and...their heartbeat and...that can also be reflected in when we start playing and improvising.*

## Adamson's Influence and Legacy

It was acknowledged that much of what Adamson represented is still relevant to all four modalities working in in-patient services at the present time, and the loss of large outdoor spaces was lamented. Therapists reflected that special interest groups are aiming to bring back the concept of 'nature' as a therapeutic environment. Nature-based arts therapy is a way for arts therapists to offer this connection away from the ward.

Adamson worked with psychiatrists and psychotherapists, and it was acknowledged by the group that working as part of a multi-disciplinary team had both advantages and disadvantages. Psychiatrists, the group felt, can be some of the most supportive colleagues for the arts psychotherapies.

> *We are there as mental health practitioners, and I think that is significant. I think that that's the legacy perhaps that we are on in-patient wards, we are in NHS Trusts, we are considered...mainstream now, we're not considered an additional extra perhaps, we are there as core parts of mental health care.*

## In Conclusion

This chapter offers a contribution to the common language of the arts therapies, covering reflections from arts psychotherapists working over the past 45 years within the NHS in-patient mental health services. The common language of the arts therapies centres on the process of using arts forms for self-expression as a way of developing the therapeutic alliance in a safe, non-verbal way that allows our service users to explore their experiences.

In talking to different arts psychotherapists and bringing together our understanding of Adamson's way of working, we can reflect that his legacy has had an impact on the development of the art therapies in mental health in-patient settings. There are many more arts psychotherapists employed now than in Adamson's time, and there is a developing understanding of the benefits of integrative approaches. The focus groups reflected that we have a lot to thank Edward Adamson for.

## References


Ammaniti, M., & Ferrari, P. (2013). Vitality effects in Daniel Stern's thinking – A psychological and neurobiological perspective. *Infant Mental Health Journal*, 34(5), pp. 367–375.

Bowlby, J. (1988). *A Secure Base: Parent-Child Attachment and Healthy Human Development*. New York: Basic Books.

Carr, C., Odell-Miller, H., & Priebe, S. A. (2013). A systematic review of music therapy practice and outcomes with acute adult psychiatric in-patients. *PLoS One*, 8(8), pp. e70252. https://doi.org/10.1371/journal.pone.0070252

Carr, C. E., Feldtkeller, B., French, J., Havsteen-Franklin, D., Huet, V., Karkou, V., Priebe, S., & Sandford, S. (2021). What makes us the same? What makes us different? Development of a shared model and manual of group therapy practice across art therapy, dance movement therapy and music therapy within community mental health care. *The Arts in Psychotherapy*, 72, pp. 101747. https://doi.org/10.1016/j.aip.2020.101747

Carr, C. E., Medlicott, E., Hooper, R., Feng, Y., Mihaylova, B., & Priebe S. (2023). Effectiveness of group arts therapies (art therapy, dance movement therapy and music therapy) compared to group counselling for diagnostically heterogeneous psychiatric community patients: Study protocol for a randomised controlled trial in mental health services (the ERA study). *Trials*, 24, p. 557. https://doi.org/10.1186/s13063-023-07232-0

Chaiklin, S. (2020). Marian Chace biography. *American Dance Therapy Association*. https://www.adta.org/marian-chace-biography

Colbert, T., & Bent, C. (Eds.) (2017). *Working Across Modalities in the Arts Therapies: Creative Collaborations* (1st ed.). London: Routledge. https://doi.org/10.4324/9781315559889

De Witte, M., Orkibi, H, Zarate, R, Karkou, V, Sajnani, N., Malhotra, B, Ho, R. T. H., Kaimal, G., Baker, F. A., & Koch, S. C. (2021). From therapeutic factors to mechanisms of change in the creative arts therapies: A scoping review. *Frontiers in Psychology*. https://doi.org/10.3389/fpsyg.2021.678397

Goodwin, C. (2016). Concepts and models: Dramatherapy. In J. Yakely, J. Johnston, G. Adshead, & L. Allison (Eds.), *Oxford Specialist Handbooks in Psychiatry*, pp. 83–85. Oxford: Oxford University Press.

Hackett, S. (2016). The combined arts therapies team: Sharing practice development in the national health service in England. *Approaches: An Interdisciplinary Journal of Music Therapy, Special Issue*, 8(1), pp. 42–49.

Hayman, N. (2016). Concepts and models: Music therapy. In J. Yakely, J. Johnston, G. Adshead, & L. Allison (Eds.), *Oxford Specialist Handbooks in Psychiatry*, pp. 83–85. Oxford: Oxford University Press.

Karkou, V., & Sanderson, P. (2006). Arts therapies: A research-based map of the field. *Arts Therapies*. https://doi.org/10.1016/B978-0-443-07256-7.X5001-3

Koch, S. (2017). Arts and health: Active factors and a theory framework of embodied aesthetics February 2017. *The Arts in Psychotherapy*, 5. DOI: https://doi.org/10.1016/j.aip.2017.02.002
Malchiodi, C. A. (2020). *Trauma and Expressive Arts Therapy; Brain, Body & Imagination in the Healing Process*. New York: The Guilford Press.
Millard, E., & Carr, C. (2021). Music therapy in psychiatry. In U. Volpe (Ed.), *Arts Therapies in Psychiatric Rehabilitation*, pp. 35–60. Springer. https://doi.org/10.1136/bmjopen-2021-051173
Mitchell, R. (1987). Dramatherapy in In-patient psychiatric settings. In S. Jennings (Ed.), *Dramatherapy. Theory and Practice* 1. pp. 257–276. London: Routledge.
NHS England. (2022). *Art, Drama and Music Therapists*. https://www.hee.nhs.uk/our-work/allied-health-professions/art-drama-music-therapists
Office for Health Improvement and Disparities. (2022, November 2). *Working Definition of Trauma Informed Practice*. https://www.gov.uk/government/publications/working-definition-of-trauma-informed-practice/working-definition-of-trauma-informed-practice
Omylinska-Thurston, J., Karkou, V., Parson, A, Nair, K., Dubrow-Marshall, L., Starkey, J., Thurston, S. Dudley-Swarbrick, I., & Sharma, S. (2021). Arts for the Blues: The development of a new evidence-based creative group psychotherapy for depression. *Counselling and Psychotherapy Research*, 21(3), pp. 597–607.
Payne, H. (1993). *Handbook of Inquiry in the Arts Therapies; One River Many Currents*. London: Jessica Kinsgley Publishers.
Perls, F. (1951). *Gestalt Therapy*. London: Delta.
Stern, D. (2010). *Forms of Vitality*. Oxford: Oxford University Press.
Van der Kolk, B. (2015). *The Body Keeps the Score, Mind, Brain and Body in the Transformation of Trauma*. London: Penguin.
Zimmerman, M. A. (2000). Empowerment theory. In J. Rappaport, & E. Seidman (Eds.), *Handbook of Community Psychology*. Boston, MA: Springer. https://doi.org/10.1007/978-1-4615-4193-6_2

# 11 Evidencing the Impact of Art Therapy Using Outcome Measures

*Runa Park and Tim Wright*

## Introduction

This chapter presents two evaluations of art therapy in acute in-patient settings using qualitative and quantitative measures. After addressing the current literature, we describe these evaluations and examine what may be learned from them in terms of practice and further research. The need for such evidence in advocating for acute art therapy is addressed in the following chapter.

Allied Health Professionals and Psychological Therapists in the NHS are encouraged to monitor outcomes (Allied Health Professions Outcome Measures UK Working Group, 2019; NHS England, 2023, 2024), and systematic research and evaluation have become a larger feature within the profession in the USA and the UK in recent years (Kapitan, 2010), though research in acute settings is still limited. Noble and Hackett (2024) reported the results of 24 completed questionnaires collected between 2013 and 2021 on patients' experiences of acute art therapy. They recommend further qualitative enquiry into the benefits of such interventions. Our literature search elicited no other articles describing the systematic evaluation of acute arts therapies or psychological interventions.

In a community context, outcome measures are used by art therapists, such as the *Clinical Outcomes in Routine Evaluation* (CORE) (Chenery et al., 2016) and *Audio Image Recordings* (AIRs) (Springham & Brooker, 2013), an art therapy-specific tool. However, many service users in the acute setting are likely to find these too cognitively or emotionally challenging to complete, and both tools are generally employed to measure change over a longer period of engagement than is common in the acute setting.

The first evaluation discussed in this chapter, titled *Implementing the Acute Arts Therapies Process and Outcome Measure*, is of an ongoing art therapy service across nine acute wards over two sites. The second, *Evaluating Art Therapy in the Acute In-patient Setting*, is a pilot study in a female acute ward and in a male Psychiatric Intensive Care Unit (PICU) at the South London and Maudsley (SLaM) NHS Trust in the UK.

DOI: 10.4324/9781003613428-14

## Implementing the Acute Arts Therapies Process and Outcome Measure (ATPOM)

The *Acute Arts Therapies Outcome and Process Measure* (ATPOM) was developed to gather quantitative and qualitative data from service users about their experiences of arts therapies groups in the acute setting and about the effects of these groups, comprising art therapy, drama therapy and music therapy. The ATPOM asks five questions about their experience of the group process. It also asks group members to rate their mood pre- and post-group. It was designed to be accessible and relevant to service users, some of whom may be in confused, anxious or suspicious states of mind.

The author developed the ATPOM in collaboration with members of the arts therapies team, based on the key benefits the team intended their group interventions to provide. These included the provision of a safe space, expression through the art form and meaningful interactions with other members. These would generally be considered process elements, while the pre- and post-rating of mood would be considered a measure of outcome (NHS, 1997).

The five questions asked in the ATPOM are as follows:

- were you able to express yourself in the session?
- did you feel safe in the session?
- did you interact with other group members in the session?
- was the art/music/drama in the session helpful for you?
- could you relate to others in the session?

The two further questions relating to mood are as follows:

- how did you feel before the session?
- how did you feel after the session?

These two questions use both a Likert scale and a space for a free-text response.

The ATPOM was designed for routine use, with therapists ideally offering it to every participant in every group. In practice, the offer has been limited by a range of factors, e.g., a chaotic or very busy group where other concerns may distract the therapists from offering the measure. Also, a therapist might judge it untherapeutic to offer it to someone in a very confused or suspicious state of mind. The ATPOM has been implemented across nine ward-based groups in two mental health units, beginning in November 2023.

A pilot audit, not registered with the Clinical Audit department, was conducted of forms returned between November 2, 2023, and May 14, 2024 (N=61). This was followed by an audit of forms returned between June 4, 2024, and November 26, 2024 (N=71), which was registered with the trust's Clinical Audit department (Ref No. 2325). This chapter reports on the registered audit, using the pilot to compare some of the results.

**Results of the Audit**

Between June 4 and November 26, 2024, there were 500 attendances and 71 forms completed, meaning that 14.2% of attendees completed a form. Forty-five forms were for art therapy groups, with no significant difference in the scores between disciplines. Quantitative and qualitative data supported each other. The 171 qualitative comments also provided nuance to the quantitative scores. Qualitative comments ranged from full sentences to single words and phrases, but even the single words mostly seemed clear in their intended meaning, with only 6 of the 171 appearing too ambiguous to interpret.

Feeling safe in the sessions received the highest score (3.57), while being able to relate to other members scored the lowest (2.91). Scores in the pilot audit (3.6 and 2.45, respectively) showed the same relationship. Free text comments (quotes are from art therapy), such as *calm environment*, *everyone felt equal* and *[the therapist] is great at keeping a calm atmosphere* supported the sense of safety. Only one comment described a lack of safety, relating to an incident of aggression. One comment was on how well the therapist dealt with difficult dynamics in the session.

Interacting with other members scored higher (3.1) than being able to relate to them (2.91). This contrasts with 2.43 and 2.45 in the pilot audit. Comments included describing the group as a collaborative space, and being able to share one's process: *communication was good* and *got to understand each other participant's perspective*. Several comments described the art therapist as listening well.

Being able to express oneself and finding the art form helpful scored almost the same (3.2 and 3.22). Comments included *Brilliant, freedom to create* and *I was able to express myself*, as well as remarks on the art being calming and inspiring. One person remarked: *found myself speaking about art.*

The figures showed higher scores for interacting with and relating to other members than the pilot audit between November 2023 and May 2024. 'Did you interact with other group members?' scored 3.1 in 2025 and 2.43 in the pilot. 'Could you relate to others in the session?' scored 2.91 in 2025 and 2.45 in the pilot. Comments alluded to sessions enabling both similarities and differences to be acknowledged: *similar emotions, experiences; we all have differences.*

Most (40) respondents rated their mood as better post-session, and the mean mood rating prior to the group was 2.5 out of 4 and after the group 3.25 out of 4: an increase of 0.75. (Pilot scores were 2.45 and 3.35: an increase of 0.85). Twenty-four respondents rated their mood the same pre and post group, and three scored lower post group. Comments were all, except in two instances, consonant with the numerical scores, indicating that respondents understood the question. One of the exceptions was the patient who commented that feeling a bit worse was part of a process of confronting difficult issues. The other exception gave a post-session comment about feeling less lonely, which seemed to contradict the decreased mood score.

Some comments in the general comments section related to the above domains. One respondent commented on how the session felt fun and a safe place to express their real feelings: *very nice lesson, felt at ease, laughed; fun convo.* One commented that they experienced more freedom of expression as a woman than in their community. One comment expressed a wish for more sessions and one for longer sessions.

## Discussion of Results

The evaluation demonstrates the viability of a mixed-method, patient-rated arts therapies-specific outcome measure in the acute context. Results show a positive response to art therapy and to the arts therapies generally. They show art therapy providing a safe, calming environment that facilitates expression and meaningful interaction with others. References to calm are particularly significant, given that groups are conducted in multi-use spaces on acute wards where there is frequently a lot of noise and where the atmosphere can be tense, agitated or chaotic. References to the positive role of the art therapist hint at the skill required to manage the required balance of permissiveness, enabling inclusivity and boundaries to maintain physical and psychological safety in the therapeutic space.

*The Allied Health Professions Outcome Measures UK Working Group* (2019) guidance suggests that clinicians consider what they wish to measure, the acceptability and utility of the measure and its measurement properties. The ATPOM has been shown to be acceptable to acute in-patients. It has not been tested for reliability, though scores were broadly consistent with those from the pilot reported in June 2024, which offer some support for the reliability and internal validity of these findings. The retrospective scoring of mood is a complex area (Barrett, 1997), but is not unusual in psychological testing.

Noble and Hackett (2024) reported themes relating to the therapy environment, the art therapist, wanting more or longer sessions, being able to express oneself, reduced symptoms and art therapy enabling talking. The data from this evaluation support all these themes, with the exception that there were no direct comments on reduced symptoms. There were also some overlap with the art therapy working alliance inventory (Bat-Or & Zichla-Mano, 2017), which included the propositions: 'my artwork in therapy promotes my progress' and 'the art work process helps me to notice inner states in myself' (p. 87).

We wished the ATPOM to be accessible to individuals in acute states and so limited it to one side of A4. Noble and Hackett asked in more detail about what was helpful and unhelpful about the group, while we included questions relating to the experience of group dynamics. Another difference is that our results pertain to groups run on the ward, while theirs are for individual and group sessions run off the ward.

## Limitations and Recommendations

The measure was offered only to those who attended groups. It may also be that forms tended to be accepted more by those who engaged more in sessions and, therefore, were more positive about the intervention. Thus, there was implicit response bias in the results, and the form could not tell us anything about why some may not engage in the arts therapies. The 14.2% completion rate by attendees was low and further limits the generalisability of the sample.

The form did not measure change over time, but this was not its primary aim. The measure is generally not completed every time an individual attends, as completing it more than once may not make sense to many service users.

The ATPOM was designed by therapists without service user involvement. However, this limitation was partially addressed when it was presented to the trust's *Lived Experience Research Network* on March 27, 2025. One of the comments from the network group was that, in addition to the current question about mood, more might be asked about the effects of the group on symptoms and patients' experience of the therapist. The question regarding safety was seen to be less central to the focus of the measure, and consequently, a revised version is being tried that replaces 'Did you feel safe in the session?' with 'Did the group help you to manage or reduce any "symptoms" you might be experiencing?' and with 'Was the therapist helpful?'. This brings it closer in some respects to Noble and Hackett's (2024) questionnaire.

One possible confounding factor in this was the number of therapists facilitating the session. This was not consistently recorded on the data spreadsheet. This information is now included.

In contrast to Park's pilot described below, the ATPOM did not collect demographic information. The gender of the wards was known, but this difference was not used to analyse results.

## Conclusion

The audit demonstrates that service users on acute psychiatric wards can engage meaningfully with qualitative and quantitative outcome measures if these are designed to be accessible. Further studies could explore differential impacts for different demographics and between different art therapy disciplines.

## Evaluating Art Therapy in the Acute In-patient Setting: A Pilot Study at South London and Maudsley (SLaM) NHS Trust

Despite the documented benefits of art therapy outlined in this book, many acute in-patient wards within the UK remain without access to it. In 2018, two acute wards within SLaM NHS Foundation Trust – a male PICU and a female acute ward – lacked such provision. Recognising the potential value, ward multidisciplinary teams (MDTs) and the Trust's Arts Therapy services initiated a pilot to evaluate potential benefits and inform future service development.

This study outlines the development and evaluation of this pilot project, highlighting the methodology, findings and clinical implications. The aim is to contribute to the evidence base for arts therapies in acute in-patient mental health and support service development in similar settings.

The pilot art therapy service was implemented in a male PICU and a female acute ward. These wards cater to adults with severe mental health presentations, including psychotic disorders, mood disorders and trauma-related conditions.

Weekly art therapy group sessions were offered to service users on both wards over the summer of 2018. The male PICU group ran for nine weeks, while the female ward group ran for ten weeks. Groups were open, allowing flexible attendance, but participation was carefully coordinated through MDT discussions and risk assessments to ensure safety, given the acute nature of the wards. Sessions typically lasted 90 minutes and included artmaking using a range of materials (drawing, painting, collage), followed by reflective group discussion facilitated by the therapist. The focus was on providing a safe, non-judgmental space to explore emotions, experiences and interpersonal dynamics through creative expression.

In total, 25 feedback forms were received from the male ward and 48 from the female ward. The population of both wards varied each week, with an average of 10 residents in the male ward and an average of 14.4 in the female ward across the duration of the study. Each resident's stay varied in length, and participation ranged from once-only to multiple weeks. Of those who attended over multiple weeks, some completed feedback forms after multiple visits.

A question about ethnicity showed that 96% of respondents in the PICU identified as Black, with 4% opting not to specify ethnicity. Gender was primarily male (96%), with 4% not specifying. Age distribution showed 28% between 18 and 24, 24% between 25 and 34, 0% between 35 and 44, 32% between 45 and 54, 8% between 55 and 65 and 8% unspecified. Length of admission varied, with 32% admitted for 1 month, 24% for 3 months, 24% for 6 months, 8% under 1 week, 4% under 2 weeks and 8% not specifying. Art psychotherapy group attendance fluctuated, with five attendees in week 1 and 2, three in weeks 3 and 4, two in weeks 5 and 6 and three in weeks 7–9.

The female ward sample was more ethnically diverse: 33.3% Black, 31.3% White, 16.7% not specifying, 10.4% Asian, 6.3% mixed race and 2.1% other. Gender was mainly female (89.6%), with 2.1% male and 8.3% not specifying. Age ranged from 10.4% between 18 and 24 years, 22.9% between 25 and 34, 20.8% between 35 and 44, 16.7% between 45 and 54, 14.6% between 55 and 65 and 14.6% unspecified. Admission duration was 35.4% for 1 month, 6.3% for 3 months, 12.5% under 2 weeks, 27.1% under 1 week and 16.7% not specifying. Attendance was higher than the male group, with peaks of 9 and 11 participants in weeks 3 and 9, respectively, out of an average of 14.4 in-patients.

A mixed-methods evaluation was employed to capture both quantitative and qualitative data about the groups' impact, whether the overall experience of art therapy was helpful for their recovery and whether the service was effective enough to merit continuing. The primary evaluation tool was a questionnaire adapted from the *Art Psychotherapy Evaluation* form (Hartland & Blair, 2003), tailored to adult in-patient populations, with added demographic questions.

A total of nine questions were asked, of which six required a 'yes, no or other' answer:

- does the group help you to reflect on your personal experience?
- does the group contribute to your recovery on the ward?
- does the group help you to reflect on your emotions?
- did you find the therapist supportive during the sessions?
- would you be interested in one-to-one art therapy sessions if they were available?
- would you be interested in attending outpatient art therapy groups in the community?

There were three further open-ended questions:

- I came to this group because...
- what did you enjoy the most?
- is there any other comment or suggestion you would like to make about this group?

Data were collected after each session. Although staff initially felt that the evaluation was too long for service users to complete each week due to the severity of their mental health conditions, service users consistently engaged well with the questionnaire.

## Results

Across both wards, the quantitative findings suggested that most service users perceived the art therapy groups as supportive environments, facilitating personal reflection and emotional processing. In the male PICU, 88% reported finding the groups supportive for personal reflection, and 92% found them beneficial for emotional reflection, with 96% feeling that they contributed to their recovery. Similarly, in the female ward, 89.58% felt the sessions supported their experiential reflection, with 85.41% feeling that they supported their emotional reflection and 89.58% feeling the sessions contributed to their recovery. The therapist was perceived as supportive by 96% of male PICU participants and 100% of the female ward.

Interest in continuing art therapy was significant, with 68% of male PICU respondents expressing interest in one-to-one therapy and 92% interested in outpatient groups. Female ward participants showed 64.58% interest in one-to-one therapy and 75% interest in outpatient groups. Enjoyment of artmaking was reported by 52% of male PICU and 68.75% of female ward participants. Enjoyment of talking and thinking about artwork was lower, at 36% in the male PICU and 50% in the female ward. Sharing artwork in groups was less frequent at 25% in the male PICU and 31.25% in the female ward.

Thematic analysis of open-ended, qualitative responses revealed several themes. Many participants described the groups as unique spaces to express difficult emotions non-verbally, especially when verbal expression was limited. This aligns with established understandings of art therapy's role in facilitating emotional release and insight, as discussed widely in this book. Participants valued the therapist's empathetic presence, which created feelings of safety and trust within the ward environment.

Creative engagement emerged as a meaningful and enjoyable distraction from ward routines and distress. Participants described the art-making process as calming and supportive of psychological processing. Suggestions for improvement included increasing session frequency and offering more one-to-one therapy to deepen the work.

## Discussion

These findings underscore the value of embedding art therapy within multidisciplinary teams and integrating routine outcome measurements to support recovery-oriented care. Outcome data can inform service development, resource allocation and clinical decision-making to optimise therapeutic engagement and benefit. Routine use of outcome measures also aligns with wider health service priorities for evidence-based practice and quality improvement, and the integration of mixed-methods evaluation within in-patient group format supports the incorporation of outcome measurement into clinical practice.

The majority of participants across both groups expressed a strong interest in continuity of therapy post-discharge, suggesting that it may be beneficial to capture their thoughts again at a later point, should they continue. Quantitative data revealed that a majority of participants across both wards found the art therapy groups supportive for emotional processing. These results align with Malchiodi's (2012) work, highlighting the capacity of art therapy to facilitate non-verbal expression and psychological insights in populations where verbal articulation may be impaired by symptoms such as trauma. The high regard for the therapist's supportive role highlights the critical importance of the therapeutic alliance, which has been demonstrated as a key predictor of treatment engagement and positive outcomes across psychotherapeutic modalities (Horvath & Symonds, 1991).

Qualitative feedback explored how artmaking provided a safe and contained space for emotional release and creative engagement. Participants described the therapy as an opportunity to communicate feelings difficult to express verbally and appreciated the non-judgmental environment fostered by the therapist. This resonates with Case and Dalley's (2014) emphasis on the therapeutic relationship and the importance of safety and containment in art therapy, particularly within acute in-patient contexts where feelings of vulnerability are heightened.

While the study demonstrates the feasibility of routinely collecting meaningful outcome data in acute settings, it also acknowledges inherent challenges, such as fluctuating attendance and symptom severity. Limitations include the small sample size, reliance on self-report and open group format, which may limit generalisability. Due to the nature of the ward, residents came and went depending on the severity of their illness, with some staying for shorter periods and others for longer. It may be that some who enjoyed art therapy and would have come back were not able to, as they were discharged. Some of those who were residents for longer came to multiple sessions and completed multiple feedback forms. Future research should explore larger samples, controlled designs and longitudinal follow-up to further elucidate art therapy's impact on clinical outcomes such as symptomatology, length of stay and relapse rates. Refinement of outcome tools to incorporate both quantitative and qualitative elements sensitive to art therapy's unique processes is recommended.

## Conclusion

This pilot study provides evidence of the impact of art therapy in adult acute in-patient mental health settings. The use of this outcome measure enabled an evaluation of therapeutic benefits from the perspective of service users. The findings affirm that art therapy can foster emotional reflection, enhancing engagement in environments often characterised by distress and communication difficulties, and service users reported feeling that participation supported their recovery.

In conclusion, this pilot audit contributes to the growing evidence base that art therapy is an effective and valued intervention in adult acute in-patient mental health care. The use of outcome measures demonstrates its capacity to promote emotional expression, therapeutic alliance and patient engagement. As mental health services strive towards holistic, trauma-informed and person-centred care, embedding art therapy with rigorous outcome evaluation offers a promising avenue for enhancing clinical practice and improving patient outcomes.

## Joint Conclusion

The combined findings from the development and implementation of the *Acute Arts Therapies Process and Outcome Measure* (ATPOM) and the pilot study of art therapy at SLaM NHS Foundation Trust underscore the feasibility and clinical value of using both quantitative and qualitative outcome measures within acute in-patient mental health settings. These studies address a significant gap in the literature, responding to long-standing calls for more systematic evaluation of art therapies in acute environments, as noted by Kapitan (2010) and Noble and Hackett (2024).

The ATPOM was designed to be accessible and sensitive to the cognitive and emotional states of service users on acute wards, allowing meaningful self-reporting even amidst anxiety, confusion or suspicion. The measure aligns more closely with the needs of acute in-patients than measures such as CORE (Chenery et al., 2016) and AIRs (Springham & Brooker, 2013). The ATPOM's inclusion of both mood rating and process questions – covering safety, self-expression and social interaction – reflects a holistic understanding of art therapy's multifaceted benefits. These dimensions echo Bat-Or & Zilcha-Mano's (2017) emphasis on the therapeutic alliance and client experience of the art process, albeit adapted for the realities of acute care.

Similarly, the pilot study at SLaM NHS Trust employed a mixed-methods approach to capture nuanced patient experiences alongside measurable outcomes. The high percentages of service users endorsing personal reflection, emotional processing and recovery support align with established evidence on art therapy's capacity to facilitate non-verbal expression and insights (Malchiodi, 2012). The strong recognition of the therapist's supportive role further highlights the centrality of the therapeutic alliance in promoting engagement and positive outcomes, as emphasised by Horvath and Symonds (1991). This therapeutic relationship creates the safe and contained environment crucial to successful interventions in acute, high-distress in-patient settings, a point reinforced by Case and Dalley (2014).

Both studies reveal challenges inherent in acute in-patient settings, such as fluctuating attendance, variable group dynamics and the difficulty of routine data collection amidst clinical complexity. These factors not only contribute to response bias and limit the generalisability of findings, but also highlight the importance of designing flexible, user-friendly measures. The ATPOM also offers the possibility of comparing different art therapies and mixed modality groups, refining ideas about what works for whom.

Adamson himself acknowledged what has been at the heart of this discussion of outcome measures: that art (and, in this case, art therapy) is increasingly called upon to 'explain in words what is essentially a matter of feeling' (Adamson, 1963, p. 53). Both studies discussed above support the case for routine, service user-centred outcome measurement in acute arts therapies, which is also consistent with the *Allied Health Professions Outcome Measures* UK Working Group (2019) recommendations. Outcome data can guide service development, for example, adjusting session frequency or expanding outpatient options, to optimise engagement and therapeutic benefit. Moreover, this evidence supports advocating for dedicated resources, affirming art therapy as an essential therapeutic modality alongside other arts modalities, psychological interventions and medication.

Future research should continue refining outcome measures tailored to art therapy in acute settings, combining quantitative scales with qualitative narratives to capture the complexity of therapeutic impact fully. Additionally, expanding sample sizes will strengthen the empirical foundation for arts therapies in acute mental health care.

The evidence presented affirms that routine outcome measures for art therapy in the acute setting can elicit meaningful quantitative and qualitative data that illuminate the value of the intervention in engaging service users meaningfully, promoting emotional processing and supporting recovery within challenging in-patient contexts. These findings bolster the case for embedding arts therapies as a vital component of multidisciplinary acute mental health services.

## References


Adamson, E. (1963). Art and mental health. *Mental Health*, 22(2), p. 53.

Allied Health Professions (AHP) Outcome Measures Working Group (2019) *Key Questions to Ask When Selecting Outcome Measures: a Checklist for Allied Health professions*. Royal College of Speech and Language Therapists.

Barrett, L. F. (1997). The relationship among momentary emotion experiences, personality descriptions and retrospective ratings of emotion. *Personality and Psychological Bulletin*, 23(10) pp. 1100–1110

Bat-Or, M., & Zichla-Mano, S. (2017) The art therapy working alliance inventory: The development of a measure. *International Journal of Art Therapy*, 24(2), pp. 76–87. https://doi.org/10.1080/17454832.2018.1518989

Case, C., & Dalley, T. (2014). *The Handbook of Art Therapy* (3rd ed.). Routledge.

Chenery, T., Fulton, J., Mellor-Clark, J., Mellor-Clark, S., & Willoughby-Booth, S. N. (2016). The routine use of evaluation by art therapists and allied health professionals in everyday clinical practice. *International Journal of Art Therapy*, 21(1), pp. 35–44.

Hartland, V. & Blair, M. (2003). Art psychotherapy evaluation form (group and individual) (with advice from N. Cosgrave & T. Tranah, updated by Hartland, V. & Blair, M., 2013). South London and Maudsley NHS Foundation Trust National and Specialist CAMHS In-patient. Unpublished internal document.

Horvath, A. O., & Symonds, B. D. (1991). Relation between working alliance and outcome in psychotherapy: A meta-analysis. *Journal of Counselling Psychology*, 38(2), pp. 139–149. https://doi.org/10.1037/0022-0167.38.2.139

Kapitan, L. (2010). *Introduction to Art Therapy Research*. New York, London: Routledge.

Malchiodi, C. A. (2012). *Handbook of Art Therapy* (2nd ed.). Guilford Press.

NHS England. (2023, October 30). *Acute In-patient Mental Health Care for Adults and Older Adults*. https://www.england.nhs.uk/long-read/acute-inpatient-mental-health-care-for-adults-and-older-adults/

NHS England. (2024, April 24). *Implementation Guidance, Psychological Therapies for Severe Mental Health Problems*. https://www.england.nhs.uk/long-read/implementation-guidance-2024-psychological-therapies-for-severe-mental-health-problems/#monitoring-outcomes

NHS Institute for Innovation and Improvement (1997). *The How to Guide for Measurement for Improvement*. https://www.england.nhs.uk/improvement-hub/wp-content/uploads/sites/44/2017/11/How-to-Guide-for-Measurement-for-Improvement.pdf

Noble, J., & Hackett, S. (2024). Art therapy in acute in-patient care. *International Journal of Art Therapy*, 28(4), pp. 196–203.

Springham, N., & Brooker, J. (2013). Reflect Interview using audio-image recording: Development and feasibility study. *International Journal of Art Therapy*, 18(2), pp. 54–66.

# Part III

# The Way Ahead

# 12 Improving Equality of Access to Psychological Therapy through Art Therapy

## A Contemporary Pilot Project in an NHS Service

*Poppy Tomkinson and Jed Jerwood*

### Introduction

The previous chapter discussed the contemporary imperative for measuring outcomes in therapeutic interventions. However, the published literature gives voice to what we instinctively know as art therapists: that finding words to communicate our internal worlds does not always feel possible for some service users and one of the consequences of this is that measuring the outcomes of therapy can be extremely difficult.

Schaverien (2000) describes how insight can sometimes be painful, and this can be especially true for individuals experiencing psychosis who may encounter great fear about participating in therapy (Wood, 1997a). Adamson too knew how less verbal forms of therapy could reduce some barriers to engagement in and increase accessibility to psychological therapies, and that art therapy facilitates experiential spaces where service users are able to connect with others, human to human, and to some extent themselves (Schaverien, 2000).

Adamson's studio-based approach emphasised *being-with* and creativity as the initial step towards self-expression. Accessing the therapeutic spaces he facilitated did not require prior knowledge or skill in the arts, nor was there a reliance on verbal communication to engage meaningfully. Instead, Adamson describes trying simply to create a 'permissive atmosphere and have the necessary pen and paper' (Adamson, 1984, p. 7). In her account of Adamson's legacy at Netherne Hospital, Wood (1997b) describes how Adamson would simply sit down next to the patients and ask them if they would like to do some painting, and this captures the relational, human-to-human ethos that underpins therapeutic work in rehabilitation settings.

This chapter will focus on a 12-month pilot project within a large UK NHS Trust. The pilot was commissioned by the Trust to introduce and evaluate the impact of broadening the range of psychological interventions within eight rehabilitation settings. Art therapy, in particular, was introduced across these settings to address inequalities of access to verbal psychological therapies for those who find these talking therapies less accessible.

DOI: 10.4324/9781003613428-16

For this client population, who often face stigma and isolation, we will argue that art therapy, and in particular the open studio model, offers a pathway to building tolerance of the therapeutic alliance, opening the doorway into further participation in other interventions and therapeutic activities, and enhancing choice and access to psychological interventions.

The chapter will also explore themes of isolation and engagement, as well as health inequalities rooted in issues around talking therapies, and ask how art therapy can mitigate some of these inequalities. Finally, we will link back to the previous chapter by reflecting upon how the pilot was evaluated and what happened following once the pilot was completed.

## Background and Context

The eight services used in this pilot project comprised seven hospital units and one community-based team. These services were developed over time to support service users with a psychosis-related diagnosis or who were recognised as having very complex needs, requiring specialist in-patient and community rehabilitation services. They provide a multi-disciplinary team approach to assessment, formulation and intervention, supporting service users to achieve their recovery goals, which for many include ending their detainment under the Mental Health Act (Department of Health, 2007) and transitioning back into the community. The services also aim to identify and address any barriers to recovery and social inclusion and support both mental health and practical daily functioning skills, with the goal of breaking long-standing cycles of acute admission and discharge.

Verbal psychological therapies with a well-established evidence base, such as Cognitive Behavioural Therapy (CBT) and Behavioural Family Therapy (BFT), existed already in the services prior to this pilot study, and while many service users engaged meaningfully with these, it was recognised that for some individuals, they were not accessible.

## Barriers to Engagement in Psychological Interventions

Maintaining engagement with services, including psychological therapies, is associated with lower risk. When service users disengage from services, risk levels can escalate quickly. People with long-term psychosis often experience multiple challenges when engaging with psychological interventions (Meaden et al., 2022), and many service users struggle to engage with solely talking therapies, so that a less-verbal approach is often more accessible.

There are a variety of identified experiences and/or influences that constitute potential barriers to engaging with talking therapies. From a medicalised perspective, active symptoms such as thought disorder and delusions impact the ability to focus and engage during sessions (Chang et al., 2014). It is also well documented that 'symptoms such as delusions and hallucinations which have not responded fully to medication can make communication and engagement difficult' (Joint Commissioning Panel for Mental Health, 2016). Attard and Larkin (2016) describe how psychotic symptoms can hinder people's ability to identify and explore their mental states. We have also seen, however, in Chapter 5 that there has been a debate in recent years about the legitimacy and utility of medicalised diagnoses (Johnstone, 2017). Art therapy in particular aligns with the premise of a psychological formulation viewed through the lens of a trauma-informed, narrative framework, and can be more accessible for some people precisely because its language is not medical. It is based on foundations of trust with the understanding that 'symptoms' can also be seen as threat responses to hostile experiences and have their own phenomenological meaning.

In recent years, the full extent of the health inequalities experienced by many groups and communities has become widely understood (Kapadia et al., 2022; Morris & Robertson, 2024; National Institute for Health and Care Excellence, 2025). The COVID-19 pandemic highlighted widespread inequity of access to health care for people from racialised communities, people with learning differences and people from the lesbian, gay, bisexual, transgender and queer (LGBTQ+) communities. In addition to inequity of access, it is now widely recognised that many groups and communities who do access healthcare services have poor experiences within services (Apodaca et al., 2022; Henriquez & Ahmad, 2021; Stonewall, 2024).

In mental health settings, these inequalities manifest themselves in the over-representation of Black men in hospital settings who are detained under the Mental Health Act (2007) (Faber et al., 2023) and the under-representation of people from diverse ethnic backgrounds and men in general in psychological services (Mercer et al., 2019; Sharland et al., 2023). People from lower socio-economic groups, often living in poverty, people who have experienced adverse childhood experiences, people who have migrated to the UK and people with complex mental and physical health problems also tend to be over-represented in UK mental health services, but may not access psychological therapies (NHS Race and Health Observatory, 2023).

These and other inequalities were, of course, also present when Adamson was practising, and many of the patients he worked with at Netherne Hospital were from extremely poor rural or urban backgrounds. Others had been traumatised in one of the two World Wars or had become excluded from their family, social or cultural group (Colley, 2024). For many of these, their response to this trauma was to become what we would now call selectively mute, so that the art studio became one of their few avenues to self-expression. In *Art as Healing* (1984), Adamson reflects upon the ways in which he worked to support the creative self-expression of service users even when they struggled to communicate. He did not define a person by their diagnosis, despite the medicalised setting, and made space for service users to bring a variety of their experiences and identities. He describes that an important part of his practice was not instructing a person what to make, but instead waiting for them to create organically.

David Gwyther, a technical assistant at Netherne in 1970, was interviewed for this book. His memories of visiting the gallery bear witness to the power of art to express in images what perhaps could not be expressed in words:

> *It was quite a revelation to witness not just the extent of the paintings but also their evident meaning, indicating state of mind at the time. Themes varied, but roads to nowhere and being lost in rough seas seemed to prevail.*

One of the patient/artists David got to know at Netherne was 'Peter'. Peter could be quite chatty, especially when helping David in his work, but:

> *There were also times when he didn't appear for a few days. I never enquired as to the reason, but when he did re-appear he would show me the scars on his arm.*

Peter gifted David one of his paintings, which we reproduce here (Image 12.1). As David says of his time working at Netherne:

> *For a nineteen-year-old like me at the time, it was a profound experience – probably the reason that I still have Peter's painting in my office 55 years later!*

In the following sections, we will explore the preparatory work involved in the pilot, what was delivered, how it was evaluated and what recommendations were taken forward.

## Delivery of the Pilot

### *Scoping and Preparatory Work with Staff*

Initially, a scoping phase was required to consider the systemic landscape and service user needs. It quickly became clear that building a shared understanding of art therapy across teams was essential to developing trust and support. Huet (1997) acknowledged the tension of working in rehabilitation services, observing 'staff are often concerned with achieving visible changes in behaviour which puts issues of success and failure high on the agenda for patients' (p. 15). Pressures such as these on staff in in-patient settings are discussed more fully in Chapters 8 and 9. The three-month scoping phase involved focus groups, shadowing, liaising with different stakeholders and participation in multidisciplinary team (MDT) meetings. *Introduction to Art Therapy* workshops were delivered to over 70 staff members from a variety of professions to increase understanding of art therapy and articulate the benefits of this intervention, and a staff survey was designed and distributed across the eight services. The observations from staff underlined the fact that many service users

*Image 12.1 A maelstrom of chaos, but with the emergence of hope in the form of a fragile boat* (c.1970).

Creator known as 'Peter'. Courtesy of David Gwyther. Image copyright: David Gwyther.

were struggling to verbalise their thoughts, feelings and experiences, with the majority navigating significant challenges with emotional regulation.

The outcome of the scoping period served to inform staff about art therapy, reduce anxiety about the introduction of a new psychological therapy, challenge preconceptions and inform referral pathways. In addition, this period led to the aims of the pilot being identified and agreed across services as follows:

- to utilise art therapy to build engagement with psychological interventions.
- to develop individual tolerance of therapeutic engagement.
- to facilitate a space for connection with self and others through art.
- to enable creative self-expression.

### *The Open Studio Model*

Building engagement had been identified as a significant initial step. The therapeutic alliance between therapist and service user is often established informally first outside of the intervention space, in recreational spaces, such as watching TV or playing pool, before formal engagement begins. In light of this and drawing on available literature and the *British Association of Art Therapists Psychosis Guidelines* (2020), an open-group studio model was developed to run weekly on each unit as the informal nature of this type of therapeutic model was designed to allow service users to engage at their own pace through developing curiosity.

Adamson's approach was influential in the development of these spaces. The studio spaces Adamson facilitated acted as an invitation to participate, but were not compulsory. He reflects in *Art as Healing* (1984) that the act of choosing to enter the intervention space and becoming involved signalled the taking of an active role in recovery and personal agency:

> The very fact that they came into the studio each day placed a responsibility on their shoulders, rather than allowing them to become passive recipients of authoritarian care.
>
> (Adamson, 1984, p. 2)

Facilitated by an art therapist alongside a co-facilitator – typically a staff member from each unit – the sessions were open to all service users and ran for 90 minutes at the same time and location each week. To foster a sense of comfort and familiarity, and as we have discussed in Chapter 4, less clinical environments were deliberately chosen, with groups held in recreational spaces or dining rooms. A range of both directive and non-directive approaches were offered, allowing everyone to engage in a way that felt accessible and appropriate to their needs. Service users were free to come and go, provided their movements did not significantly disrupt the group. This flexibility was a key feature, supporting a paced and responsive approach to participation without imposing restrictive boundaries. The groups provided an expressive space for service users to connect with others and explore feelings and experiences in a way that did not rely solely on verbal communication.

### *Attendance and Demographics*

Over a six-month period, 485 clinical contacts were completed across seven units. Sixty-eight service users engaged with group interventions, with 443 group clinical contacts being completed. Seven service users engaged in individual art therapy, with 42 individual clinical contacts completed. All units saw a steady increase in attendance in groups each month, and therapists observed that time spent within the sessions also increased.

A higher proportion of service users were male (c. 65%), which was higher than the previous level of engagement for men in psychological interventions across the seven units. Around a third of service users attending were Black/Black British (30%), a third White (30%) and a third Asian (33%), with a small minority (7%) of other ethnicities recorded. In terms of age, the range of service users attending was more evenly spread: 27% were aged between 25 and

34; 30% between 35 and 44; 12% between 45 and 54 and 27% between 55 and 64. A small number of service users aged over 65 took part, and this was reflective of the demographic in the units. One of the aims of introducing less verbal therapies was to reach service users not previously engaging in psychological therapies, so these data were encouraging.

### *Evaluation of the Pilot*

Feedback was gathered through written narratives, outcome measures and clinical observations. Validated tools such as the *Recovering Quality of Life* questionnaire were selected with input from clinical psychologists and Peer Mentors. Peer Mentors noted that formal measures, as we saw in Chapter 11, often hinder engagement due to difficulties verbalising feelings and past negative experiences with mental health services/professionals. This was a pattern subsequently observed across the units. As a result, qualitative methods such as verbal feedback, staff forms and therapist observations were used to better capture service user experiences.

### *Service User Views*

Service users were invited to share their reflections on the art therapy groups, offering insights into what they had valued. Their feedback drew attention to themes of psychological safety, connection and creative self-expression. This was significant as the experiences closely aligned with the initial objectives of the groups. Many described the sessions as *calming* or *peaceful*, with some attributing this sense of ease to the use of certain materials or the supportive presence of facilitators. Service user comments below are recorded in italics:

> *I wanted to join the group because I thought it was a good idea and that it might be calming.*
>
> *I have found the group peaceful.*

Service users noted a range of personal benefits, including increased confidence, improved concentration and a sense of satisfaction from feeling able to demonstrate dedication through regular attendance.

> *Coming to the group has helped me build my confidence...I have also shown myself I can concentrate and be dedicated to something.*

The informal studio approach invited service users to utilise the space in a way that felt tolerable to them, often requiring the freedom to come and go as required, and feedback suggested that the structure of the groups helped to establish routine. Individuals often described the group space as *inclusive* and allowed for genuine involvement. Engaging with others through art was frequently mentioned as a positive and enjoyable experience. For some, the group setting served as a stepping stone, leading to further engagement in individual therapy.

> *The most important thing about the group to me was the company and having my friends around me. We interact with each other through art, and it is fun to look at each other's drawings.*

### *Clinician's Views*

Clinicians working in the services observed a range of positive outcomes resulting from the art therapy groups. Clinicians' comments below are recorded in italics.

The sessions were described as *friendly* and *accessible* and staff reflected that, over time, service users would look forward to attending. It was observed that the groups encouraged service users to interact with one another through creative expression, offering a less verbal avenue for sharing thoughts, feelings and experiences.

> *It encourages people to start interactions through the work of art, as well [as] expressing their inner feelings.*

Staff noted that the groups supported the development of coping strategies and contributed to a calmer, more connected ward environment. Significantly, clinicians reported gaining deeper insights into service users, with many expressing and communicating their experiences more openly through the artwork.

> *Patient's artistic side is quite fascinating to see their imagination and interpretation, [I] gained an insight.*

In line with discussions in Chapter 9, an outcome of the pilot included the impact on staff well-being. Nursing staff, in particular, reported that co-facilitating the groups had increased their well-being at work, provided a space to express themselves and provided time alongside service users to reflect upon collective experiences on the units. It was something they went into work looking forward to attending.

> *Beautiful, pleasant friendly environment. Brought the best out of my inner self.*

## Case Study: 'Curtis'

To exemplify the impact of the pilot, a brief participant case study is presented here. All identifying information has been changed to ensure anonymity, and a pseudonym is used.

Curtis had no known engagement with psychological interventions before entering a long-stay in-patient recovery service, despite frequent contact with mental health services. Before engaging with art therapy, Curtis had completed one psychology initial assessment and tentatively participated in a group facilitated by a psychologist on the unit before withdrawing, stating that it was *too much* and *too confusing*.

Curtis initially began to engage with art therapy through the group sessions, which were available on the unit. To begin with, his participation was brief, often leaving the room and returning on several occasions. Over the 17 sessions he attended, both the longevity and quality of Curtis's engagement increased, with him beginning to recognise, reflect upon and share his thoughts and feelings.

As discharge from the unit grew closer, Curtis expressed concern about the transition and agreed to engage in individual art therapy sessions. During the assessment process, Curtis reflected that he wanted to use the sessions to think about *staying on the right path* after discharge and to think about emotional regulation, such as finding ways to self-soothe. Curtis completed three assessment sessions and six therapy sessions.

In the final session, Curtis reflected that he had felt able to get his *point across* during the intervention and expressed feeling more hopeful about the future post-discharge. He also shared that he would like to continue engaging with psychological support.

## Reflection on the Pilot

Running a pilot is a complex process. The units were scattered across a large city, with the therapists themselves spread across four units each, which challenged their own sense of belonging and containment, and this initial disorientation could be said to mirror at least in part the experiences of disconnection and uncertainty often felt by the service users themselves. As one therapist put it in their reflective journal:

> *Each location has its own rhythm which must be learnt, but this is difficult when I feel the daily disruption of arriving and pain of leaving.*

The therapists worked to consistently hold the groups in open communal spaces to foster connection. Bion (1961) highlights that the setting of the group is fundamental in providing a containing framework for any psychotherapy work. Making engagement tolerable requires the therapists first to work with the service: understanding its rhythms, its psychological landscape and unspoken dynamics. Only then can they begin to build trust and offer a space where creativity might gently invite connection. Nitsun (1998) also finds that 'the eventual aim of the therapy group is intimate sharing in an atmosphere of trust and safety' (p. 50).

For individuals with histories of being marginalised, creating tolerable and relationally safe spaces is a nuanced process. To support participation, the therapeutic frame was adjusted to consider the unit not only as a group, but also as an independent community. This drew on psychodynamic theories around group processes, acknowledging that no matter how isolated individuals were from the group, they still hold an active position in the collective psyche (Bion, 1961). This perspective allowed the therapists to view each setting as its own therapeutic community, with each individual held in mind during the groups, regardless of whether they attended or for how long.

Given that many service users had spent much of their lives feeling excluded or unseen, simply entering a group space could be a profound and challenging step. As one staff member commented:

> *It [Art Therapy group] has had an impact on the ward, as service users sit together and enjoy the artwork doing of their choice.*

Being in a group often brings up questions around identity, and although the thought of the group caused some anxiety, once within it, the group appeared to allow greater self-exploration, and the use of artmaking amongst participants became more experimental. In some units, service users began to use their artwork to communicate their past identities and the journey that had led them to hospitalisation. Clay, in particular, as a tactile and malleable medium, seemed to evoke deeply personal and often painful narratives – echoing the *remembrance and mourning* phase of the trauma-informed framework (Herman, 1992):

> *I felt really nervous about coming but I found it calming – especially using the clay.*

## Evaluation

The aim of the pilot was to explore how art therapy could complement existing psychological therapies and address inequity of access by people underrepresented in those psychological therapies. The evaluation demonstrated significant impacts across recovery services, enhancing the accessibility of, and engagement with, psychological therapies.

> *Lots of service users have given very positive and endorsing feedback, some have clearly gained therapeutic value from them [art therapy interventions], and found that these groups have supported their recovery, helped with anxiety and distress and acted as positive distraction through occupation.*
>
> (Staff Member)

As the evaluation highlights, there was a significant engagement in art therapy by men and for people from diverse ethnic backgrounds. In addition, engagement in psychological therapies was increased generally with the addition of art therapy groups and some individual interventions. For some service users, the art therapy intervention served as a gateway into other psychological therapies, which had previously not been accessed.

Throughout the pilot, engagement steadily increased, with service users attending more consistently and for longer durations. Group sessions fostered greater interaction and connection, and as attendance grew, so did the volume of artmaking. The space also facilitated interactions between staff and service users in a way that encouraged curiosity and understanding. These connections with self and others are particularly significant for individuals who have experienced marginalisation or discrimination. For these service users, feeling psychologically safe with others was especially challenging. Clinicians also observed a rise in participation in other ward activities and a strengthening of relationships across the units.

> [Something I would keep the same about the group is]...*getting along with other members of the group. I can be social when I want but keep to myself when I need to.*
>
> (Service User)

## Challenges and Limitations

During the pilot, several challenges and limitations emerged. Having limited time on each of the eight units – just one day per week – slowed down the process of building familiarity with service users, and with hindsight, focusing on a smaller number of units may have allowed for deeper engagement. Group engagement developed slowly, revealing that the 12-month timeframe was too short to capture the depth of the therapeutic process unfolding. Therapists noted difficulties in evidencing interventions that were only just beginning as well as naming and meaningfully communicating to other professionals what was happening during the interventions. Measuring the unspoken and unconscious processes also proved difficult and, often, therapeutic impact only became clear in retrospect. Finally, high-quality supervision was essential in managing well-being and feelings of isolation. Peer supervision became a valuable resource, offering space for reflection and connection. Ongoing attention to support structures will be crucial in the future for therapists working in these complex settings.

## Conclusion

Adamson's legacy shaped the way in which art therapy was introduced to the units, favouring an open studio model, which allowed for user-led engagement and a safe and consistent therapeutic container in which trust could be slowly built. Improved engagement, more meaningful relationships, reduced isolation, enriched ward environments and increased access to psychological therapies were all documented outcomes of the pilot. These important findings emphasise how art therapy offers a way into accessing psychological therapy for many service users who may have otherwise faced significant barriers, and addresses inequities of access to psychological therapies.

Introducing a new modality of therapy to an established service area was seen to be a complex process; however, what has been evident throughout this pilot is that engagement in art therapy must always be led by the individual and shaped by their needs. Initial attendance was rarely motivated by an explicit desire for therapeutic intervention, connection or emotional expression, but tended to emerge organically, following the development of a therapeutic alliance outside the therapy space. In addition, it was important to help staff understand how a less verbal therapy might help service users who struggle to engage with existing therapies and other activities on the units.

Adamson's approach of being in relation to a person who struggles with connection, in a way made tolerable through art, has been central to this pilot. Adamson described his early days at Netherne hospital and how he felt like he was working in the dark, and working intuitively (Adamson, 1984). His reflections helped the therapists running the pilot to tolerate uncertainty, to work intuitively and to allow the therapeutic frame to develop in partnership with the service users through attuning to their needs and meeting them where they were, rather than imposing a predefined model upon each unit.

Following evaluation of the pilot, a full-time, permanent Senior Art Therapist post was created to support three high-dependency units, where the need for less verbal interventions was perceived to be the greatest. An art therapy provision is now well established across the three units, with the service continuing to evolve. Due to budget constraints, not all the services have permanent access to art therapy yet; however, the demand continues to be evidenced. The groups provide relationally safe spaces, enabling connection and supporting self-expression:

> *Under such conditions, it was not surprising that the studio gradually became an oasis for each person to express…individually.*
>
> (Adamson, 1984, p. 2)

The following chapter takes up some of the themes developed here to discuss the role and impact of art therapy within an ever-evolving health service.

## References

Adamson, E. (1984). *Art as Healing*. Coventure.

Apodaca, C., Casanova-Perez, R., Bascom, E., Mohanraj, D., Lane, C., Vidyarthi, D., Beneteau, E., Sabin, J., Pratt, W., Weibel, N., & Hartzler, A. (2022). Maybe they had a bad day: How LGBTQ and BIPOC patients react to bias in healthcare and struggle to speak out. *Journal of the American Medical Informatics Association*, 29(12), pp. 2075–2082. https://doi.org/10.1093/JAMIA/OCAC142

Attard, A., & Larkin, M. (2016). Art therapy for people with psychosis: A narrative review of the literature. *The Lancet Psychiatry*, 3(11), pp. 1067–1078. https://doi.org/10.1016/S2215-0366(16)30146-8
BAAT. (2020). *Guidelines on Art Therapy for People with a Psychosis Related Diagnosis.* The British Association of Art Therapists in association with Salomon's Institute for Applied Psychology. Canterbury Christchurch University.
Bion, W. R. (1961). *Experiences in Groups and Other Processes.* London: Routledge.
Chang, N. A., Grant, P. M., Luther, L., & Beck, A. T. (2014). Effects of a recovery-oriented cognitive therapy training program on in-patient staff attitudes and incidents of seclusion and restraint. *Community Mental Health Journal*, 50(4), pp. 415–421. https://doi.org/10.1007/S10597-013-9675-6.
Colley, A. (2024). *In-patient Mental Health Care from the Asylum System to the Present Day. A lived experience of policy and practice.* London: Routledge.
Faber, S., Khanna Roy, A., Michaels, T., & Williams, M. (2023). The weaponization of medicine: Early psychosis in the Black community and the need for racially informed mental healthcare. *Frontiers in Psychiatry*, 14, p. 1098292.
Henriquez, N., & Ahmad, N. (2021). The message is you don't exist: Exploring lived experiences of rural Lesbian, Gay, bisexual, transgender, queer/questioning (LGBTQ) people utilizing health care services. *SAGE Open Nursing*, 7. https://doi.org/10.1177/23779608211051174
Herman, J. (1992). *Trauma and Recovery.* New York: Basic Books.
Huet, V. (1997). Challenging professional confidence arts therapies and psychiatric rehabilitation. *International Journal of Art Therapy: Inscape*, 2(1), pp. 14–19. https://doi.org/10.1080/17454839708413040
Joint Commissioning Panel for Mental Health. (2016). *Guidance for commissioners of Rehabilitation Services for People.* www.jcpmh.info
Johnstone, L. (2017). Diagnostic Alternatives; Psychological Formulation as an Alternative to Psychiatric Diagnosis. *Journal of Humanistic Psychology.*
Kapadia, D., Zhang, J., Salway, S., Nazroo, J., Booth, A., Villarroel-Williams, N., Bécares, L., Esmail, A., (2022). *Ethnic Inequalities in Healthcare: A Rapid Evidence Review.* NHS Race and Health Observatory
Meaden, A., Fox, A., & Hussain, H. (2022). *Team-Based shared Formulation for Psychosis.* London: Routledge.
Mercer, L., Evans, L., Turton, R., & Beck, A. (2019). Psychological therapy in secondary mental health care: Access and outcomes by ethnic group. *Journal of Racial and Ethnic Health Disparities*, 6(2), pp. 419–426.
Morris, L., & Robertson, R. (2024). *Tackling Health Inequalities | Seven Priorities for the NHS.* https://www.kingsfund.org.uk/insight-and-analysis/long-reads/tackling-health-inequalities-seven-priorities-nhs
National Institute for Health and Care Excellence. (2025). What are health inequalities. *NICE.* https://www.nice.org.uk/implementing-nice-guidance/cost-saving-resource-planning-and-audit/nice-and-health-inequalities/what-are-health-inequalites
NHS Race and Health Observatory. (2023). NHS 'talking therapies' review identifies barriers in accessing care. *NHS – Race and Health Observatory.* https://nhsrho.org/news/nhs-talking-therapies-review-identifies-barriers-in-accessing-care/
Nitsun, M. (1998). *The Anti-Group Destructive Forces in the Group and Their Creative Potential.* London: Routledge.
Schaverien, J. (2000). The triangular relationship and aesthetic countertransference in analytical art psychotherapy. In A. Gilroy & G. McNeilly (Eds.), *The Changing Shape of Art Therapy: New Developments in Theory and Practice*, pp. 55–83. London: Jessica Kingsley Publishers.

Sharland, E., Rzepnicka, K., Schneider, D., Finning, K., Pawelek, P., Saunders, R., & Nafilyan, V. (2023). Socio-demographic differences in access to psychological treatment services: evidence from a national cohort study. *Psychological Medicine*, 53(15), pp. 7395–7406. https://doi.org/10.1017/S0033291723001010

Stonewall. (2024). *LGBTQ+ Facts and Figures.* https://www.stonewall.org.uk/resources/lgbtq-facts-and-figures

Wood, C. (1997a). Facing fear with people who have a history of psychosis. *International Journal of Art Therapy: Inscape*, 2(2), pp. 41–48. https://doi.org/10.1080/17454839708413046

Wood, C. (1997b). The history of art therapy and psychosis (1938–95). In K. Killick & J. Schaverien (Eds.), *Art, Psychotherapy and Psychosis*, pp. 144–173. London: Routledge.

# 13 Art Therapy and the Changing Face of the NHS

*Maggie Batchelar and Tim Wright*

## Introduction

This chapter will consider how art therapists are adapting their practice to fit within the changing landscape of the NHS. We begin by reviewing how society, the NHS and art therapy have changed and developed since Adamson's day, and we then proceed to examine the current situation. This will encompass clinical approaches, demonstrating value and the evidence base, training and strategic and organisational issues. Some developments in art therapy are embedded in those of the wider families of arts therapies and allied health professions and we will refer to these when appropriate.

We refer to the strategic context of the NHS Long Term Plan and also to the trauma-informed frameworks, NHS mental healthcare strategy, the National Institute for Health and Care Excellence (NICE) and British Association of Art Therapists (BAAT) guidelines when referring to the future direction of travel for art therapy in in-patient settings.

## Changes in Society

By the end of Adamson's career as an art therapist at Netherne Hospital, which ran roughly from 1946 to 1981, the context of his work had changed considerably, and social, political and technological changes over the decades since Adamson retired mean that art therapists today inhabit a significantly different world. This brings different benefits and challenges, with the pace of change appearing to be ever-increasing.

We now inhabit a digitally networked world. Enhanced communication and the ready availability of data bring a range of benefits, greatly broadening access to information, facilitating connectedness locally, nationally and globally, and changing the way healthcare professionals work. Social attitudes have shifted in many ways; notably, recognition and respect for diversity have increased over the past 40 years in relation to sexuality, culture and ethnicity, leading to the NHS actively addressing the inequalities of access and experience for racialised people (NHS England, 2023b). Stigma regarding mental health problems has greatly decreased, with mental health now a mainstream

DOI: 10.4324/9781003613428-17

conversation. The challenges to authoritarian psychiatry that surfaced in the 1960s (Whitley, 2012) have, in some respects, found a more accepting audience in the contemporary NHS, where the contribution of 'experts by experience' (Care Quality Commission, 2025) is increasingly written into policy.

On the other hand, increased global instability, climate crisis, widening economic and health inequality and economic decline mean that the for the first time in living memory, the young often hold a bleaker view of the future than their parents (Broome et al., 2023; Wills, 2024). Overall economic inequality rose sharply between 1979 and 1990 and, despite some fluctuation, has remained high since (Equality Trust, 2025). Digital connectedness has also been seen not to be only beneficial but also to have disruptive and demoralising effects, fuelling distrust, aggression and anxiety (Huesman, 2009). The impact on the United Kingdom's mental health of the 2019 COVID-19 pandemic and associated restrictions continues to be felt (Watson & Rowles, 2021).

## Changes in the NHS

Over this period, the NHS has reflected these social changes as well as undergoing more specific shifts. The widespread introduction of psychotropic drugs in the 1960s led to a dissolution of the old asylum system and a move away from institutional care in general. The Victorian asylums targeted in Powell's 1961 Water Towers speech (Colley, 2024) are now gone and their grounds have been sold. Not many mourn the passing of the drab, imposing and often sinister-seeming edifices so hauntingly evoked by David Bowie in his song *All the Madmen* (1970), though one loss entailed in this change is that the kinds of studio space available to Adamson and many art therapists who followed him are not available to contemporary art therapists. As space on contemporary in-patient wards has become more limited and there is a higher risk to the in-patient population, much art therapy provision has moved onto the ward itself, where groups may be held in dining areas or other multi-use spaces. This is explored in depth in Chapter 4 and elsewhere in this book.

The National Health Service and Community Care (1990) Act was a significant step in the process of de-institutionalisation, placing a duty on local authorities to assess the need and ensure support for those requiring it, as well as establishing hospital trusts and encouraging provision from the private sector. The initiation of Home Treatment Teams (Department of Health, 2001) led to fewer psychiatric admissions and bed stays have gone down, though the acuity of individuals on psychiatric wards is seen to be higher now. More recently, the Community Mental Health Framework (NHS, 2019) and the NHS Long Term Plan have promoted greater integration between health and social care and between primary and secondary and the third sectors. The term 'place-based care' is employed to refer to an approach that values community as a resource and aims to be sensitive to local needs. Sadly, however, the influence of government austerity policies since 2010 has depleted community mental health resources (Brown, 2024), often making for a fragile transition between ward and community.

The NHS has seen changes in the population it serves and the disorders it treats. Personality Disorders are now more widely recognised as treatable (Snowden & Kane, 2003) and the term itself is increasingly replaced by the less stigmatising term Complex Emotional Needs. Autism spectrum condition is now more frequently diagnosed, with the Royal College of Psychiatrists (2024) stating that it applies to around 10% of people admitted to psychiatric wards. In the twenty-first century, the NHS has actively incorporated some ideas from the service user movement, notably the Recovery Model and co-production. Service users now frequently occupy paid roles or research roles in NHS mental health services as peer support workers or Experts by Experience. The NHS also demonstrates increased sensitivity to the impact of power differences in mental health and wellbeing from institutional racism or gender bias. Mental health inequalities persist but are more openly discussed than in Adamson's day (Kings Fund, 2024). Some minority ethnic groups are shown to be overrepresented amongst detained psychiatric patients, and services are increasingly alert to the need to address this and other inequalities (NHS England, 2023b).

Models of mental health and illness have changed, for example, with a movement towards trauma-informed care (Rothwell & Grandison, 2016) and the appreciation of social factors. The Power Threat Meaning Framework (Johnstone et al., 2018) makes explicit links between power differentials, trauma and mental illness. There are also initiatives to reduce the use of restrictive practices through models of practice such as Safewards (Bowers, 2014). Many trusts have at least in principle embraced psychological formulation as a means of broadening out from a simply diagnostic understanding and most clinicians at least theoretically subscribe to a biopsychosocial model. Chapter 5 explores this change in more detail. The growing influence of the digital across society is reflected in the NHS with shared online clinical records, an increased use of ever-growing data sets to plan strategy and monitor the quality of care and treatment and the growth, especially since the 2019 Coronavirus pandemic, of online health provision.

## Changes in Art Therapy

Art therapy grew as a profession during Adamson's career and continued after his retirement, frequently spurred by the professional body he helped to found in 1964: the British Association of Art Therapists (BAAT). The national arts therapies career structure in the NHS that had begun in the 1980s has developed further, assisted by statutory regulation. This began with the Council for Professions Supplementary to Medicine (CPSM) in 1997, which ultimately became the Health and Care Professions Council (HCPC). This provided increased accountability with protection of title. The titles Art Therapist and Art Psychotherapist can only be used by HCPC-registered practitioners, and only these can claim to offer art therapy or art psychotherapy. Alongside these developments, art therapy trainings have multiplied from the first in 1969 to 11 HCPC-validated trainings in 2025, covering each nation of the United Kingdom.

With state registration, BAAT lost its disciplinary role and developed other strategic roles in collaboration with the British Association of Dramatherapists and the British Association of Music Therapists. A welcome recent development is the recognition of art, drama and music therapy within the Psychological Professions Networks (NHS England, 2023a).

Theoretical and clinical approaches have developed from Adamson's day, but what is retained of his approach is the skill of creating 'an atmosphere sympathetic to self-expression' (Cunningham-Dax, 1953, p. 20) and an understanding that individuals' artworks are intensely personal, unique and a means of externalising emotional landscapes. As later art therapists, unlike Adamson, began to take on an explicitly psychotherapeutic role, they looked to psychoanalytic therapy to help them navigate this. The enormous influence of that approach has, in the twenty-first century, receded and a wider range of research and theory now informs art therapy practice generally and in acute settings. This includes a range of recent trauma-focused models drawing on neuroscience and on social theory, e.g., the Power Threat Meaning Framework (PTMF). The PTMF and high-profile social movements such as Black Lives Matter have influenced art therapists to reframe psychological distress as a social issue and to see the importance of a reflexive attitude and to be more open to conversations with clients about power and identity. Sensory- and mentalization-based approaches have become more prominent and adapting practice to neurodiversity has also been a prominent theme in recent years.

Historically, art therapists have often struggled to help employers appreciate how their contribution differs from Occupational Therapy and from arts in health. This distinction has arguably become more widely understood and the profession's increasingly secure identity has enabled it to develop good working relations with the arts in health and arts for wellbeing field, which is seen as complementary. Community arts resources can be a recommended continuum for patients who have found art therapy helpful whilst in hospital.

Art therapy trainings have generally incorporated new models and broadening of understanding, such as intersectionality, trauma-informed approaches and systematic research methodology. In 2017, the beginning of the process of setting up arts therapies' apprenticeships offered a new way to train that promised to bring more social and ethnic diversity to a predominantly white and middle-class profession. The apprenticeship 'standard', i.e., the framework for training, was developed by a 'trailblazer group' that included large and small employers of arts therapists as well as representatives of the professional bodies for art, drama and music therapy. An apprenticeship course was set up at Teesside University in 2024 and recruited two cohorts of apprentices, all of whom will potentially complete the apprenticeship and qualify. However, the removal of funding from level 7 apprenticeships in May 2025 makes the future of these apprenticeships extremely uncertain and art therapy may need to find alternative ways to increase diversity amongst its practitioners.

Art therapy's evidence base has developed from mainly therapist point-of-view case studies to more use of empirical methodologies, both qualitative and quantitative. BAAT has been active in leading this change via the International Journal of Art Therapy (formerly Inscape), which began to employ double-blind peer review in 2008.

No UK Randomised Controlled Trials (RCTs) have been conducted on art therapy in the acute setting, though an RCT of acute music therapy (Talwar et al., 2006) was influential in the arts therapies as a whole, gaining a place in the National Institute for Clinical Excellence Guidelines (NICE, 2010) on the treatment of Psychosis and Schizophrenia. These recommend the arts therapies for the reduction of negative symptoms. Further research in the acute field includes Montag, whose RCT (Montag et al., 2014) of art therapy with in-patients with a schizophrenia diagnosis showed a positive impact on positive and negative symptoms and on psychosocial functioning. Noble and Hackett's (2023) qualitative study explored patients' perceptions of the benefits of art therapy. There has also been a growth in UK-based randomised controlled trials involving art therapy (Van Lith, 2016).

The BAAT has also produced professional guidance on art therapy in a number of clinical areas, including *Guidelines on Art Therapy for People with a Psychosis Related Diagnosis* (2020), which drew on a wide literature and consultation base. This advised a flexible, collaborative practice that acknowledged the service user's organisational and social context.

Provision of art therapy in the acute setting generally comprises open, drop-in groups run on wards, studio-type groups run off-ward and individual art therapy. BAAT guidelines on art therapy for people with psychosis (Wright & Holttum, 2020) advise that the art therapist offers a flexible response to individuals' needs and that they work closely with the ward team. Noble and Hackett's (2023) description of an off-ward acute art therapy group shows how the art therapist makes sessions as inclusive as possible, notably offering a succinct explanation of the purpose of the group and emphasising that attendees are not compelled to make art, while also helping them to overcome anxiety in starting to use the materials.

Noble and Hackett propose a Venn diagram model in which the three circles of space and environment, art making and reflection overlap. They quote Edward's (2004) description of the importance of the art therapy room in holding feelings to facilitate creativity and emotional growth. Art therapy groups run on the acute ward itself present a different sense of space and environment.

More research is needed into the benefits and challenges of on-ward groups. Work in this setting maximises inclusivity; no permission to leave the ward is required, so newly admitted and 'high-risk' patients can be included. In this context, it is relevant that although NHS data do not indicate the proportion of psychiatric patients detained under the Mental Health Act (with consequent restrictions on their ability to leave the ward), the authors' anecdotal experience is that it is around three quarters. Ward staff may also participate in on-ward groups, bringing some equality and creative sharing to the nurse–patient relationship. On the other hand, there are limitations, notably on the range of materials, on confidentiality and the ability to create a space free from disruption. Chapters 4 and 5 explore the benefits and challenges of this fluid and temporary space.

The acute setting can be a challenging one for training placements, and consequently, the trainees have tended to be on their second placement. This is one of the issues that the National NHS and HEI strategic leads forum has addressed in its work in developing understanding and clarifying expectations between these two groups, and some progress has been made in offering openings to first years. The authors and some of their peers find anecdotally that trainees can experience challenges in seeing how the therapeutic models they are learning can be adapted to enable them to connect with individuals in acute states and in the fluid environment of the ward. However, many trainees find that work in the acute environment provides a rich and deeply rewarding experience.

## Demonstrating Value

As we have seen in Chapter 11, to maintain and develop the support of NHS organisations, art therapists need to demonstrate their value and to show how their interventions support service priorities. One way to do this is through measuring clinical outcomes, but other considerations such as accessibility, inclusivity and user satisfaction are also relevant. Art therapists may also demonstrate how their interventions support service priorities such as reducing risk, reducing restrictive practice, embedding positive behaviour support and ensuring purposeful admission and safe discharge. In addition to this, art therapists contribute to supporting staff wellbeing and facilitate reflective practice.

It is now more common for art therapists to report on activity and outcome data at a local level and to employ standardised outcome measures, although the development of suitable outcome measures in the acute context is at an early stage. Chapter 11 offers two examples of routine outcome measurement in this setting, as well as examining the literature on art therapy outcomes in acute settings.

Art therapists can maximise accessibility via a range of means, including using their communication skills to gain the support of ward staff, to engage a diverse range of in-patients and to help them manage any challenges that arise in the group process. Providing a range of materials and helping patients overcome anxiety about using materials is part of this. Providing groups on the ward opens the offer to those who may arguably be in greatest need. People in acute states can connect with art at times when formal conversation is too much, a theme that is elaborated in Chapter 4. The art therapist needs to be skilful in communicating the relevance of service users' artwork to their presenting difficulties and, in supporting the team to treat it in a respectful manner. The artwork can be a medium for improving understanding between the multi-disciplinary team (MDT) and the service user.

Art therapy can also contribute to reducing clinical risk, though offering patients a means of self-expression and alleviating distress by facilitating communication amongst patients and between patients and staff (especially when staff participate in on-ward groups), fostering a sense of self-worth through creativity. For similar reasons, art therapy can also contribute to reducing restrictive practice and art therapists can also contribute to safe transition out of hospital. This may be by referral onward to community art therapy, where this is available, or through signposting to community arts provision or alternative therapy provision. This continuum of influence is included in Chapter 5.

There is a growing literature about how art therapy skills have been adapted to offer organisational interventions using creative methods in this area and some of this occurs in the in-patient setting. For instance, Huet's (2012) pilot study included a group with staff from a secure in-patient learning disabilities unit. Staff wellbeing and reflective interventions are addressed in detail in Chapter 10. As that chapter points out, supporting staff with such interventions can help staff to cope more effectively with the complexities and stresses of the caring task.

## Organisational Context

NHS England states that there are over 20,000 psychological professionals working in NHS-commissioned health care in England. The psychological professions include art, drama and music therapists who:

> *often identify as both allied health professions (AHPs) and psychological professionals. Art, drama and music therapists will continue to be represented by AHP leadership nationally and regionally. Psychological Professions and AHP leadership are committed to working together to ensure these professions thrive.*
>
> (NHS England, 2025)

There are fourteen Allied Health Professional Groups, but Art, Drama and Music Therapy are the only AHP groups that are psychological therapies. This underpins the need for these professions to have dual identity and to be recognised as psychological therapies to ensure that they are in the services that can be accessed by those who need them. This dual identity was the subject of a project funded and supported by Health Education England, aimed at producing a shared career framework supporting Art, Drama and Music Therapists to work across both its aspects. Individual interviews and focus groups were held with arts therapy practitioners and representatives from a range of people in senior organisational roles, to understand the issues at stake locally and nationally. The project summarised that art, drama and music therapists are the bridge between AHPs and psychological therapies, as they work holistically and are skilled at working with service users from marginalised groups and diverse populations, who find using words difficult to process their mental health needs. The priority is to ensure that patients receive the right intervention, at the right time, to meet their needs (BAAT, 2023).

The project also produced a range of material, including films to improve understanding of art, drama and music therapy in services and to support better career pathways and progression, including at more senior levels. The report suggested that these professions need to be encouraged to take up leadership roles, including representing other professions. In the survey that furnished this report, a high number (92%) of respondents confirmed that they supervise staff of their own and other disciplines. Some NHS mental health organisations have an established and well-populated art, drama and music therapy (and dance movement psychotherapy) workforce, with good career progression. More commonly, there appears to be a less strategic approach to employment from one organisation to the next, possibly largely influenced by the lack of NHS benchmarking for workforce ratio per patient population, as there is for psychologists. It is positive that the Standards for Acute In-patient Services for Working Age Adults (Royal College of Psychiatrists, 2019) recommend that each ward receive dedicated input from what they term 'creative therapists' though this title is inaccurate as the one used by the HCPC and recognised in law is 'art therapist/art psychotherapist', and the suggestion that input is sessional is unhelpful, and does not support their inclusion within the MDT. Art therapists are not included in the Workforce Development Plan in the British Psychological Society Guidelines for Psychological Services (NHS, 2021) within the Acute Adult Mental Health Care Pathway. This is despite the document stating that: 'Art psychotherapists offer alternative, non-verbal, creative ways of enabling engagement and reflection, which can complement or provide choices when more verbal ways of working are difficult for people' (p. 15).

Similarly, although an art therapist was on the expert reference group for the Acute Mental Health Competence Framework for Adults and Older Adults (University College London, 2022), the BAAT was not among the professional bodies included in devising it. This was limited to psychiatry, nursing and psychology professional bodies. Such limited representation can disadvantage arts therapists seeking to develop or protect their services.

The NHS Long Term Plan (NHS England, 2019) suggests that acute wards are often not safe, therapeutic or conducive to recovery. One of its key recommendations is to improve the delivery and quality of acute mental health in-patient care. The plan identifies the need to improve the therapeutic offer for in-patients by enhancing access to therapeutic interventions and increasing the skill mix on wards.

The need for patients to have access to a range of group and individual interventions is recognised in the aforementioned Acute Mental Health

In-patient Competence Framework, and this book proposes that art, drama and music therapists' provision of safe, effective, therapeutic interventions in in-patient wards should be more recognised in workforce planning. The absence of these professions from the in-patient workforce mix highlights the need for a focused and strategic approach from the arts therapies to improve this. There is no doubt that more robust and consistent outcomes are needed to demonstrate efficacy of arts therapies in in-patient settings, including amplifying the service user experience and voice. Chapter 11 offers examples of how meaningful data can be collated. Mental health services are now beginning to work more attentively with people with lived experience who report the need for and benefit from having access to art therapy: 'The mental health service user voice has been too long neglected on the basis of "lack of insight". The result is a dearth of research into the service user perspective on psychological therapy' (Woods & Springham, 2011, p. 60)

In response to the lack of strategic workforce planning for art therapists in in-patient settings, a new Special Interest Group (SIG) was set up in February 2025, as part of the British Association of Art Therapists (BAAT). The purpose of a SIG is defined by BAAT as a chance for art therapists to meet and focus on clinical specialty, focus on research, networking and CPD. Developing a SIG for art therapists working in in-patient settings provides a timely opportunity to enhance the profile of the arts therapies. The SIG can establish a clearer national picture of where and how art therapists are employed in in-patient settings and work towards developing best practice guidelines, gathering more systematic evidence of current practice to support in-patient workforce benchmarking, ensuring that patients have equal access to art therapy in all NHS in-patient settings. This will improve equality of access to psychological therapy for those who would otherwise struggle to engage in a more verbal and dominantly cognitive approach, an issue that is explored in chapter fourteen. This book is also contributing towards these aims, in bringing an overview of the art therapy profession in acute in-patient services and highlighting the skills and contributions brought by art therapists, both clinically and organisationally.

## Conclusion

This chapter has reviewed the changes that are relevant to in-patient art therapy, in society and within the NHS, since Adamson's day. We have addressed developments in theoretical and clinical approaches and in the research context and in training. We have looked at how art therapists can demonstrate the value of their contributions. Lastly, we have offered an outline of the strategic context within which art therapists are working and key issues within that. Art therapists have come a long way since they were paid less than refuse collectors (Adamson, 1970, p. 151), but there is, as always, much work to be done. We have pointed to the continuing need to develop the evidence base and to develop art therapy's profile amongst the psychological professions and its presence in workforce planning.

The final chapter in the book will take many of the discussions from this book into the wider context of society and explore the development nationally of arts and wellbeing.

## References

Adamson, E. (1970). Art for mental health. In J. Creedy (Ed.), *The Social Context of Art*, pp. 147–162. London: Tavistock.

Bowers, L. (2014). Safewards: A new model of conflict and containment on psychiatric wards. *Journal of Psychiatric Mental Health Nursing*, 21(6), pp. 499–508. doi: http://dx.doi.org/10.1111/jpm.12129

Bowie, D. (1970) *All The Madmen, on Man Who Sold the World*. Mercury Records.

British Association of Art Therapists. (2020). *Guidelines on Art Therapy for People with a Psychosis Related Diagnosis*. London: The British Association of Art Therapists in association with Salomon's Institute for Applied Psychology Canterbury Christchurch University.

British Association of Art Therapists. (2023). *Supporting Art, Drama and Music Therapists as AHPs and Psychological Professionals*. https://baat.org/publications/insight/summer-2023-24/supporting-art-therapists-as-ahps-and-psychological-professionals/

British Psychological Society. (2021). *Psychological Services within the Acute Adult Mental Health Care Pathway*. https://www.bps.org.uk/guideline/psychological-services-within-acute-adult-mental-health-care-pathway

Broome, M., Corlett, A., Hale, S., McCurdy, C., & Pacitti, C. (2023). *An Intergenerational Audit for the UK*. Resolution Foundation.

Brown. (2024, September 9) *Austerity Hit Young People's Mental Health*. https://www.understandingsociety.ac.uk/blog/2024/09/09/austerity-hit-young-peoples-mental-health/

Care Quality Commission. (2025, February 10). *What Do Experts by Experience Do?* https://www.cqc.org.uk/about-us/jobs/experts-experience

Colley, A. (2024). *In-patient Mental Health Care from the Asylum System to the Present Day - A Lived Experience of Policy and Practice*. London: Routledge.

Cunningham-Dax, E. C. (1953). *Experimental Studies in Psychiatric Art*. London: Faber and Faber.

Department of Health. (2001). *Crisis Resolution /Home Treatment Teams: The Mental Health Policy Implementation Guide*. London: Department of Health and Social Care.

Edwards, D. (2004). *Art Therapy*. London: Sage UK.

Equality Trust. (2025). *How Has Inequality Changed?* https://equalitytrust.org.uk/how-has-inequality-changed/

Huesman, L. R. (2009). The impact of electronic media violence: Scientific theory and research. *Journal of Adolescent Health*, 41(6), pp. S6–13

Huet, V. (2012) Creativity in a cold climate: Art therapy-based organisational consultancywithin public healthcare. *International Journal of Art Therapy*, 17(1), pp. 25–33, DOI: http://dx.doi.org/10.1080/17454832.2011.653649

Johnstone, L., & Boyle, M. with Cromby, J., Dillon, J., Harper, D., Kinderman, P., Longden, E., Pilgrim, D., & Read, J. (2018). The power threat meaning framework: Towards the identification of patterns in emotional distress, unusual experiences and troubled or troubling behaviour, as an alternative to functional psychiatric diagnosis. *British Psychological Society*. https://www.bps.org.uk/news-and-policy/introducing-power-threat-meaning-framework

Kings Fund. (2024). *Mental Health 360: Inequalities.* https://www.kingsfund.org.uk/insight-and-analysis/long-reads/mental-health-360-inequalities

Montag, C., Haase, L., Seidel, D., Bayerl, M., Gallinat, J., Herrmann, U., & Dannecker, K.N. (2014). A pilot RCT of psychodynamic group art therapy for patients in acute psychotic episodes: feasibility, impact on symptoms and mentalising capacity. *PloS One*, 9(11), p. e112348.

National Institute for Health and Care Excellence. (2010). *Schizophrenia: The NICE Guidelines on Core Interventions in the Treatment and Management of Schizophrenia in Adults in Primary and Secondary Care* (Updated edition). London: The British Psychological Society and the Royal College of Psychiatrists.

Noble, J., & Hackett, S. (2023). Art therapy in acute inpatient care. *International Journal of Art Therapy*, 28(4), pp. 196–203.

NHS. (2019). *The Community Mental Health Framework for Adults and Older Adults.*

NHS England. (2021). *Workforce Training and Education: Art, Drama and Music Therapists.*https://www.hee.nhs.uk/our-work/allied-health-professions/art-drama-music-therapists

NHS England. (2023a). *Art, Drama and Music Therapies and Dual Identity as Allied Health Professions and Psychological Therapies.*

NHS England. (2023b, October 30). *Patient Race Equality Framework.* https://www.england.nhs.uk/mental-health/advancing-mental-health-equalities/pcref/

NHS England. (2025). *Workforce, Training and Education, Art, Drama and Music Therapists, Background.* https://www.hee.nhs.uk/our-work/mental-health/new-roles-mental-health/psychological-professions-roles

Rothwell, K., & Grandison, S. (2016). Notes on service design for art psychotherapists working in time – limited group programmes on adult mental health inpatient wards. In Hughes, R. (Ed.), *Time Limited Art Psychotherapy*, pp. 118–193. London: Routledge.

Royal College of Psychiatrists. (2019). *Standards for Acute Inpatient Services for Working Age Adults.* Royal College of Psychiatrists centre for Quality Improvement.

Royal College of Psychiatrists. (2024). *Autism and Mental Health.* https://www.rcpsych.ac.uk/mental-health/mental-illnesses-and-mental-health-problems/autism-and-mental-health

Snowden, P., & Kane, E. (2003). Personality disorder, no longer a diagnosis of exclusion. *Psychiatric Bulletin*, 27, pp. 401–403.

Talwar, N. et al. (2006) Music therapy for in-patients with schizophrenia Music therapy for in-patients with schizophrenia. *British Journal of Psychiatry*, 189, pp. 405–409.

University College London. (2022). *Acute Mental Health Competence Framework for Adults and Older Adults.* https://www.ucl.ac.uk/brain-sciences/pals/research/clinical-educational-and-health-psychology/research-groups/competence-frameworks/delivering-adult-and-older-adult-acute-mental-health-inpatient-care

Van Lith, T. (2016) Art therapy in mental health: A systematic review of approaches and Practices. *The Arts in Psychotherapy*, 47, pp. 9–22.

Watson, E., & Rowles, S. (2021). Patient experiences of the pandemic; exploring the effect of COVID-19 on patients detained under the mental health act. *BJPsych Open*, 7(1). pp. S299–S300. https://doi.org/10.1192/bjo.2021.793

Whitley, R. (2012) The antipsychiatry movement: Dead, diminishing, or developing? *Psychiatric Services*, 6(10), pp. 1039–1041.

Wills, E. (2024). *The Climate Crisis: A Critical Threat to Mental Health.* https://www.kingsfund.org.uk/insight-and-analysis/blogs/climate-crisis-critical-threat-mental-health

Woods, A. & Springham, N. (2011) On learning from being the in-patient. *International Journal of Art Therapy*, 16(2), pp. 60–68. DOI: http://dx.doi.org/10.1080/17454832.2011.603697
Wright, T., & Holttum, S. (2020). *BAAT Guidelines on Art Therapy for People with a Psychosis-Related Diagnosis.* London: British Association of Art Therapists.

# 14 The Wider Context

## Growth in Arts and Wellbeing Provision Nationally and Internationally

*Maggie Batchelar and Andrew Colley*

This chapter will begin by briefly reviewing some of the key points raised in the preceding chapters. It will then summarise the now overwhelming body of academic and empirical evidence demonstrating that participating in the arts and having access to artworks can dramatically improve clinical outcomes and mental and physical health for all. We will then go on to discuss how, despite financial constraints and the prevalence of what has become known as the 'business model' across the public services in the UK and elsewhere, recent policy and other initiatives have brought about a new impetus for the provision of creative activity and will show that this gained momentum during and after the COVID-19 pandemic. The chapter will conclude with an appeal for even greater access to the creative arts across all sections of society in line with Adamson's own assertion in *Art as Healing* (1984) that 'art has a vital part to play in the quest for mental health' (p. 56).

This book began by introducing Edward Adamson himself and discussing his pioneering work at Netherne Hospital in Surrey from 1946 to 1981, before looking at the complex and at times controversial issues around collecting and exhibiting artworks made by service users from mental health in-patient settings. The main body of the book took a largely academic and research-led approach to exploring to what extent the gentle but highly effective practice of art therapy Adamson developed in the now almost entirely lost environment of the Victorian-era psychiatric hospital is viable in the very different environment of the modern and highly controlled in-patient mental health unit.

A very strong case has been made in these pages for the vital role art psychotherapy and indeed all the arts therapies play in the wellbeing and recovery of service users in in-patient settings, and in doing so, an equally strong case has been made for the essential and undeniable role of the arts in improving our wellbeing. This final chapter will move beyond the in-patient ward and delve more deeply into this wider context.

There has always been an acknowledgement that there is an essential link between access to the arts and human wellbeing and that the arts are linked

DOI: 10.4324/9781003613428-18

to wellbeing throughout the lifespan, a concept developed by Dissanayake (2003):

> We must not forget that although 'Art' as a concept seems to have been born of and continues to be sustained by a commercial society, and is therefore only roughly two centuries old, … the arts have always been with us. And so have ideas of beauty, sublimity, and transcendence, along with the verities of the human condition: love, death, memory, suffering, power, fear, loss, desire, hope, and so forth. These have been the subject matter of and occasion for the arts throughout human history.
>
> (p. 15)

Art, then, is a universal human behaviour, with evidence of arts activity in all cultures. In *What Art Does: An Unfinished Theory* (2025), Eno and Bette propose that 'we make art all the time, but we don't usually call it that' (p. 13).

Creativity, we accept, is an essential part of childhood development, but just as children use play to learn and make sense of the world, the arts in their widest sense are an essential way for people of all ages to make sense of themselves and others. Eno and Bette describe art as 'how adults play' (p. 72) and that this continuation of play into childhood helps us to keep learning, to "research our feelings"' (p. 72). John Timlin in *Art as Healing* (1984) articulated just this:

> Arts is a form of play, not an idle occupation; quite the contrary; play is learning at a natural tempo; facing up to new problems and working out the answers. Each solution is an advance in knowledge and growth in consciousness… why not extend some of these ideas into the wider 'normal' society, with it's overcrowded prisons and where so many hospital beds are occupied by the mentally ill?
>
> (p. 65)

Pablo Picasso (1881–1973) is usually cited as being the first person to say that *every child is an artist. The problem is how to remain an artist once he grows up*, but why has that become a 'problem'? Edward Adamson himself acknowledged that 'creative therapy has, in this country, been distinguished by the inverse ratio of lip service to official recognition' (Adamson, 1963, p. 53). Arguably more than 60 years later, there is an even harsher climate within health services brought about by public sector policies dominated by what was known in the 1980s and 1990s as the 'business model', though today, the terms 'business plan' or 'business case' are used more commonly, especially in official documents relating to the use of public resources. This has been further exacerbated by Government policies around austerity following the 2008 financial crash as well as systemic funding cuts to the arts and financial pressures on schools to privilege sciences over the arts, so that there is potentially now less access to artmaking for everyone and Eno and Bette (2025), who also understand that arts activity is a 'key attribute to being human', suggest that:

> We shouldn't be surprised when governments marginalise the arts and humanities in education, or when the 'brighter' students are directed away from the arts into science and tech, or when support for theatres, libraries and concert halls is the first thing to be withdrawn in a financial squeeze.
>
> (p. 5)

And yet, it is undeniable that there have been recent Government policy initiatives in the UK and elsewhere, which have acknowledged the importance of the arts to social cohesion and wellbeing, and this offers hope for a better future for us all.

Arguably, this more proactive approach to arts provision and to the widening of access to the arts to improve wellbeing was initiated in the UK at least as far back as 2007, when an arts and health working party set up by the Department of Health published a report jointly with the Arts Council of England: *A Prospectus for Arts and Health*. In 2014, an All-Party Parliamentary Group on Arts Health and Wellbeing (APPG AHW) was formed, and from 2015 to 2017, the group led a two-year inquiry which resulted in a report, *Creative Health: The Arts for Health and Wellbeing* (2017). Among other things, the report not only recommended that the transition from in-patient services to the community can be smoothed through the arts but also recommended art therapy as part of a combined therapeutic approach to a number of conditions including stroke, post-traumatic stress disorder (PTSD) and cancer patients. The first recommendation at the end of the report was as follows:

> We recommend that leaders from within the arts, health and social care sectors, together with service users and academics, establish a strategic centre, at national level, to support the advance of good practice, promote collaboration, coordinate and disseminate research and inform policy and delivery.
>
> (p. 154)

In response to this, the National Centre for Creative Health (NCCH) was established as a registered charity in July 2020 and was officially launched on March 9, 2021. The NCCH advances good practice and research, informs policy and promotes collaboration, helping foster the conditions for creative health to be integral to health and social care and wider systems.

From 2022 to 2023, the APPG AHW conducted a review, chaired by Lord Howarth of Newport and informed by a panel of esteemed commissioners, parliamentarians and leaders in public life, healthcare and culture, and in

December 2023, it published *The Creative Health Review: How Policy Can Embrace Creative Health.* Key messages from the review were that creative health is fundamental to a healthy and prosperous society and that it should be an integral part of a 21st-century health and social care system with a focus on reducing inequalities and supporting people to live well for longer. The NCCH's Creative Health Associate (CHA) programme also supports the ambition to foster the conditions for creative health to be integral to health and care and demonstrate the power of culture and creativity to benefit the lives of individuals and communities. The July 2024 UK General Election brought in a new government and although initially all APPGs were dissolved, a new APPG on Creative Health was launched on November 26, 2024.

Policy initiatives in some other countries over the last 20 years have acknowledged that the arts have a beneficial effect on wellbeing and that there is a will to enhance arts provision across the public sector and across society as a whole. In 2019, the World Health Organisation (WHO) in its scoping review *What is the evidence on the role of the arts in improving health and wellbeing?* acknowledged the growing evidence base for the role of the arts in improving health and wellbeing and the added health value of engagement with the arts. The arts, the report finds, can be cost-effective solutions since they can frequently draw on existing assets or resources, and could help countries reach the integrated targets of key global frameworks, such as the 2030 Agenda for Sustainable Development and the Thirteenth WHO General Programme of Work, 2019–2023, which aims to increase human capital, reduce inequity and promote multisectoral action for health and wellbeing.

We have already heard in Chapter 6 from Australia, where arts health programmes have been developing since the 1990s, and an increase in programmes is now possible because of support at the federal and state levels. In the USA, although in 2025 mental health services are being exposed to the harsh realities of government shutdowns and the mass firing of federal employees, the National Endowment for the Arts continues to fund a range of initiatives, including its *Creative Forces Programs*, which bring creative arts therapies to military patients and veterans in association with the Department of Defence and Veterans Affairs.

In the Netherlands, although there is little public policy around the arts and wellbeing, the *Arts in Health* programme aims to make a permanent place for artmaking in Dutch health care, and the programme published a report in 2025 *Arts Health in Other Countries*, which found that EU countries working on arts and health projects and policy include Bulgaria, France, Luxembourg and Portugal. Scandinavian countries are particularly active in integrating arts in health into social systems, and Finland, for instance, has a coordinated national effort to publish local cultural wellbeing plans. Arts on Prescription pilot programmes have also been started in cities and regions in Denmark, Germany, Poland, Latvia and Sweden.

These initiatives are very much in line with the social prescribing model, which has been developing in the UK for a number of years. Link workers, often employed in Doctors' surgeries, 'prescribe' patients – usually with non-medical issues that are impacting their health – access to a range of activities – from physical activity, crafts, singing and green volunteering, with an October 2024 report by the BBC finding that in some areas social prescribing referrals tripled in three years.

Part of the reason for this increase in social prescribing can be attributed to the impact of the COVID-19 pandemic from 2021 onwards. The fear, uncertainty and restrictions COVID-19 brought to the world have given rise to a shift in understanding and valuing of how the arts can offer imaginative life and connection to others. The pandemic reinforced for many people forced to stay at home during successive lockdowns the importance of creative activity. Creative engagement offered solace, assurance and a means of expressive communication when the usual support systems and contacts were not possible.

This clear shift in understanding of the necessity for creative experience and engagement for the population's wellbeing offers context for Adamson's premise that engaging with the imagination through creative means has the potential to 'heal' and can offer so much more than an aesthetic pastime. Adamson confessed 'to be one who makes large claims for the curative effects of art' (Adamson, 1963, p. 274), and perhaps we are now realising in our disconnected digital and virtual age how true that is, and how much we all need to cultivate our imaginative lives and connections with others through shared creative experiences.

Evidence shows that in the aftermath of the pandemic, engagements with the arts and creative activities in the UK and in other countries have been maintained and in some cases increased, and there are a number of national initiatives, some of which pre-date the pandemic, which aim to bring the benefits of the arts to as wide and diverse a cohort as possible, enhancing equality and inclusion and bringing together cultures and communities creatively. An article by Martegani (2020) in the magazine *artnet* about artist responses to the world in crisis proposes that

> Art can open up dialogues that are based in shared experiences, instead of anger, and it can create meaningful connections and understandings between people with different experiences. Art can bring people together physically, but more importantly, emotionally. And it can help bridge dangerous divides. Public art, in particular, can do this in a way that is safe and meaningful. Most importantly, the connection is open and free for everyone to partake.

Museums and other heritage environments are increasingly seen as hubs for creative engagement, which can respond to some of the issues discussed above and in other parts of this book, and The Baring Foundation Report, *Creatively Minded at the Museum: Creative and Mental Health Activity in Museums* (Cutler, 2020), was 'written to highlight targeted work by museums to engage people with mental health problems, especially using participatory arts' (p. 5).

In another report, *Museums as Spaces for Wellbeing* (Desmarais et al., 2018), published shortly before the COVID-19 pandemic, the National Alliance for Museums, Health and Wellbeing, which receives public funding from Arts Council England (2007), states:

> The relationship between culture and health has achieved new visibility through the activities of the All-Party Parliamentary Group for Arts, Health and Wellbeing. Alongside this development, social prescribing is increasingly envisaged as an effective and economically viable response to psychosocial difficulties not best addressed in primary care. The heritage sector provides sympathetic terrain for emerging asset-based cultures of co-creation, community building and green wellbeing.
>
> (p. 53)

In New York, the Museum of Modern Art's (MOMA) Alzheimer's Project, which ran from 2007 to 2014 developed training resources intended for use by arts and health professionals on how to make art accessible to people with dementia. More recently, the museum has hosted events with community health workers from the New York public health system and developed a podcast called *How Art is Helping Teens Find Their True Selves.*

The therapeutic impact of art on wellbeing is now acknowledged across the lifespan. The Research Centre for Arts and Wellbeing at Edge Hill University in Birmingham is funded by sources within the public, private and charitable sectors as well as from the European Union. The stated aim of the Centre is to 'engage in purposeful interdisciplinary research with people across their life span in creative ways, that are participatory, ethical and of demonstrable value' and it supports and evaluates arts initiatives such as *Arts4us*, a place-based arts initiative supporting the mental health of children and young people.

We also saw in Chapter 4 how art therapy is used to help older people in in-patient settings.

This is celebrated by the charity Arts for Dementia[1] which finds that

> The role of the arts in combating loneliness and cognitive decline is now widely recognised as providing vital benefit to patients. The arts help people with dementia preserve their brain health, and keep active, connected and inspired in community life for years longer.

There is also an increasing awareness of the role of the arts in enhancing the wellbeing and independence of young people with special educational needs (Colley & Tilbury, 2021), though London-based consultant in special educational needs and disabilities (SEND) Nana-Kofi Okyere, interviewed for this chapter, explained that accessing art-based therapies for children with SEND or those not engaging in education because of emotional needs can be complex. Typically, parents make a request to the local authority, but are often turned down if they cannot demonstrate an educational benefit. However, if a need can be proved, the Local Authority then has an obligation to provide funding. An art therapist, for example, will then come into the school or into the home, with the quality and outcomes of the therapeutic intervention usually evaluated by the commissioning team. Some special schools in the independent sector employ their own arts therapists – often in art or music – though these are becoming increasingly rare in the state sector because of systemic cuts to funding.

In 2023, an editorial piece in *The Guardian* newspaper reported on the 'creativity crisis' in arts education and identified the concerning health inequality divide in children's access to the arts in schools, with the government at that time reducing the opportunities available to state school pupils, whilst private schools increased investment in music and art provision. However, an editorial in the same newspaper in 2025 points to a more hopeful shift contained in the UK Government's *Curriculum and Assessment Review Interim Report of English Schools* (2025), which is reported as likely to boost music, art and drama. Despite this, there continues to be a need for more equitable and open access to the arts for any child or young person, and The Baring Foundation Report in 2020, *Creatively Minded and Young*, showcases the role arts organisations can have in meeting the gaps in the creative needs of children and young people. One arts project in the report proposes this:

> We would like to see art sessions embedded in educational institutions as a place of play, experimentation, expression, reflection and contemplation, nonjudgement and of voice. We feel this would allow young people to reduce stress and see value in themselves as unique creative individuals. We believe that creativity plays a huge part in life as it offers transferrable skills in creating something from what resources you have.
>
> (p. 61)

John Timlin, writing in *Art as Healing* (1984), draws on his experience as a teacher, to propose that the arts should be an integral part of every child's educational experience and that this could have profound implications: 'The imaginative use of spontaneous art in schools might prevent many people from ever needing psychiatric care in later life.' (p. 66). If, as proposed by Eno and Bette (2025), art has the propensity to 'help us identify the sources of feelings and anxieties and give us a way of locating them and sharing them' (p. 99), then the preventative impact of enabling children to have a safe, expressive creative outlet is ever-more relevant in current times, as it was when John Timlin in *Art as Healing* (1984) suggested that 'The educational system could seize a wonderful initiative to prevent a good deal of the rising generation from ever needing community care in later life'. (p. 68).

## Conclusion

Edward Adamson, interviewed in 1989 by ITV for *Night Network*, said this:

> *I'd like to see the hospitals being built now having studios attached to them.*

Nearly 40 years later, Adamson's wish for modern hospitals clearly has not been realised, but this book has, we hope, brought to light the long and continuing history of art therapy in mental health in-patient provision and shown that all the arts therapies have profound and continued relevance in the very different setting of the modern in-patient unit, especially when applied within the evidence-based relational framework we know to be so helpful for people in distress.

Learmonth (2005) stated that 'art is one of the deepest and oldest of human resources. All times, all cultures have made art' (p. 18). The editors of this book believe that this universal truth is finally being recognised and that there has been a real and lasting shift in understanding of the necessity for creative experience and engagement for the population's wellbeing. This belief offers a

*Image 14.1* Ink drawing *(Man Painting*, Netherne art studio). Edward Adamson. 1954.

Ink on paper. Edward Adamson Archive, Wellcome Collection. Courtesy of Wellcome Collection.

much wider context for Adamson's premise that engaging with the imagination through creative means has the potential to heal and that 'art has a vital part to play in the quest for mental health' (Adamson, 1963, p. 56). In 2001, John Timlin put it like this:

> *The act of creation makes the person feel better.*

It seems appropriate to conclude this book with a drawing made by Edward Adamson himself in 1954 of a man painting at an easel in one of the many studios at Netherne Hospital (Image 14.1).

We will never know who this man is, why he became a patient at Netherne in the first place or how long he spent there. He seems to be middle aged and is wearing a jacket, but other than that we know nothing about him. What we can say though with some certainty is that when he first came – possibly reluctantly – into the studio space at the hospital, he will have been greeted warmly by a balding man with a kind face wearing a smart suit and a tie. This man, Edward Adamson, would have sat down next to him, chatted about inconsequential things and then, perhaps on that day or maybe a few days later, would have said:

> *Would you like to do some painting?*

## Note

1 www.artsfordementia.org

## References

Adamson, E. (1963). Art and mental health. *Mental Health*, 22(2), 53.

Adamson, E. (1984). *Art as Healing*. London: Conventure.

All-Party Parliamentary Group on Arts, Health and Wellbeing (2017, July). *Inquiry Report: Creative Health: The Arts for Health and Wellbeing*. London: APPG.

Arts Council England. (2007). *A Prospectus for Arts and Health*. Arts Council England.

BBC. (2024, October 10). *Social Prescribing Referrals Triple in Three Years*. https://www.bbc.co.uk/news/articles/cdrjmn1zjjro

Colley, A., & Tilbury, J. (2021). *Enhancing Wellbeing and Independence for Young People with Profound and Multiple learning Difficulties: Lives Lived Well*. London: Routledge.

Cutler, D. (2020, February 18). *Creatively Minded: An Initial Mapping Study of Participatory Arts and Mental Health Activity in the UK - the First Report of Our New Arts & Mental Health Funding Theme*. https://baringfoundation.org.uk/resource/creatively-minded/

Desmarais, S., Bedford, L., & Chatterjee, H. J. (2018). *Museums as Spaces for Wellbeing: A Second Report from the National Alliance for Museums, Health and Wellbeing*. www.museumsandwellbeingalliance.wordpress.com

Dissanayake, E. (2003). The core of art making *Special Journal of the Canadian Association for Curriculum Studies*, 1(2), 13–38.

Eno, B., & Bette, A. (2025). *What Art Does: An Unfinished Theory*. Faber.

Learmonth, M. (2005). Changing our minds. *Open Mind*, 134, 18–19.
Martegani, M. (2020). *Artists Are Finding Inspiring Ways to Adapt Their Work to a World in Crisis.* Arts Organizations Must Do the Same. https://news.artnet.com/art-world/micaela-martegani-op-ed-1897492
National Centre for Creative Health. (2023). *The Creative Health Review: How Policy Can Embrace Creative Health.* London: The Baring Foundation.
The Guardian Newspaper. (2023, February 7). *The Guardian View on Arts Education: A Creativity Crisis.* Editorial. London.
Timlin, J. (2001 July 9). Unreleased video interview with Ed Lawrenson & Pia Borg.
World Health Organisation (WHO). (2019). *What Is the Evidence on the Role of the Arts in Improving Health and Well-Being?* https://www.who.int/europe/publications/i/item/9789289054553

# Index

Pages in *italics* refer to figures and pages in **bold** refer to tables.

For Product Safety Concerns and Information please contact our
EU representative GPSR@taylorandfrancis.com Taylor & Francis
Verlag GmbH, Kaufingerstraße 24, 80331 München, Germany